Frederic Nicholls, A. W. Wright

Report of the Demonstration in Honour of the fortieth Anniversary

Of Sir John A. Macdonald's Entrance into Public Life

Frederic Nicholls, A. W. Wright

Report of the Demonstration in Honour of the fortieth Anniversary
Of Sir John A. Macdonald's Entrance into Public Life

ISBN/EAN: 9783337194826

Printed in Europe, USA, Canada, Australia, Japan

Cover: Foto ©ninafisch / pixelio.de

More available books at **www.hansebooks.com**

1884

REPORT

OF THE

DEMONSTRATION

IN HONOUR OF THE

FORTIETH ANNIVERSARY

OF

SIR JOHN A. MACDONALD'S

ENTRANCE INTO PUBLIC LIFE.

PROCEEDINGS AT TORONTO AND MONTREAL.

COMPLETE LIST OF DELEGATES APPOINTED TO ATTEND TORONTO CONVENTION.

COMPILED BY
FREDERIC NICHOLLS AND A. W. WRIGHT.

TORONTO:
PRINTED BY THE CANADIAN MANUFACTURER PUBLISHING CO. (LIMITED).
1885.

CONTENTS.

	PAGE
Preface	1
Sir John A. Macdonald, P.C., G.C.B.	3

THE CONVENTION.—FIRST DAY.

Local Committees	5
Nominating the Chairman	8
The Chairman's Speech	8
The Secretaries	10
Moving the Address	10
Handing in the Addresses	11
Sir John's Arrival	15
The Address to the Premier	15
Speech of Sir John Macdonald	18
The Proposed Liberal-Conservative Association	37
The Resolutions	38

SECOND DAY.

Speech of Hon. Alex. Morris	38
Speech of Hon. J. A. Chapleau	40
The Manitoban Tribute	40
Address from Assiniboia	42
The Premier's Reply	43
Speech of Hon. Mr. Norquay	44
The Conservative Union	45
Speech of Mr. Robillard, M.P.P.	45
Speech of Mr. Solomon White, M.P.P.	46
Speech of Mr. J. J. Hawkins	46
Draft of Resolutions	46
Election of Officers	47
The Boundary Question........Mr. G. T. Blackstock	47
The Alleged Conspiracy........Mr. N. A. Coste	48
The National Policy........Mr. R. McKechnie	49
The Canadian Pacific Railway........Mr. Thomas Cowan	50
Frontenac's Splendid Tribute	52
Fidelity to the Empire	53
Speech of Sir Leonard Tilley	54
Speech of Sir Hector Langevin	63
Speech of Sir D. L. Macpherson	64
Speech of Hon. Mr. Caron	65
Speech of Hon. Mr. Blanchet	66
Thanks to Mr. Manning	66
Thanks to the Chairman	67

THE BANQUET.

	PAGE
Descriptive	69
Reading Letters and Telegrams	70

TOASTS AND REPLIES.

The Queen	71
The Governor-General and Lieutenant-Governor	72
The Army and Navy :	
Speech of Hon. Mr. Caron	72
The Toast of the Evening	75
Speech of Sir John Macdonald	76
The Ministry :	
Speech of Sir Hector Langevin	85
" Sir D. L. Macpherson	86
The Senate :	
Speech of Sir Alex. Campbell	86
The House of Commons :	
Speech of Hon. J. A. Chapleau	87
" Mr. Thomas White, M.P.	91
The Legislative Assemblies :	
Speech of Mr. Patterson, M.P.P.	93
" Hon. Mr. Norquay	93
" Hon. Mr. Blanchet	94
The Manufacturing Industries :	
Speech of Mr. Thomas Cowan	95
Trade and Commerce :	
Speech of Mr. Robert Henry	96
The Ladies :	
Speech of Senator Turner	97
" Mr. W. R. Meredith, Q.C., M.P.P.	97
The Press :	
Speech of Mr. Creighton, M.P.P.	98

THE MONTREAL BANQUET.

Descriptive	99
Speech of Sir John Macdonald	99
Speech of Sir Leonard Tilley	106

EXTRACTS FROM A SPEECH OF HON. JOHN CARLING.................. 109

APPENDIX.

List of Delegates appointed to attend Toronto Convention (containing nearly eleven thousand names.)

PREFACE.

The following report of the proceedings at the late Liberal-Conservative Convention and of the Banquet to the Right Honourable Sir John Macdonald, G.C.B., although of much interest at the present time, will, the compilers think, be looked upon in years to come as a volume of historic interest, as it contains not alone a full report of the proceedings of the greatest and most enthusiastic political convention ever held in the Dominion of Canada, but a valuable collection of able and instructive speeches, delivered by some of the most prominent leaders of the Liberal-Conservative party, which deal comprehensively with the past, present and, to some extent, the future of the Dominion.

The original intention was to confine the scope of this pamphlet to chronicling the proceedings at the Toronto demonstration, but the importance of the Banquet at the Windsor Hotel, Montreal, tendered Sir John by the Junior Conservative Club of that city, could not be overlooked, and accordingly the speeches of Sir John Macdonald and Sir Leonard Tilley, delivered on that occasion, have been reproduced in these pages. It would have been a pleasure to the compilers, and of profit to the subscribers to this work, had it been possible to give the admirable speeches of the other leaders which were delivered at the Montreal Banquet, but the magnitude of the undertaking has already exceeded our estimate, and we have had, though reluctantly, to omit them.

That part of the speech delivered by the Honourable John Carling before a meeting of his constituents, which deals with the progress of Canada during the past decade has been appended, as the tabulated statements will prove a valuable record for future reference.

The list of delegates appointed to attend the Toronto Convention from every electoral district in Ontario, is very full and complete, containing upwards of ten thousand names. This long list testifies in a mute but eloquent manner of the widespread desire to do honour to the Chieftain, on the celebration of the fortieth anniversary of his entrance into public life.

The compilation of this work has not been unattended with difficulties and drawbacks, but it has been prosecuted with as much haste as was compatible with proper revision, and is now presented to the public with the assurance that any delay in its publication will be readily excused.

Our thanks are due to Mr. F. D. Barwick, the Secretary of the Convention, to Mr. W. Baillie, Assistant Secretary, and to the Toronto *Mail*,—to the two former for their willingness to afford us every assistance and for permission to examine the records in their possession, and to the latter for the use made of the excellent reports which appeared in that paper.

FREDERIC NICHOLLS,
A. W. WRIGHT.

Toronto, February 1st, 1885.

SIR JOHN MACDONALD,

P.C., G.C.B., ETC.

To attempt here to give a complete or at all extended review of Sir John Macdonald's remarkable career would be to unduly extend the limits of this volume. Yet in a history of the honours paid by his countrymen to a statesman who had just completed forty years of arduous and faithful public service, something in the way of a reference to his public career may naturally be expected. Scarcely in the pages of history will there be found another whose name is so intimately interwoven with the records of his country. When Mr. John A. Macdonald first entered public life as the member for Kingston, the history of Canada—the constitutional history at least—had scarcely begun, and while it would be invidious and unfair to claim for him the entire honour of the building of the constitutional edifice which has since been erected, to the ignoring of the services of others—services which he never denied or sought to belittle—yet it may fairly be said that he assisted in placing in position almost every stone and beam "from turret to foundation stone." While devoting himself to the service of Canada he has never forgotten that services rendered the whole empire are services rendered to the Dominion, and the honours which have been showered thickly and ungrudgingly upon him by Her Majesty, whether her advisers at the time being belonged to one or other of Britain's great parties, testify eloquently of the high estimation in which his imperial services are held.

The biography of the Conservative chief since his arrival here at the tender age of five years, on through his student days, through his brief but brilliant career at the bar, and through his parliamentary and ministerial history would read almost like a romance, so full would it be of thrilling incident and of the record of great purposes wisely formed and faithfully and tenaciously carried out. It is not ours in this place to attempt to trace his career, nor is it necessary ; not only in Canada, but by British and American writers it has been sketched on a more or less pretentious scale and always in an appreciative tone indicative of the enviable position he has achieved in the esteem of every intelligent person who speaks the English tongue. Wherever that tongue is spoken his power as a debator, his ability as a man of affairs, and the grasp and wisdom of his statesmanship are recognized. True he has not escaped the attacks of his enemies ; the shafts of malice and envy have fallen thickly around him. If no one has ever been so loved and admired by the great majority of Canadians ; if no colonial statesman has ever been so highly and deservedly honoured by the sovereign—no one has ever been so bitterly, so savagely assailed by faction. If he has found that the sunshine of his country's love and trust, and of his sovereign's favour falls on him in his high position undimmed and unobstructed he has also experienced the truth of the proverb, "high winds blow on high hills." But the attacks and the calumnies of his enemies—it would be a misnomer to call them opponents—only serve as a background to bring out in more vivid relief the attachment and regard of his friends. It would be unfair to say that all who oppose or have opposed the policy by which Sir John has raised the Dominion to its present high position, and which if carried out will achieve for it yet greater eminence, are the enemies of Canada; but it is a fact that all who decry, and by spoken and printed words seek to injure her, are numbered among his political antagonists.

Since the formation of the Macdonald-Cartier administration in 1854 Sir John has been the most prominent figure in Canadian politics, even during the brief periods in which he was in opposition the eyes of the people were turned on him rather than on the leader of the government, his superiority being recognized by friend and foe alike. In general if not in detail the events of his long and remarkable career are familar to the Canadian people, by whom they have been observed with a pride and pleasure that has made their contemplation a labour of love. That those who know him best love him most; that the people who have closely scanned his career have assembled to do him honour in numbers and with an enthusiasm almost if not altogether unparalleled, is perhaps the most flattering thing that can be said of a statesman, and it is the sufficient answer to all the calumnies that have been levelled at him.

Lacking space to fully indicate the why and wherefore of the personal attachment of the vast majority of Canadians to the great Conservative chief, we must content ourselves with saying that his success in vanquishing every opponent, in overcoming every difficulty, and in eventually consummating every part of his policy, his faithfulness to his friends, his broad patriotism, combined with his prophetic and abiding faith in the future of his country, and his implicit reliance in the justice and wisdom of the ultimate verdict of the Canadian people, all have endeared him to every man who admires ability, force of character, and high, patriotic aspirations. He is, in brief, one with a head to think and a heart to feel, and such have ever been the men who have enshrined themselves in the hearts of their countrymen.

The reconciliation of Upper and Lower Canada, the Confederation of British North America, the negotiation of the Washington Treaty, the acquisition of the North-West, the inauguration of the National Policy, and the construction of that great national highway—the Canadian Pacific Railway—are lofty summits in a high range of public services during forty years of political life. Upon those summits will gleam the sunlight of fame throughout that glorious future which he has predicted and prepared for his country, and which will no doubt be hers.

THE CONVENTION.

The seventeenth and eighteenth days of December, 1884, will always be remembered as red letter days in the history of the Liberal Conservative party. Some months previously the great leader of the party had gone to England to consult leading physicians there regarding his health; immediately some of the most prominent organs of the Grit party began a series of attacks, in which the hope that his illness might be sufficiently serious to terminate his political career was but poorly disguised. The attacks were coarse to the very verge of brutality, but if the makers of them, or the political leaders, whose instructions these makers seemed to be obeying, hoped to weaken the influence of the Conservative chief among his friends and supporters, if they thought to lessen in any degree that affectionate regard and esteem in which he is held by the masses of the Conservative party, they were grievously mistaken. Instead of the abuse heaped upon him having the desired and hoped-for effect, the indignation of the Conservatives was roused, and they determined to give him such a hearty and enthusiastic welcome on his return that there should in the future be no room to doubt that Sir John Macdonald was supported by a party loyal to the great principles which had guided his long public career, and devoted to himself. At first it was proposed to tender him a banquet at Toronto, on the occasion of the fortieth anniversary of his entrance into public life. Then the necessity for effecting a better organization of the party which had long been recognized by leading and thoughtful Conservatives, suggested the holding of a convention of delegates chosen from the various constituencies. Finally, both convention and banquet were decided on. A meeting was held in St. Lawrence Hall, at which eight efficient committees were appointed to carry out the necessary arrangements. These committees were :—

FINANCE.

ROBT. HAY, ESQ., M.P., *Chairman.*
GEO. GOODERHAM, ESQ., *Treasurer.*

Christopher Robinson, Esq.
John Bain, Esq.
Hon. Wm. Cayley.
Fred'k Wyld, Esq.
J. D. Henderson, Esq.
W. R. Brock, Esq.
W. H. Beatty, Esq.
James Tilt, Esq.
J. H. Morris, Esq.
Patrick Burns, Esq.
William Ince, Esq.
W. G. Falconbridge, Esq.
Walter S. Lee, Esq.
J. O. Kemp, Esq.
Hector Cameron, Esq., M.P.
Dalton McCarthy, Esq., M.P.
Elmes Henderson, Esq.
Frank Turner, Esq.
Alderman Walker.
Alderman Crocker.
Alderman Davies.
Alderman Lobb.
Alderman Allen.
Alderman Irwin.

Alderman Turner.
Alex. Manning, Esq.
E. O. Bickford, Esq.
John Shields, Esq.
Hon. Alex. Morris.
Hon. G. W. Allan.
J. N. Lee, Esq.
John Hague, Esq., F.S.S.
D. R. Wilkie, Esq.
Arthur Lepper, Esq.
R. H. Trotter, Esq.
S. M. Jarvis, Esq.
Edgar J. Jarvis, Esq.
C. H. Ritchie, Esq.
J. A. Worrell, Esq.
James Graham, Esq.
H. J. Scott, Esq., Q.C.
Thomas Ogilvy, Esq.
W. J. Ramsay, Esq.
Thomas Shortiss, Esq.
J. A. Macdonnell, Esq.
John J. Davidson, Esq.
John Small, Esq., M.P.

ROOM AND DECORATION.

D. B. DICK, ESQ., *Chairman*.

J. Pape, Esq.
Ex-Ald. Dill.
Dr. Pyne.
John Thompson, Esq.
J. S. McMurray, Esq.
W. R. Brock, Esq.
A. R. Denison, Esq.
John Stewart, Esq.

John Chambers, Esq.
A. A. Staunton, Esq.
Ald. Crocker.
E. Coatsworth, Esq.
James Fulton, Esq.
George Jarvis, Esq.
Henry Pellatt, Esq.
Dr. George Wright.

CONVENTION.

HENRY E. CLARKE, ESQ., M.P.P., *Chairman*.

Dalton McCarthy, Esq., M.P.
Hon. Alex. Morris.
C. W. Bunting, Esq.
J. J. Foy, Esq.
John Shaw, Esq.
A. Boultbee, Esq.
Major Gray, M.P.P.
Robert Hay, Esq., M.P.
James Beaty, Esq.
J. B. Bickle, Esq.
N. Murphy, Esq.
Arthur Tiffin, Esq.
E. Gurney, Esq.

Hon. John O'Donohue.
E. F. Clarke, Esq.
Geo. T. Blackstock, Esq.
F. D. Barwick, Esq.
John Small, Esq., M.P.
N. C. Wallace, Esq., M.P.
R. Birmingham, Esq.
E. O'Keefe, Esq.
B. Tomlin, Esq.
John Poucher, Esq.
Robert T. Sutton, Esq.
J. A. Macdonnell, Esq.

MUSIC AND TOASTS.

EX-ALD. JOHN BAXTER, *Chairman*.

R. H. Bowes, Esq.
T. McMullen, Esq.
Thos. Bickerstaff, Esq.
Robert Hay, Esq., M.P.
Wm. McSpadden, Esq.
Elijah Westman, Esq.
John Cornell, Esq.
Ald. C. L. Denison.
David Dunlop, Esq.
William Hynes, Esq.

John Greer, Esq.
Richard Harper, Esq.
Wilbur Grant, Esq.
Ald. Sheppard.
Thomas Thompson, Esq.
Jos. C. McMillan, Esq.
Thomas N. Gearing, Esq.
Ed. Medcalf, Esq.
R. L. Cowan, Esq.

PRINTING AND INVITATIONS.

EX-ALD. G. M. EVANS, *Chairman*.

F. Rolph, Esq.
E. F. Clarke, Esq.
J. B. Bickle, Esq.
Major Gray, M.P.P.
James Tilt, Esq.
J. S. Williams, Esq.
Wm. Hambly, Esq.
J. E. Robertson, Esq.
J. S. Fullerton, Esq.
Ald. Allen.

Hon. Alexander Morris.
Jos. C. McMillan, Esq.
Ald. Sheppard.
Geo. Chesman, Esq.
R. F. Walton, Esq.
E. P. Roden, Esq.
John Mills, Esq.
R. A. Barton, Esq.
J. E. Winnett, Esq.

RECEPTION.

Marcellus Crombie, Esq., *Chairman.*

E. Pearson, Esq.
A. M. Browne, Esq.
Ald. Hynes.
Alf. Medcalfe, Esq.
Ex-Ald. William Bell.
E. H. Boddy, Esq.
Ex-Ald. John Woods.
J. M. Munro, Esq.
Follis Johnstone, Esq.
Ald. Piper.
T. R. Whiteside, Esq.
John C. Noble, Esq.
E. P. Roden, Esq.

J. G. Gibson, Esq.
Thos. Colby, Esq.
Finlay MacDonald, Esq.
Ald. Irwin.
J. C. Swait, Esq.
P. H. Drayton, Esq.
Edward Gearing, Esq.
Ed. Medcalfe, Esq.
R. A. Barton, Esq.
Jas. Graham, Esq.
John E. Winnett, Esq.
H. K. Dunn, Esq.
C. A. B. Brown, Esq.

REFRESHMENT.

Dr. McCollum, *Chairman.*

Geo. J. Foy, Esq.
Ald. Defoe.
Ald. Irwin.
Ald. Blevins.
Ald. B. Saunders.
Ald. Walker.
Ald. Adamson.
Geo. Chesman, Esq.
Alex. Patterson, Esq.
Frank Somers, Esq.
J. H. Beatty, Esq.
John Massey, Esq.
John Pearson, Esq.
John Lamb, Esq.
Geo. D'Arcy Boulton, Esq.
Henry Pellatt, Esq.
Thos. Kerr, Esq.

John Thompson, Esq.
J. D. Henderson, Esq.
J. Pape, Esq.
Mayor Boswell.
J. A. Macdonnell, Esq.
C. W. Bunting, Esq.
John Wright, Esq.
Ex-Ald John Dill.
Ald. Jones.
C. W. Brown, Esq.
R. A. Barton, Esq.
Napier Robinson, Esq.
Hon. Frank Smith.
Hon. Wm. Cayley.
John Munroe, Esq.
Geo. A. Boomer, Esq.

EXECUTIVE.

Mayor Boswell, *Chairman.*

John Small, Esq., M.P.
A. Boultbee, Esq.
Dr. McCollum.
H. E. Clarke, Esq., M.P.P.
Major Gray, M.P.P.
James Tilt, Esq.
J. E. Robertson, Esq.
Ex-Ald Pape.
F. Somers, Esq.
J. B. Bickle, Esq.
Wm. Ince, Esq.

J. S. Fullarton, Esq.
W. R. Brock, Esq.
E. F. Clarke, Esq.
C. W. Bunting, Esq.
J. A. Macdonnell, Esq.
Dalton McCarthy, Esq., Q.C., M.P.
Hon. Alex. Morris.
Ald. Allen.
Ald. Adamson.
Ald. Blevins.
Ald. Defoe.

These committees, composed as they were, of Toronto's leading citizens, went to work with a will ; invitations were sent to the Conservatives of the various constituencies to co-operate, and soon throughout the Province the Conservative party was in a blaze of enthusiasm in anticipation of the coming event. Just when the bustle of preparation had fairly begun the gratifying intelligence was flashed across the Atlantic that the Queen had conferred on the Conservative Chief an honour never before bestowed on a colonial statesman. It did not need this to assure the success of the demonstration; but the enthusiasm now knew no bounds. Long before the day of the convention drew near, it became clear, from the long lists of delegates appointed and the number of applicants for tickets for the banquet, that Toronto did not own a building large enough to accommodate the thousands who were flocking to the city, and no hall which would suffice to seat the multitude who desired to do honour to Canada's most illustrious statesman by attending the banquet. The committee in charge were therefore reluctantly compelled to limit the number of tickets to the capacity of the pavilion of the Horticultural Gardens, the largest hall available. Through the kindness of Mr. Alexander Manning, one of Toronto's most public-spirited citizens, the Grand Opera House was placed at the disposal of the Convention. Rooms had been secured adjacent to the Opera House for the use of the committees where the credentials of the delegates were received and tickets of admission issued. On the night of the 16th the delegates began to arrive in the city, and every train on all the roads centering in Toronto continued to come in laden with delegates. By one o'clock on the 17th the enormous work of receiving credentials had been completed and the delegates proceeded to the Opera House. In less than half an hour the vast auditorium was filled to its utmost capacity. The stage too was crowded. Never before had the Opera House been so densely packed, and yet hundreds had to go away, unable to obtain even standing room. The enthusiasm was unbounded; never had a Canadian public man received such a magnificent ovation. It was evident that the great heart of Ontario conservatism beat as true as ever to the great principles which had brought the party into existence, and that the conservatives of the premier province had lost none of their enthusiastic loyalty to the chief who had led them so faithfully and patriotically for so many years. The assemblage was far larger than former conventions, large and enthusiastic though those conventions were. At the convention of 1878, which was held at Shaftesbury Hall, there were estimated to be six hundred present. This convention was the preliminary to the great National Policy victory of that year. At the gathering of 1881, which was also held in Shaftesbury Hall, there were 1,400 present. At the convention in September, 1883, there were said to be three thousand present. The attendance, it will be observed, has increased as convention has followed convention, and no better evidence could be given that the party is one of the future as well as of the past and the present.

THE PROCEEDINGS.

MR. DALTON MCCARTHY, Q.C., M.P., rose, the great audience breaking out into enthusiastic cheering. He said:—Gentlemen, the hour has arrived when, I think, the business should commence which you, in your strength and in your might, have met here from every township—almost, at all events, every township—in the province of Ontario to transact. In order that our business may be regular, the first thing we have to do, is to appoint a chairman. As you are a grand meeting and a great assemblage I desire that you should have a great chairman, and I have to present to you for that position the man that we would honour most after the great chieftain himself, Mr. W. R. Meredith, leader of the Opposition in the Legislature of Ontario. (Loud applause.) I think I may take it for granted that the nomination is unanimous. (Renewed cheering.)

THE CHAIRMAN.

MR. W. R. MEREDITH, on coming forward, was received with loud cheering, the entire audience rising. He said:—Gentlemen, in assuming the temporary chairmanship of this magnificent meeting, gathered from all sections of the Province of Ontario, the leading men of the Conservative party, I desire to thank you most sincerely for the high honour you have conferred upon me in placing me in this position. It would be a position of honour on any occasion, but on an occasion such as this, a red letter day in the annals of the Conservative party, I consider it a doubly high honour to be placed in this position. We are met to-day for the purpose of hearing an address from our great chieftain—(cheers)—and the proceedings must close at five o'clock, therefore it would be impossible for us to occupy much time in the preliminary proceedings of the meeting. I may state briefly in a few sentences the object for which we are gathered here. We are met here for a party purpose, and may I say also for a national purpose. (Hear, hear.) We are met here for a party purpose, with a view of organizing a Liberal-Conservative Association for this great Province of Ontario. (Cheers.) We have a great chieftain to lead us—(cheers)—we have a great cause to support—(renewed cheering)—and we have a great assemblage of those prepared to support that cause. (Loud cheers.) Gentlemen, as in a more bitter warfare, it is necessary that we should have organization in order that our battalions should be organized when the day of battle comes. It has long been felt that in the Province of Ontario our organization has been defective, and those that have taken a great interest in the affairs of the party have thought that upon this occasion, when the leaders of the party throughout Ontario are met together, that we should sit down in council and devise a scheme by which our forces, when the occasion makes it necessary to go into battle, shall be in proper array, and produce the most effective work. Therefore, one of the objects for which we are met will be to form a grand association, one of the cardinal principles of which shall be that there shall not be the slightest interference with the rights of localities in the selection of candidates or in dictating the policy of the party. Those who have had the honour of bringing it to your attention believe that the objects will be best served by forming the organization which will have the duty of looking after the registration of voters, which most important duty will be probably more important in the near future, when by the extension of the suffrage there will be a large addition to the number of voters throughout Ontario, and when the hour of battle comes, having matters so arranged that our efforts may be effectively felt throughout the country. That is the political object for which we are met here to-day. The national object to which I have referred is that which brings this magnificent attendance from all parts of the province here to-day to do honour to the man of all the men who have held foremost positions in Canada for well nigh half a century now. (Cheers.) I do not think that upon an occasion such as this, which, as I have said, may be considered a national one, that it would be fitting that we should deal with that question from a purely party standpoint; but on an occasion like this we should look at it on higher and more national grounds. (Hear, hear.) We are met to honour the man who for forty years has occupied a high position in the affairs of Canada, and for a quarter of a century, with but one or two slight intervals, has practically ruled the affairs of Canada. Gentlemen, when we look back during those forty years and see the progress made since Sir John Macdonald entered Parliament, we see that it had to do with the affairs of a comparatively small province, and one that was not very populous. To-day he is in the proud position of being Premier of a Dominion comprising one-half a continent, extending from sea to sea, and containing within its limits nearly five millions of people. For Sir John Macdonald during all that time to have occupied the position he has in the councils of the nation is the reason why every man, whether Conservative or Reformer, should feel it a duty to turn out and do honour to him. I observe that in one of the public newspapers something has been said about why it should be given. I say that those who put that question should look for an answer in the faces of the men who are here to-day—(hear, hear) —men who have come from every quarter of the province, engaged in every walk of life—and see in their faces an answer to the question. Have these men left their avocations, have they gathered here with such enthusiasm for no purpose? The answer will be read in the faces and in the enthusiasm of those gathered here to-day. (Cheers.) But I do not believe such feelings animate the great Reform party. We ask if Sir John is not the man we claim him to be how has he ruled Canada so long? The answer is that Providence sometimes permits people to be afflicted for their sins. (Laughter.) That, I think, gentlemen, is something like it. There is a certain section, I believe a small section, of the people of Canada who have sinned, and if Providence is desirous of punishing them for their sins I believe the gentleman whom we have met to honour has administered a good deal of the castigation. (Hear, hear.) But, gentlemen, I think that section is still in its sins, and will require castigation still. (Laughter.) Then it is said, that Sir John Macdonald is an essentially corrupt man. I say that that is an insult to the people of Canada. (Cheers.) I say that it is an insult to the people who, during that time, have delighted to honour Sir John Macdonald by placing him in the high positions which he has occupied. (Cheers.) Then the people who have chosen and put him in these positions must also be corrupt. But I say these are charges which ought not to be made. These people who make them do not believe them, but they are addressed to the young men of the country with the object of giving them the idea that corruption exists in high places, and that for a man to enter public life he has to defile himself. I do not believe there is any truth in such a charge, and the men who make it insult the public life of Canada and the whole people of the Dominion. (Applause.) We have here in the presence of this audience to-day an answer to the query made by these gentlemen, and the effect of this magnificent gathering will be felt, not only throughout the length and breadth of Ontario, but of the Dominion. I am proud to see representatives of the different provinces of the Dominion here, among them being, from Manitoba, the Hon. John Norquay, the Premier. (Applause.) We have also here the Speaker of the Legislative Assembly of that Province, and members of the Cabinet and members not in the Cabinet from the neighbouring Province of Quebec. I think the presence of these men indicates what has been the guiding star of Sir John Macdonald throughout his career. He has recognized that we are a people composed of persons of different nationalities, race, and religion, and has devoted his energies to the purpose of welding them into one great Canadian nationality. (Cheers.) In order to carry out such a magnificent enterprise he joined hands with that patriot who has long since gone to his grave, Sir George Cartier, in uniting and forming and building up, upon a new and more liberal basis, the Conservative party, and concentrating their energies upon this scheme. I am convinced that coming here as you do, to evince your appreciation of Sir John Macdonald, there is no effort in his career which you will appreciate more or so much as his consolidation of the provinces of the Dominion. (Cheers.) I have spoken longer than I intended, and now declare the meeting open for the transaction of the business of the convention. (Cheers.)

THE SECRETARIES.

Mayor BOSWELL here came forward and was received with loud applause. He said :—" I have been requested to make a motion before this large audience in regard to the election of secretaries of the convention, because we shall not be able to do the business we have before us with only one secretary. As Mayor of Toronto I extend to the Conservatives of this great province a hearty welcome to the Conservative city of Toronto. (Cheers.) I beg leave to move that Messrs. Carruthers, of St. Thomas, Maguire, of Kingston, and Pepler, of Barrie, be the secretaries of this convention." (Applause.)

Mr. GUILLETT seconded the motion.

The resolution was carried.

MOVING THE ADDRESS.

HON. J. B. PLUMB then came forward to address the meeting, and was received with loud cheers. He said :—It is difficult to express to you the feelings with which an old soldier of the line comes forward to-day to meet so many of his comrades in the victories which have been won by the Conservative party, and in which he fought side by side with them. (Cheers.) It is truly an occasion upon which the Conservative party can congratulate itself when it meets here to-day to do honour to the chieftain who has led it so often to victory, and also while doing honour to him to do honour to itself. I did not suppose when I came on the platform that I would be permitted to take any part as a speaker to-day, but I am asked to perform a duty which I shall do in a very few words, and which will be preliminary to the opening of the regular business of the convention. I again say I congratulate you upon having responded to the call by which you are assembled here to-day. I believe this is a most important occasion for the Conservative party, and that it will have the effect of hurling back upon the heads of those who have uttered them, the vituperations they have poured out for the last four months upon the great leader of the party, and show that the great heart of the Conservative party is unmoved and untouched by their slanders. (Cheers.) It will have the effect of rebuking the slanderers. But we do not want to silence them, but rather prefer that they should go on, because I believe they are playing our game as well as it could be possibly played by them. I have been charged with the duty of presenting for adoption by this great meeting an address to be given to the thrice honoured chieftain who is soon to be amongst us. (Cheers.) That address has been printed and is in your hands. In order to avoid the necessity of reading it twice, because it will be read to our chieftain, I propose that it be accepted as read, and adopted as the sense of this meeting and a reflex of the opinions of the Conservative party. This address in brief is a recognition of our feeling towards him as our chosen leader, and I trust in the providence of God that, having returned with renewed health and added honours from the Mother Country, he may long be spared to lead the Conservative party ; and not only the Conservative party but the people of Canada onward in a path of prosperity.

> "Like that far famous sea whose tideful flow
> Ne'er knows retiring ebb, but keeps due on,
> Through the Propontis and the Hellespont,
> To feed and swell the illimitable deep."

(Cheers.) He moved that the address be received and adopted.

Mr. H. E. CLARKE, M.P.P., said :—I have very great pleasure, indeed, in seconding the resolution for the adoption of this address, as presented by the Hon. Mr. Plumb. I have just one or two remarks to make and won't detain you for two minutes, as I know you are anxious to hear our veteran chief. (Applause.) We are here to welcome him on his return home to us laden with fresh honours from our Sovereign Lady the Queen, and in bestowing the Grand Cross of the Bath on Sir John, I think Her Majesty has paid a high compliment to the Dominion whose great representative he is. (Applause.) We meet also to show that the Conservative party of Ontario is ready to repeat the lesson of 1872 and 1882—(cheers)—if there is anyone blue-moulding for want of the lesson. (Laughter and cheers.) I have very great pleasure, indeed, in seconding the resolution.

The CHAIRMAN—You have heard the resolution, is it your pleasure that the motion be adopted ?

The motion was adopted unanimously, amid loud applause.

HANDING IN THE ADDRESSES.

The CHAIRMAN—While we are waiting for Sir John I will ask that the addresses from the different constituencies be handed in now, so that we may save time.

Addresses were accordingly handed in from the various constituencies. Many of them were beautiful works of art, more particularly those of Algoma and Cornwall. The following are selections from them :

ALGOMA.—"To shield the weak, was one of the virtues inculcated of old by the bards of your native land, and in the mystic language of Ossian, the King of Morven is represented as better satisfied that 'the neck rested behind the lightning of his steel,' than with the victories he had gained. Among the many laurels you have deservedly won in forty years of public life, those which the native races are sure to twine may not perhaps be the least enduring."

BROCKVILLE.—"It is a great satisfaction to the loyal people of this country that the Premier of the Dominion, and the leader of the Conservative party, is one whom our beloved Queen delighted to honour. For nearly half a century you have been the guiding star of the party, leading them on through times of difficulty and danger, even when they seemed but the forlorn hope."

SOUTH BRANT.—"At much personal sacrifice you have done more to promote and advance by your wise counsel, patriotism, and statesmanship, the material interests, welfare and happiness of the people than any other statesman who has had a controlling power in the administration of its political affairs."

WEST BRUCE.—" We beg to tender our congratulations upon the honourable distinction which her Most Gracious Majesty the Queen has recently been pleased to confer upon you, and we are proud as a party in the possession of a great leader whose services have so often called forth in a distinctive manner the appreciation of the authorities in the Mother Country."

CARLETON.—" For forty years you have devoted yourself to the service of your country. Not among the living, nor of those who have passed away, is there one who has done so much to mould its destinies. We believe that if God spares you to add another decade to the service of your country, your half century may end in the consummation of the great triumph of the age—the grand union of every country, and every clime where floats the British flag."

CORNWALL.—" The members of the association take a pardonable pride in pointing to the fact that, ever since its formation the principles of the great constitutional party have triumphed in the constituency, and members thoroughly in accord with those principles have been returned to represent the constituency in the Federal Parliament. We beg to assure you that the same spirit of fidelity which has secured triumphs in the past still exists to guarantee them in the future."

EAST DURHAM.—" Under your guiding hand an affectionate and loyal devotion to the Crown has been permanently established, the resources of this vast territory developed, and the best interests of the country and its people promoted."

WEST DURHAM.—" The history of Canada during your long tenure of power has nothing but the most gratifying reminiscences for the great Liberal-Conservative party, of which for thirty years and upwards you have been the acknowledged and undoubted leader. With its aid before Confederation you settled justly and satisfactorily most difficult and disturbing questions, national and religious, such as the clergy reserves, seignorial tenure, schools, etc. ; with its aid you succeeded in creating out of a number of uninfluential, scattered, and detached provinces a grand Confederation, destined to be the greatest and most valuable appanage of the British Crown ; with its aid you have carried to completion some of the greatest and most important works on this continent, namely, the Intercolonial and Pacific railways; with its aid you have given to Canada her most useful legislative enactments, and her most successful financial policy."

FRONTENAC.—"We consider the present occasion a fitting one to express our sincere respect for you as the leader of our party, and our admiration for the statesmanlike and loyal qualities you possess, and which have been so fully recognized, not only by all parties in the Dominion, but by the Mother Country and the neighbouring Republic. We wish you, sir, to kindly accept from us the accompanying testimonial as a slight token of the respect and esteem in which you are held by the Liberal-Conservatives of the old county of Frontenac and as a political birthday gift, on this the fortieth anniversary of your entering public life." Mr. — Wilmott here handed Sir John A. a magnificent silver epergne.

HAMILTON (Junior Conservative Association).—" Your proposed legislation on the subject of the extension of the franchise whereby those engaged in mechanical pursuits will possess the same rights and privileges as those enjoyed by farmers' sons, and the humanitarian provisions of your proposed Factory Act commend themselves to the approval of all the members of our association."

HAMILTON.—" Forty years of work in the public service of the country, marked by wisdom in design, skill in execution, and lofty patriotism."

WEST HASTINGS.—" We also, with feelings of profound pride, congratulate you upon the fresh honours worthily won and graciously conferred upon you by Her Most

Gracious Majesty the Queen, in recognition of your long and eminent public services to this the most important of her Majesty's colonial possessions, and earnestly pray that you may long be spared to enjoy them."

WEST HURON.—" We congratulate you upon your long and successful career as the foremost statesman of this our common country and land of adoption. We also beg leave to tender our congratulations upon the present satisfactory state of affairs, brought about in a great measure by those wise and beneficial fiscal changes inaugurated under your present administration. The rapid completion of our transcontinental railway, with the furtherance of which undertaking your name and policy will ever stand identified, is one of the most significant features of your latest *regime;* and we hail with satisfaction the fact that your services in that direction have been gracefully recognized and appreciated by the Imperial authorities. The cementing together of the provinces of Canada into one homogeneous whole, through the completion of that great project, would seem a fitting prelude to that greater union forshadowed in your recent utterances in England. We beg to express our entire concurrence with and appreciation of the principles enunciated in those utterances, and we hasten to give expression to our full approbation of any scheme looking toward a closer connection with the Mother Land."

KINGSTON.—" The task of confederating the provinces which now form this Dominion was accomplished chiefly through your energy and influence, and your name will live in history as the promoter of that great and desirable work. To you also is chiefly due the merit of having inaugurated a policy which has had and will have the effect of building up our country and fostering our manufacturing interests. Though conservative, you have been ready to adopt all useful reforms, and your administration of public affairs has been characterized by energy and vigor. The great majority of the people of Canada, sir, are fully aware of the extent of the debt which this country owes you for having devoted your life to its service. They recognize the fact that, disregarding the attractions of wealth and comfort, which your great talents placed easily within your reach, you have unreservedly given your whole time and abilities to the interest of the public."

LONDON.—" The completion of Confederation is the crowning triumph of your statesmanship. While your opponents trembled and fainted by the way your own high courage enabled you to recognize the giant strength that was in the people of Canada to accomplish this task, and to cheer them on to its consummation."

EAST MIDDLESEX.—" We trust that you, our tried and trusted leader, may, with renewed health, be spared for many years to witness the result of the great measures for the welfare of Canada, in the production of which you have taken the leading part, and in doing this we re-echo the sentiments of the leading statesmen of both parties in Great Britain, as evinced by their recent utterances, in which your services to Canada and the Mother Country have been so flatteringly recognized."

SOUTH LANARK.—" To your labours, under Providence, we owe all the great and manifold advantages which as Canadians we now enjoy."

SOUTH SIMCOE.—" May you long live to see the happy results of your wise legislation."

PERTH.—" We congratulate you on your being spared to see the practical consummation of the three great achievements of your political life—the Confederation of the Provinces, the introduction and carrying out of the National Policy, and the virtual completion of the Canadian Pacific Railway."

PETERBOROUGH, WEST RIDING.—" Connection with the British Empire being one of the most important articles in the creed of Liberal-Conservatism, your supporters, unlike their opponents, heartily appreciate the distinguished honours which Her Most Gracious Majesty has from time to time been pleased to bestow upon you, and they feel more than ordinary pride in the recent addition to these honours."

RENFREW, NORTH.—" We as Conservatives of North Renfrew are proud to own you as our political chieftain, and we point with pride to the fact that North

Renfrew has been loyal to you through cloud as well as through sunshine. We feel it a high privilege to be represented here to-day in this grand gathering of Conservatives assembled in your honour. Trusted by your Queen, beloved by your friends, feared, yet respected, by your enemies, you can well look back with pride and pleasure upon the last forty years as well spent in the service of your country."

ST. THOMAS.—"We desire to congratulate our chief on the completion of the fortieth year of his public life. As the veteran statesman who has controlled and guided the destinies of Canada for the greater part of the last half century; as the framer of the great scheme of Canadian Confederation, and as its steadfast protector from its inception until now; as the statesman who has carried to the verge of completion that great national undertaking, the Canadian Pacific Railway; as Canada's chief statesman and Prime Minister, we recognize in Sir John the one most deserving of honour, whether at the hands of the Crown or of the people."

SOUTH VICTORIA.—"We have learned with feelings of the deepest gratification of the honour Her Majesty the Queen has been pleased to bestow upon you, and regard it as a graceful and fitting tribute to your ability and loyalty, and an appropriate recognition of the many years' service in the cause of good government in your adopted country."

WELLINGTON (CENTRE).—"During your forty years of public life there have been few great measures in the policy and government of our country which have not received their first impulses from your foresight and wisdom, and their final consummation under the guidance of your genius.

"The union of the Provinces in the Confederation of the Dominion of Canada will ever stand as a monument of your wisdom and high statesmanship, and the hitherto harmonious working of that union amid so many conflicting interests is another evidence of that liberal and high-minded policy which has ever actuated you as the head of the Government.

"Under the fostering influences of the wise tariff, framed and carried into effect by your Government, dying industries have been infused with fresh life, new manufactories have been successfully established, a flagging trade has been revived, and the general prosperity of our country largely increased.

"Your expressions of firm attachment to the British throne and loyalty to our beloved Queen find an echo in the heart of every Canadian Conservative."

WROXETER VILLAGE.—"It is our earnest prayer that you may long be spared in health and happiness to witness the fruits of your labours, and that the day is far distant when you will cease to be the ruling mind of the Dominion and the trusted guardian of its best interests."

WEST LAMBTON.—"We congratulate you on being spared to see the practical consummation of the three great achievements of your political life—the Confederation of the Provinces, the introduction and successful carrying out of the National Policy, and the virtual completion of the Canada Pacific Railway—all of which great schemes have been initiated and perfected by administrations of which you were the head."

HALTON.—"We regard the Grand Cross of the Order of the Bath conferred upon you by Her Majesty as a graceful and fitting tribute to your ability, loyalty, and worth, and an appropriate recognition of your forty years of faithful service to your country. We congratulate you that at the end of your fortieth year of public life you still retain the admiration and confidence of the great majority of your fellow-countrymen."

NORTH LEEDS AND GRENVILLE.—The legislation of forty years, in which you have borne so conspicuous a part, is the most fitting tribute to your ability, loyalty, and patriotism, and when the history of Canada comes to be written your unselfish devotion to your country's interests will be an important factor of it, and long after those who have vilified and traduced you are forgotten your life-service to Canada will remain as one of its brightest pages."

Prince Edward.—" The men of the county of Prince Edward feel a glow of family pride when they remember that you are one of them. Though not born among them you grew to manhood in their midst, and formed among them the character that has given you success in life. The memory of our youth together has added a feeling of kinship to our patriotic pride, as we have watched with unvarying interest and increasing confidence your public career."

Hastings, East.—" Your advocacy of equal rights to all parties irrespective of creed or society arouses a kindly feeling towards you in the hearts of all."

Prescott.—" For forty years you have been favourably conspicuous in active political life in Canada, ever prominent in conciliating, amalgamating, and consolidating the various representative elements of the people of this great and important country."

Russell.—" Beg to assure you of their continued confidence in your leadership, marked as it has been throughout by wise, patriotic, and successful statesmanship, and blessed by advancement and prosperity."

The presentation of these addresses was provocative of numerous interesting incidents. Glengarry, Kingston, London, and Toronto were received with enthusiastic applause. Halton evoked the exclamation, " That's the Scott Act county," and laughter. North Bruce handed in a handsome blue silk banner, made by the ladies of that constituency, on one side of which appeared in letters of white silk, " North Bruce venerates forty years of statesmanship and patriotism," and on the reverse, " For Canada and the Empire."

SIR JOHN'S ARRIVAL.

Shortly after two o'clock Sir John Macdonald entered the building, and his appearance on the platform, accompanied by Sir Hector Langevin, Sir David Macpherson, his Worship the Mayor, and other gentlemen, was the occasion of indescribable enthusiasm. The vast audience cheered itself hoarse, hats were thrown up, delegates rose in their seats, the banners from the dress circle fluttered, while, to add to the interest of the occasion, the fair ladies in the boxes waved their handkerchiefs as demonstratively as any of those in the audience. The cheering was again and again taken up, it finally subsiding after a venerable looking farmer in the audience had stood up and called, " Let's give him a tiger." The tiger was given in due course, and then the audience resumed their seats.

THE ADDRESS TO THE PREMIER.

The Chairman addressing the Premier, then said—Sir John Macdonald, I have been directed by the unanimous voice of this meeting to present to you this address:—

To the Right Honourable Sir John Macdonald, M.P., P.C., L.L.D., D.C.L., G.C.B.:

Right Hon. Sir,—At the close of the fortieth year since your entrance into public life, your friends and supporters in Ontario—assembled in convention from every constituency of the Province, and representing alike those who have followed your fortunes from old times and those who have grown into manhood and increased in political knowledge during your career—desire to address to you this public expression of their cordial congratulation.

This greeting comes not alone from those Conservatives with whom your earlier years were associated, but also from those later Conservatives whom you educated to newer views of the needs and duties of their political school, and from those Liberals who saw in your acts and policy the noblest of reasons for joining their force to yours in the formation of the triumphant and now historical body of Liberal-Conservatives, and who in 1878 and 1882 renewed the expression of their confidence by giving your Administration their support.

It is with the pride becoming British subjects that we find this happy event coincident with an increase in those distinguishing honours by which the Crown has, on this as on so many former occasions, recognized and rewarded the services of a life devoted to the advancement of British interests and the strengthening of the bulwarks of British power on this continent, by the foundation, government, and development of the Dominion of Canada.

It is with satisfaction we have learned that the ceremony of conferring these new honours was assisted at by the illustrious Liberal Premier of Great Britain, and that the chiefs of the historic Conservative party joined with their distinguished rivals—even in the midst of a political conflict in which the future of the Imperial Constitution is involved—in doing honour to our own chief, whose best thought was always for the good of the Empire, whatever party was uppermost in the Imperial councils.

And it is with a feeling of prideful exaltation that we reflect that these added honours and this happy occasion occur at a time when, by the voice of the electors of Canada, you have been, for the fourth time since the foundation of the Dominion, called to guide its destiny and to govern its people. While all parts of the Dominion and all sections of the people have been faithful to your banner, we shall be allowed at this time to record our satisfaction in thinking that your friends in Ontario have been in an especial manner faithful to your fortunes and jealous for your fame.

The germs of power sprang early from your political labours, and have grown with your increasing years. The forty years during which you have laboured in our service, and for our good, may seem short to you, as all men's lives do when looked back upon from the summit of high accomplishment, after years of labour that have been too full of events to allow of thought as to their length ; but within that space there have occurred all the political and national triumphs of which the present and the departing generation are proud ; and with all of these memorable events the historians of Canada must always most honourably connect your name.

The happy results of British rule in North America, begun when the policy of Pitt was accomplished by the valour of Wolfe, would have been imperfect, if not frustrated, but for the cordial relations which you have nearly for half a century maintained, in spite of unjust and unpatriotic criticism, with the loyal men of genius who have been the chiefs of the loyal Canadians of Quebec ; and on this occasion we would mingle with our felicitations to yourself a tribute of grateful remembrance of Cartier, whose statue rises in another city to bear witness to his public deeds and to keep his memory green.

The hopes of Imperial, and the policy of Canadian statesmen to found a strong and lasting confederation of the British North American Provinces might have been prevented from early accomplishment but for your unselfish conduct, your generous recognition of the sincerity of political opponents, your willingness to admit to your counsels men of genius and skill when the service of the nation was paramount to the service of party. And history will recall with impartial admiration your agreement in policy and your continuance in friendship with Brown, and Howe, with Hincks, and McGee, representing phases of opinion which, with the quick sympathy of genius, you conciliated at a time of crisis to the service of the State.

In a Confederation in which the people are divided by very earnest and sincere differences of opinion in race, religion, and political sentiment, unity of action and harmony of thought have been maintained with striking success by the wisdom, tact, and true liberality with which you have made alike the Cabinet, the Provincial Executives, the Bench, the Bar, and the Public Service, bear witness to your forethought and care for the interests of races, creeds and opinions as part of the forces by which nations are governed, and by the wise conduct of which they grow strong, united, and prosperous.

By the side of the Great Republic which revolted from British rule, you have been mainly instrumental in raising up another British Dominion, with a constitution founded upon the British model, and framed in express avoidance of the weakness which time had discovered in the Republican Constitution of the United States; and for the space of twelve out of the seventeen years of its existence, you have laboured to prove that this British experiment could be a brilliant success. Those who have most wisely considered the ill effects which flowed from the want of a balanced constitution with a strong central government, in the United States, will most earnestly defend the wisdom of your policy, and most sincerely admit the success of the Canadian Constitution.

While those who were for a brief period entrusted with power in your stead refused, in times of public distress, to risk their political fortunes in any experiments for the relief of industry and the employment of labour, your Administration has been remarkable for the number and the courage of its national experiments and enterprises. The building of the Pacific railway, the encouragement of national industries, and the development of the North-West have been undertaken with an energy in which your opponents, who did nothing, have discovered recklessness and haste, but in which labour and capital, commerce and manufactures, agriculture and mining, parliament and the people, have recognized spirited and statesmanlike efforts for the increase of public prosperity.

While your opponents have been deceptively proclaiming their own alleged success in obtaining a judgment from the Privy Council favourable to the territorial claims of this province, the public records show, and the public memory indelibly records, that you strongly insisted, more than ten years ago, on an appeal to the Privy Council for a final, legal and permanent settlement of the boundaries of Ontario; that your opponents then refused your advice, and did for ten years thwart the appeal, thereby depriving Ontario of her just rights during that time, deceiving the people with false cries, making vain pretence of seeking for a settlement which they, in fact, wished to prevent, and unfairly flinging on your shoulders the blame of their own needless, factious, and unpatriotic delay. Your advice when taken at last, under the stress of legal proceedings, resulted in a territorial gain for Ontario. Had it been taken earlier the gain would have been greater; your opponents' policy resulted in ten years' of loss and delay which can hardly be recovered and made good to this province in the lifetime of the present generation.

The Empire has witnessed your efforts to make it greater still; and our Empress-Queen has royally rewarded you with honours which all men prize.

British statesmen have recognized your genius, and have extended to you that fraternal recognition and friendship which will link your memory with theirs in the splendid traditions of public life.

The Dominion of Canada has appreciated your statesmanship, and has bestowed on you the highest gift in its possession—the right to control its fortunes.

The provinces of the Union have approved of your policy, and have sent their best leaders to support you, with the majority of their followers.

The individual citizen has recognized in you one whose interest in even personal rights has not been lessened by the continual contemplation of national problems.

And we, your followers, your friends—counting our years from old time, and counting them only long enough to qualify us for giving you the support of citizenship—wish on this occasion to express to you our joy in your restored health, our gratitude to the Crown for the honours bestowed upon you, our prayers to Heaven for length of days for you and yours, for continued health and prolonged power, and renewed opportunities of benevolent and brilliant statesmanship. We conclude by expressing our conviction, in language which it was your privilege of genius to employ, "that there has never been in this land a man who has given more of his time, more of his health, more of his heart, and more of his intellect, to the service of the people of Canada."

THE PREMIER.

SIR JOHN A. MACDONALD :—Mr. Meredith and gentlemen, I would indeed be unreasonable if I did not receive this address and this cordial greeting with feelings of the deepest emotion. I can assure you, gentlemen, that during my long and varied career no moment of my life can approach to the culmination of all the various kindnesses and all the honours that have been bestowed upon me from Crown and people—no instance in my life, I say, can at all approach to the gratification with which I receive this greeting. (Cheers.) To have been in Parliament and in public life for forty long years ; to have fought the various battles of the party ; to have struggled with strong, able and earnest opponents ; to have been the object of attack, of insult, of contumely and of obloquy ; to have with all this, and after all this, at the end of my career a greeting such as this ; to receive such assurances of your kindness—I may say, of your affection—(loud cheers)—to hear the eloquent language in which my services have been spoken of in the address you have just read, make me indeed a proud man. (Hear, hear.) At the same time, Mr. Chairman and gentlemen, I must say that my feelings are commingled. This is not only a great and glorious incident in my career, but it is a very solemn one. When I look back through my forty years of public life ; when I remember how few remain of those who with me entered full of hope, life, and the earnestness of youth; when I bear in mind that those who do remain are like myself, feeble old men—(cries of "No, no,")—when I think I am now approaching, if I have not already approached, the culmination of my career—(cries of "No. no," and a voice, "You'll never die, John A.") — when I think of all this, feelings of a most solemn nature are awakened in my mind. But if most of the friends of my youth have departed I still have the gratification of knowing that they are succeeded by their sons and their grandsons—some, indeed, by their great grandsons—and that in addressing these I speak to men thoroughly imbued with the feeling of patriotism, the devotion to Liberal-Conservative and Conservative-Liberal principles which marked the characters of their ancestors forty years ago, and I have the further consolation as a Canadian and as a party man of knowing that the country and the party are safe in the hands of such men and of those other supporters of mine who are so nobly represented in this present meeting. (Cheers.) I heard a cry just now from one of my friends saying, "You will never die." (Laughter.) Gentlemen, I really do believe that those who are in political opposition to me think so too—(renewed laughter)—and I fear though they pray for me and all other like sinners, that in their supplications there is no pious expression of the desire that my life may be long spared. (Loud laughter.) They have no objection that I should go to another and a better world, so that I should not prolong my stay in this. (Loud laughter.) I am happy, gentlemen, to state to you that your good wishes with respect to the renewal and the continuance of my health, have been to a very great extent realized. (Loud cheering.) Thanks to a good conscience and Sir Andrew Clark, I come back to you nearly as good as new (cheers and laughter)—a little the worse for wear to be sure—(laughter)—but still able to stand the battle for a few years longer. (Cheers.) I was much amused, gentlemen, when in England, to read a sentence in a Toronto newspaper stating that the position of the Opposition was simply this, "If John A.'s stomach gives in, then the Opposition will go in—(loud laughter)—but if John A.'s stomach holds out, then we will stay out. (Continued laughter.) You will be glad to know that there are strong indications that they will stay out." (Hear, hear.) I think, gentlemen, it will be admitted that since 1844, when I entered Parliament, Canada has made some progress. (Hear, hear.) Even those who malign Canada, who belittle its resources, who have retarded its development, who have praised up other lands to the disparagement of our own, will admit that there has been great progress in Canada one way and another since 1844. (Hear, hear.) Now I may say that during the time that progress has been going on—during the forty years in which I have been in Parliament,

I shall have been in May next twenty-five years in the Government. (Cheers.) There are, then, fifteen years left during which, though in Parliament, I was not in office. In 1847 I became a Minister. But for two years before I became a Minister, Canada was governed by a Conservative Administration, which I was elected to support. So that of the whole of the forty years during which I have been in Parliament, there are only thirteen years in which the Liberals or Grits have held the reins of power. (Hear, hear, and a voice, "Good.") Therefore, if this country has made any progress ; if it has been developed ; if it has grown from a collection of small feeble provinces into a great Dominion, its advancement must to some degree be dependent upon the legislation and the administration of the various Governments of which I have been a member. (Applause.) Thirteen years of the forty years are all the years for which the present Opposition can claim any share of the development of the Dominion or of the old Province of Canada ; and gentlemen, even of these thirteen years the Grit party cannot claim the whole. They can only claim five—(hear, hear)—the years during which Mr. Mackenzie was Premier—for before that time, Canada's destinies were swayed by a Government of which I was not a member, viz. : the Baldwin-Lafontaine Administration, which was not a Grit, but a Conservative-Liberal Government. (Hear, hear.) We were afterwards ruled by the Hincks-Morin Government, which was also a Liberal—a Reform Government if you will—but not a Grit Government. (Hear, hear.) Therefore, when we read of the development of Canada, and of the great progress it has made in numbers and in area, we must remember that but an insignificant portion of that development and of that progress can be at all attributed to the present Opposition in the Canadian Parliament—(hear, hear).—And of those various Liberal Governments what can I say ? What can I tell you in looking back ? To the Baldwin-Lafontaine Government I was opposed. I was elected to vote against it. But we respected each other's differences of opinion, giving credit to opponents for their conscientious support of their own cause, as they gave us credit for acting as we believed to be best in the interests of our country. We respected each other, although we were opposed to each other ; and by slow degrees Mr. Baldwin, who was the leader of the Government which I opposed, ended by giving his cordial approbation to the coalition which was formed with the best and the ablest of his party in 1854. (Cheers.) And so, Mr. Chairman and gentlemen, with respect to the Reform Government which succeeded the Baldwin-Lafontaine Government—the Hincks-Morin Government—so strong were our principles, although we were really opposed, so much did we respect each other's opinions, so much confidence had we in each other's honesty, that when the time came both Mr. Morin—the leader of the French-Canadian Conservatives, of whom you have spoken so justly in this address—became my colleague, and, in after years, when Sir Francis Hincks, after considerable service in other colonies as representative of the Queen, came back to Canada—our relations had been so pleasant, our confidence in each other was so strong that I did not hesitate to ask him to become Finance Minister of a Conservative Administration. He came to us, and in the future we acted cordially together, because both in the case of the Baldwin-Lafontaine Ministry and in that of the Hincks-Morin Administration, we believed in each other, and whenever we differed we differed honestly in opinion, and whenever we agreed we could act cordially together. (Cheers.) Mr. Chairman and gentlemen, when I entered Parliament in 1844, the prospects of the old Province of Canada were not brilliant. The embers of the old hostility between the races still caused a strain, the events of 1837-38 and '39 still existed in the peoples' mind, the peoples of the two provinces were drawn up against each other, the two races were formed into hostile armies ready to fly at each other's throats. The French-Canadians in Lower Canada had their constitution taken away from them, they were forced into the union without their consent. The assent of Upper Canada had been obtained, but by no very great majority. When they were assembled together in 1841 in the town of Kingston they met as if they were drawn up in battle array, and not for the purpose of peaceable legislation for the good of the country. By slow degrees this feeling has been dissipated and has disappeared, and now what do we see ? We see the Conservative party of Lower Canada, the French-Canadian Conservatives—true Conservatives by their instincts, by their antecedents, and by their institutions—joining cordially hand in hand with the Liberal-Conservatives of the other provinces, giving us a Conservative Government in 1878, maintaining it at the polls in 1882, as they will give us a Conservative majority in 1887. (Cheers.) Gentlemen, when I spoke to you of the growth of this country, of the development of every portion of it in all that constitutes progress and prosperity, all that constitutes advancement of civilization—(a pause)—Gentlemen, you must excuse me, I am sometimes overcome by the emotion which arises in my mind from this cordial greeting which you have given me. (Loud cheers.) But in speaking of the development of this country, I did not mean to say that it was altogether attributable to our great genius, to our great wisdom, to the great energy, or to the great power of the Administration. I claim for the various Administrations of which I have been a member that they have at least materially assisted and had a share in all this development and progress. (Cheers.) In order to show you, gentlemen, the nature and extent of that progress, I shall read to you some returns, instances of the development of the country. In 1844, the population of British North America, leaving out Newfoundland, which is still a separate province, was 1,600,000 ; in 1884 we may fairly call it 5,000,000. The progress in education, which of course, since 1867 has belonged to the different provinces, has been equally great. During the past forty years the expenditure has grown from $700,000 to nine and a-half millions. The pupils have increased from 174,000 to close upon one million, and the teachers from 5,300 to nearly 20,000. The Government which I supported in 1844 increased the grant for education by $235,000. At the same time they increased the annual grant in aid of the agricultural societies by $25,000, and the amount for public works by $350,000. The Government of 1844 cut down expenses in several directions by nearly $25,000. And yet, gentlemen, we have been called extravagant. (Cheers.) Ever since I have been in the Government, the Governments with which I have been connected have been charged with being wasteful of the public resources. We commenced, at all events, in 1844 by cutting down $25,000 in order to give money directly for the people's benefit. It is true that if you compare the payments shown in the public accounts forty years ago with those of to-day there is an enormous difference, and the total amount is hugely greater than it was. So it is, I must confess, with the expenditure, which has largely increased, but at the same time the expenditure has all been for the good of the country. (Cheers.) It is very easy to pick out a large sum expended in one year and contrast it with a small sum expended years before, and then cry out, " See what an extravagant Government this is." We might just as well charge Baron Rothschild with being extravagant. The founder of the family commenced by collecting second-hand corks and selling them at a profit. His expenditure was probably a few cents a week. Before his career was ended his expenditure was some hundreds of thousands of dollars, but then his fortune was perhaps millions. Commodore Vanderbilt commenced his operations by running a ferry through to Brooklyn at a cost of a few dollars per week. Afterwards his expenditure increased to hundreds of thousands of dollars, but at the same time his credit and fortune increased proportionately. So with Canada. As we grew from a few scattered provinces into a great country we grew in wealth and resources. As we expanded into one united and important nation great responsibilities and expenditure were called for, and this is my answer to the charge that we have been guilty of extravagance. Strange to say, notwithstanding all the enormous expenditure of the funds of the country with which we have been charged, both the wealth and credit of the Dominion have steadily increased. I remember well that the old Province of Canada could not borrow a farthing in England or the capitals of Europe at a less percentage than 6 per cent. To-day, although we have incurred large obligations and the national debt has been increased, and although we have been charged with extravagance of every kind, yet by slow degrees—well, perhaps, not so very slow— our credit has risen, and we were able to borrow at five per cent., then at four per cent., until at the present time we could go into the English market and obtain all the money we wanted at three and a-half per cent. (Cheers.) During the period in which I have been connected with the Government, we have not always been so extremely prosperous. There are times of shrinkage and depression, and there are times of expansion. There are times of great enterprise and commercial activity, and those of little enterprise and little activity. We have had during the last forty years many vicissitudes to encounter in this variable world. But during all that time, whether in the height of prosperity or in the despondency of temporary depression, we have never lost confidence in the future of Canada. (Cheers.) We knew that the prosperity of this country was based upon a solid foundation of good laws, a good climate, a fertile soil, and a law-abiding and industrious population, and we knew that these seasons of adversity could be only temporary in their nature, and that the invaluable resources of Canada must in the long run place her where she has been ever since 1867, with the exception of the five years of Grit rule. (Laughter.) But we began well, for we had a surplus of $340,000 in our treasury. In 1874-75 Sir Richard Cartwright would have been very happy even then to have had so large a surplus. But to go on with a statement of the development of Canada in all its material source of wealth, I would call attention to the marine of the country. The increase in the number of steam and sailing vessels during the forty years has been 3,233, or in tonnage 951,829 tons. Canada has 38 tons carrying power to every hundred inhabitants. The United States has 17, Australia 20, Europe 10, Norway 95, the United Kingdom 51. Canada stands third in regard to its population as to the tonnage which it floats on every sea. (Cheers.) In close connection with this subject is the lighting of the coasts. We, in our northern latitude of tempestuous seas must, of course, take care that our sailors and vessels are protected from shipwreck by an efficient and sufficient system of lighthouses. In 1840 Canada as now constituted had 41 lighthouses, while she has now 569 lighthouses, 36 fog alarms and 10 automatic buoys, being excelled among the nations by only two, the United Kingdom and the United States. When we took office in 1854, when the provinces were united, the lighthouses were very indifferent and insufficient, and required immediate increase. I had the good fortune to have for Minister of Marine and Fisheries an active and zealous colleague, who was himself a ship-owner and ship-builder, and knew exactly the wants of our commercial marine. I allude to the Hon. Peter Mitchell. (Applause.) To him we owe the protected state of our coast along the Atlantic shore. With respect to trade in 1844, the imports and the exports of the provinces now constituting Canada amounted in the aggregate to thirty-three and a half millions of dollars. That sounds very large. But in 1883 it was over 230 millions. According to the last census of the United States the aggregate trade of that country in merchandise amounted to about $30 per head of the population. In our last census year the same trade was equal to $47 per head in the Dominion of Canada. (Cheers.) Now, as to our exports, as to what we send out of our country to foreign countries to pay for the goods that we import; during forty years the exports of the products of the mines of Canada have increased—how much do you think, gentlemen? One hundred per cent? Is that too much. During forty years the exports of the products of the mines of Canada have increased 990 per cent.—(loud cheers)—of the forests 196 per cent.—(cheers.)—of the fisheries 719 per cent.—(cheers)—of animals and their products 8,452 per cent.—(cheers)—of agriculture 721 per cent., and the export of our manufactures had increased from $6,229—that was all we exported of manufactures in 1844—to $3,500,000. (Loud cheers.) Take one article which will interest the agriculturists of Canada more especially, take the single article of cheese. The export of cheese in 1844 amounted to $5,250 in all, and in 1883 to $7,252,000. (Cheers.) The export of cattle in 1844 amounted to $1,440, in 1883 to $3,900,000. (Loud cheers.) I need not say much about the evidences of increasing prosperity in our postal communication, as my good friend and colleague Mr. Carling has lately expatiated on the subject. I will, however, only say that in 1844 there went through the post-offices of the several provinces 1,400,000 letters, of which 1,200,000 were sent not beyond 400 miles of the senders' residences because of cost, the rates of postage being 4½d. for 60 miles, and running up according to a scale to 2s. 3d. a letter if carried a thousand miles. In 1883 the number of letters carried was 90,000,000, and the postage from the Atlantic to the Pacific is but 3c. per letter. (Cheers.) I well remember myself when I had to pay 1s. 6d., 2s., and 3s. a letter under the old system of older Canada. Now, gentlemen, as regards the cost of transport, and as you know, the value of our agricultural crop, especially, depends greatly on the cheapness of the price at which it can be carried to the market to which it is destined. The freight rate in 1844 for a bushel of wheat from Kingston to Montreal was 12½c., and from Chicago to Montreal 28c. For the last ten years the average freight rate on a bushel of wheat from Kingston to Montreal has been a little over 2c., and from Chicago to Montreal a little over 9c. (Cheers.) Now, gentlemen, about the great arteries of transport, the railways. When I entered public life there were 16 miles of railway in operation in Canada. (Laughter.) There are now nearly 10,000 miles. (Cheers.) Canada has $104 invested in railways for each inhabitant, being only excelled by the United Kingdom, which has $107, and by the United States, which have $112. Now as to railway rates. The charge in 1844 was equal to $1.92 per ton and passenger; last year the charge was equal to $1.45. If the rate of 1844 were applied to the passenger and freight traffic of 1883, the result would be the addition of 10¾ millions to the cost of transport. By our railway and canal policy we have reduced the cost of transport so greatly that the saving effected would not only pay the whole interest on our public debt and all the cost of schooling in Ontario, but give the people, through cheapened transport alone, three quarters of a million for pocket money. In all British North America, not including Newfoundland, the deposits of the people in the savings and other banks amounted to six and a-half millions. They are now 151 millions. (Cheers.) In 1844 the total bank circulation was under six millions, in 1884 the circulation, Government and bank, is 45 millions. The value of farm property in Ontario in 1844 was 41 million dollars. In 1883 it was 654 millions. As to our progress since confederation, the deposits of the people have increased in banks, building societies, etc., since 1868, by 127 million dollars. There were 8,500 miles of telegraph wire in 1868 and 39,350 miles in 1883. The messages sent in 1868 numbered 690,000, and in 1883 they were over four millions. The net amount insured by fire policies in 1883 was 384 million dollars more than in 1868. The total amount of life insurances in 1883 was nine million dollars more than in 1868. The total premiums paid for fire and life insurances in 1883 were over five million dollars more than in 1868. (Cheers.) Compared with 1878 the increase in 1883 in vessels entered and cleared was 18,917, and the increase in tonnage arrived and departed was 6½ million tons, the increase in the number of men employed in this branch of industry was 80,000. In 1883 the tonnage arrived and departed in connection with the coasting trade was over 4½ million tons more than in 1878. In 1883 the freight carried by railways was nearly six million tons more than in 1878. (Cheers.) These, gentlemen, are some of the instances of the progress of the country, which, at the risk of being tedious, I thought it well to communicate to you, showing, among the many other indications of the great progress during my political life, the wonderful advance that Canada has made. (Cheers.) In 1844 when I entered Parliament, Responsible Government had been carried. I personally had no act or part in the carrying of that great principle. I must say here that the carrying of that all-important principle of responsible Government, of the people being governed by the advice of a ministry responsible to the people, and supported by the majority of the people, was due in great measure to the persistent efforts of the Reform party in Upper and Lower Canada. They deserve that that credit should be given to them. In the old Province of Upper Canada, Wm. Lyon Mackenzie, Dr. Baldwin, and afterwards his more illustrious son, Robert Baldwin, were the champions of the great principle of responsible government. All Lower Canada was in favour of the same principle, as you know. At the same time we must remember that responsible government was established in 1843 by certain resolutions carried in the united Parliament at Kingston, and those resolutions were introduced and carried by Attorney-General Draper, the leader of the Conservative party of Upper Canada. (Cheers.) So with respect to our municipal institutions, which are, I think, in a very perfect state in Ontario. That system was introduced in a tentative form by Mr. Draper in Upper Canada under the government of the late Lord Sydenham. It was introduced, as the older members of my audience will remember, in a very cautious way. There were no township councils, there were only county councils, and the wardens were in the first instance appointed by the Crown. That system was a great advance, and marks the progress of this country in municipal institutions and local self-government in a most remarkable degree. Why, gentlemen, at this moment England has not such institutions. (Cheers.) At this moment England is trying to obtain such powers of self-government, the present Administration of Mr. Gladstone having promised such a measure, but it has not yet been carried. We are forty years ahead of even our beloved old Mother Country in this matter. (Cheers.) While the merit of initiating this system is due to the late Chief Justice Draper, it was carried out to its present stage of perfection by the labour, the genius, and the ability of Robert Baldwin. (Cheers.) If that statesman had done nothing else, in all his long and illustrious career, than to carry the Municipal bill, which he did in 1848 and 1849—if he had carried no other measure that alone would have been sufficient to render his name illustrious and to entitle him to rank among the greatest statesmen of Canada. (Cheers.) That system is still existing with occasional amendments as experience has shown were necessary ; but the basis, the substance, the groundwork of our municipal system rests upon the united labours of Messrs Draper and Baldwin, the two great leaders of the Liberal-Conservative and the Reform parties of Ontario. When I came into Parliament, therefore, those were settled questions. They did not arise in my time, and I had neither the merit of supporting them nor the demerit of opposing them. But as I have already stated to you, when I entered Parliament the two races were drawn up as it were in hostile array. The future of Canada looked dark. One scarcely saw how we were to escape from the angry feeling—I may say the antipathy—existing between the two races. However, by patience, by moderation, by a desire for conciliation, the two races arrived at a *modus vivendi*, a means of governing this country by united action and in a united Parliament. Still the mutual dislike and distrust continued until it culminated in that most lamentable event, the burning of the Parliament house in Montreal in consequence of the Rebellion Losses bill. The younger men here can scarcely know that such an event happened in our history. I need not speak particularly as to the unhappy causes which ended in the Montreal riots. There had been a rebellion in Lower Canada, and the two races had been fighting. The feeling in Montreal was intense. The English-speaking inhabitants had been drawn up in one camp, the French-Canadians in another. There was a great feeling among the former against the Rebellion Losses bill, and that feeling, fanned as it was by some political agitators, ended in riot, and the destruction of the parliament house. Great was the regret among all law-abiding men at that event. Yet I believe that, under Providence, it was the main cause of the junction of the two races afterwards. Both parties were appalled at the consequences that were imminent. The English-speaking people and especially those in Upper Canada, were shocked at the violence of their own people, and the French people saw that the feelings and prejudices of the English must be respected. They therefore said :—" Here we are in one country ; we see that we cannot be severed ; we must pull in harness together, whether we like it or no." And just here, looking back at that decision, I say I really think the very outrages which took place, the very extremes to which party feeling went, and the shock that was caused by the violence then displayed, helped to bring about the final union of the Conservatives of Upper and Lower Canada. (Cheers.) I, as a humble member of Parliament did all I could to promote that union—(applause)—I cultivated, as far as I could, the acquaintance and friendship of my French-Canadian fellow subjects, and I am happy to tell you, as Canadian history shows, that I did not work in vain. (Cheers.) And although, gentlemen, I am proud to have you as my supporters, and to have the people of Ontario as represented by you at my back, I tell you that no more faithful or loyal friends and supporters are to be found than are to be found among my French-Canadian friends. (Loud cheers.) I have two of them sitting by me at this moment. My lieutenant, Sir Hector Langevin—(cheers)—and my friend the Minister of Militia—(renewed cheering)—both of whom are here to-day giving evidence by their presence of the loyal support of those they represent in Quebec—the majority of the people in that province. (Cheers.) You can well understand the importance to the Conservative party all over the Dominion of that support. (Hear, hear.) The Province of Quebec has sixty-five members, and of those sixty-five members I believe all but fifteen support the present Government. (Cheers.) Gentlemen, long may that union exist. (Renewed applause.) Long may the Conservatives of Ontario and of the Maritime Provinces work in union with the loyal Conservative majority in the Province of Quebec. For, so long as that union exists the constitution—the connection with the mother country—is safe. (Loud and prolonged cheering,) the advancement of this country is safe—law. order and constitutional liberty will continue—(cheers)—and I may add that when a severance takes place, if it ever does take place, I believe it will not be the fault of the French-Canadians. (Loud applause.)

Well, gentlemen, after being only three years in Parliament I was asked in 1847 to join the administration of Mr. Draper. I had but little hopes when I took office that it would be for a long period, but I was told by my party that it was my duty. I have been a party man, gentlemen, as you know. (Laughter.) I was told by my party that it was my duty to join the Government, although the prospects were gloomy, and although there was but little chance that they would be able to hold their majority at the next election. I was told that having put my hand to the plough I should not draw back, because I was a young man, for gentlemen, I was a young man once. (Laughter.) I was told that having taken the responsibility of coming to Parliament and leading the young men in it I must stand or fall by my party. I took office with the idea that my career as a minister would be a very short one. I went through an election believing that in a few months, or in a year or two, at the next general election, my term of office must cease. I think it was my duty to take office, and looking back I am proud of that step, although every feeling of prudence and self-interest was against it, and although it involved the sacrifice of my business, which for a young man was large. Although it was against my pecuniary interest I felt it my duty to yield, and I yielded to the cry of my party. That I did right you, gentlemen, 37 years after I took office have affirmed. (Cheers.) During the short time I was in the Government, a little less than a year, I introduced three measures which, if carried, would most likely have made a great difference in the educational system of Ontario. At that time the University here at Toronto then known as King's College, was governed under an old constitution from England. Under the royal charter it was purely and entirely a Church of England institution. That was attacked most fiercely by the Reform party in Upper Canada and by a great many Conservatives. The measures which I introduced, if carried at that time, would have had a most beneficial effect on the educational system of the people of Ontario. It was proposed that a certain portion of the endowment, (which at that time was large, with a large sum in the treasury) and the whole of the magnificent property known as the University Park, should be settled on King's College which should remain a Church of England institution. It was proposed that an endowment should be given out of the same fund to Victoria College, as representing the Methodists ; to Queen's College, as representing the Presbyterian body ; and to Regiopolis College, as representing the Roman Catholics, and the balance—and there would have been a considerable balance if it had been well administered—was to have been given to the support of grammar and common schools. When I introduced the measure I was in hopes that it would have been carried, and if it had been carried I think the cause of religious education would have been greatly promoted. (Hear, hear.) However, the measures did not receive support from Parliament, and shortly afterwards we retired, and from 1848 until 1854 I was in the cold shades of opposition. At the same time, gentlemen, I am proud to say that our opposition was a legitimate one. It was an honest one, and it was acknowledged to be an honest one by the leaders of the Administration, Messrs. Lafontaine and Baldwin. Again and again have I been thanked by Mr. Baldwin on the floor of the House, because no matter what the temptation in a party sense might have been to vote with the Grit party, which was at that time just raising its head, united to the Rouge party, which had lately been revived in Lower Canada for the purpose of defeating the Government, we never did so. We refused to do so. We were Conservatives, not in a party sense, but in a real honest sense. (Cheers.) We would not sacrifice our principles for the sake of a temporary party triumph. Messrs. Baldwin and Lafontaine could rely upon the Conservative Opposition as well as upon their own followers when any extreme democratic measures were attempted to be forced upon them by the radical republican wing. (Cheers) Well, gentlemen, I wish to speak of the Rebellion Losses bill. The feeling of irritation among my friends of the same race and lineage as myself in Montreal was so extreme that an annexation movement took place in Montreal. It was nearly altogether confined to that city, and you can well understand why the feeling existed there, and why it did not extend much further. The whole of the British race in Montreal had been in arms in 1837-38-39 facing the insurgents. They had been out in the battle field, and some had been killed and their property destroyed. Therefore there was a great feeling of irritation, and that irritation culminated in a strong annexation feeling. The English-speaking people in Montreal said, " Well, if we are to be governed in this way we had better join the United States, for at all events they are of our own blood, lineage, and language." That was a very dangerous feeling, but it met with no response from the Conservatives of Upper Canada—(cheers)—and there was a strong minority in Lower Canada among the British race opposed to them. We had to find out a safety valve, some means of quieting this feeling, some means of carrying on the government of the country in peace and quietness, and that safety valve was found in the establishment of the British North American League. From all parts of Upper Canada and from the British section of Lower Canada, and from the British inhabitants of Montreal representatives were chosen. They met at Kingston for the purpose of considering the great danger to which the constitution of Canada was exposed. A safety valve was found. Our first resolution was that we were resolved to maintain inviolate the connection with the Mother Country. (Cheers.) The second proposition was that the true solution of the difficulty was the confederation of all the provinces. That was in the year 1850. The third resolution was that we should attempt to form in such confederation, or in Canada before confederation, a commercial national policy. (Cheers.) The effects of the formation of the British North American League in 1850, were marvellous, and as I speak I see a gentleman looking at me—I mean the Hon. Alexander Morris—who had as much to do in framing the conclusions to which the League came, as any man now living. (Cheers.) The solution was found. The annexation feeling died away, the feeling of irritation died away, and the principles which were laid down by the British North American League in 1850 are the lines on which the Conservative Liberal party has moved ever since. (Cheers.) After that, as I have already explained, the accord between the Conservatives of Lower Canada and Upper Canada increased, until in 1854 they were perfectly ready for a coalition with us. The Liberal party who, very strong in opposition, are but a rope of sand when in Government, had one after the other cut off the heads of their leaders. The factious opposition of the Grits disgusted Mr. Baldwin, and he retired The factious opposition of the Grits drove out Sir Francis Hincks. Looking later on, the same factious course of the Grits has driven out one of the most respected, perhaps the most respected, leader of the Reform party, Mr. Mackenzie, who has been deserted at his utmost need by those whom he had

... so ably, earnestly, and disinterestedly. And I may say here that I glory in the fact that entirely different was the course pursued towards me, when in 1873 I was covered with a storm of obloquy, when false charges based upon stolen documents were brought against me, and I was accused of every crime in the calendar. When public indignation was excited against me by these false representations, what was the course of my party in and out of Parliament? When we resigned in consequence of the Pacific railway slander, I felt that as leader of that party and the person most attacked, and most liable to be attacked, I might be in the way of the future prospects of my party, We called the members of the party from all the provinces together and I said, "Do not consider me; make me the scapegoat if you think the good of the country demands it. Choose a younger man one not calumniated with all these charges, and I will fight in the ranks as I have done before." (Cheers.) What was their answer? They indignantly refused. (Cheers.) But I said "Gentlemen, I know your good hearts and your sympathy for me; and that you do not wish to humiliate me and would like to save my feelings, but you are not doing your duty to the party and the country if, truly believing that you can do better, you do not elect a new leader. I will give you time to consider the matter, and you can meet me to-morrow." When I went to meet them the next day there was not a single man about. (Laughter.) I walked into the House of Commons with the consciousness and proud feeling that at all events my friends in Parliament, who knew what I had done, had sifted the evidence and knew the futility of the charges make against me, would stand by me, and I believed that those whom they represented would do the same, and I got an answer to my appeal in 1878. (Cheers.) The contrast between this course and that of those opposed to us is marvellous. The Grits deserted Mr. Baldwin, and drove out Sir Francis Hincks. What course did they pursue towards Mr. Mackenzie? When he went to Parliament in Ottawa knowing that he was leader of his party he received a printed paper asking him to attend a meeting for the purpose of electing a leader of the Reform party. (Laughter.) I have alluded to this because it is one of the proudest incidents in my career that in the days of my adversity, when I almost thought that I might never rise again, when it was said that, like Lucifer, I had fallen, never to rise again, the members of Parliament representing the Conservative party stood by me, and when an appeal was made to the country the people approved of the course taken by their representatives, placed me where I am now, and repeated their favourable verdict after I had another term of office. (Cheers.) Well, a coalition government was formed in 1854 and we got the support of the leading Baldwin Reformers. The union which took place with the Baldwin Reformers has existed ever since. The vast body of the Baldwin party who came over and supported us in 1854 never repented their action, and we now have in our ranks not only dyed-in-the-wool Tories like myself, but Liberal-Conservatives, Conservative-Liberals, and Baldwin Reformers, who have all combined in forming one great constitutional party. What were the consequences of this union? The consequences were most happy, as we had a strong, and therefore a vigorous Government, and in 1854, in our very first session, we settled some of those questions which were the most dangerous to the future of this country. (Cheers.) Chief among those which culminated in the rebellion in Upper Canada, as Wm. Lyon Mackenzie declared in 1837, was the clergy reserves bill. We all remember what an agitation there was about that. All remember how religious feeling, how denominational feeling, how sectional feeling was aroused on that question. But we settled it, gentlemen, and settled it on rational grounds. We yielded to the opinion of the people of Ontario that the clergy reserves should be secularized, and while holding to the pledge of the Imperial Government we took care that those men who had gone into holy orders on the faith of their incumbencies being secured to them should be protected. (Cheers.) Notwithstanding that that question had been a matter of so much agitation, notwithstanding that it was one threatening the peace of Upper Canada, notwithstanding the necessity that it should be settled, we had the opposition of Mr. George Brown against the settlement of that question. He said, "No; you must take away the last shilling; drive out these men to starve, although the faith of the British Government had been pledged, although they had been drawing their salaries for years, they must be deprived of every farthing." And because these interests were respected, the rights of property respected, Mr. Brown voted against that bill, as also did the mass of the Reform party. What have been the consequences of our action ? You never hear of it to-day. The clergy behaved in a most Christian manner. They could have gone to the foot of the throne, but they said, "We do not desire to be self-seeking, do with us as you will;" and in carrying that measure I had the support of the clergy of the Church of England. (Cheers.) The question was settled forever and the ministers enjoy their pittances, for in some cases they are little more than pittances, in peace, the balance was handed over to the municipalities to do with it as they pleased, and that which threatened war, and, in fact, was one of the causes of war, is now never heard of. This was one of the effects of the coalition of the Baldwin Reformers and the Conservative party of Canada. And, gentlemen, when I state that this measure was opposed by Mr. Brown and the Reform party, it has so happened with almost every measure we have introduced. No matter what bill has been laid before Parliament for the development of the country, no matter what great measure we have pledged ourselves to, and succeeded in carrying, we have had not only to meet the difficulties of the question itself, but right or wrong, the blind, senseless opposition of the Opposition of the day, simply because it was proposed by a Conservative Administration. (Cheers.) Then, gentlemen, there was a question which affected the Province of Lower Canada as much, perhaps more than the clergy reserves question in Upper Canada, and that was the Signorial Tenure Bill. There, gentlemen, the people were in a state of quasi-serfdom, there the feudal system with all its antiquated privileges existed. The people were resolved to throw them off, and we were resolved that the farmer of Lower Canada should stand on the same footing of freedom as the farmer of Upper Canada. (Cheers.) We were convinced that it was a question of so much importance that we would not ask where the money should come from, but put our hands in the common chest as we knew that Upper Canada would be willing to free the Lower Provinces from this feudal tyranny. (Cheers.) We therefore charged the general expense on both provinces. That was opposed to the death by the Opposition of the day, but you gentlemen, hear of it no more. The French Canadians, however, remember their obligation. They are a grateful people, a thinking people, and they remember what party it was that freed them from their bondage, and no longer obliged them to undergo those humiliating services which the feudal law enjoined on them. They remember what is due to the Conservative party. (Cheers.) I fear I am tiring you— ("No, go on,")—with this long retrospect of forty years, but I am trying in my humble and inefficient way to give an account of my course of action during that period. In 1854, gentlemen, among other measures we had to carry in this coalition Government was the Reciprocity Treaty with the United States. We do not claim, we may not claim, the merit of having negotiated that measure. That is due altogether to the Hincks-Morin Government. It lasted, as you know, for eleven years. It was a great benefit to Canada, and of great service to all her interests. We had only the accidental glory of carrying the bill, all the measures which led to the treaty are due to the Baldwin Reform Government of that day, headed by Sir Francis Hincks. And here, speaking of reciprocity, gentlemen, you must all remember the feeling of dismay that went over the whole country, especially among our farmers, at the closing of that treaty. Why it was closed you all know. It was no fault of ours. I do not think there was any objection in the United States to the treaty, but the feeling of hostility between England and the United States was very great at that time. And because we were a portion of the British Empire, and because we were supposed to be governed by hostile feeling towards the North, although no supposition was more unjust and unwarrantable, during that great contest in the United States, in consequence of that feeling they gave notice that the treaty should be abrogated. There was dismay in our ranks. It was thought we should have no market for our products. It was thought that the cause of the farmer was lost. We did all that we could to renew that treaty but without success. After a little while we found out we were more frightened than hurt; we found that Canada could obtain other markets. We discovered that no country, large as this is, fertile as this is, can be crushed by the action of any foreign country whatever. (Cheers.) If then we are true to ourselves, if we are a law-abiding people, if we are industrious, if we seek new markets as we lose old ones, if we change our industries as old ones fail us, the country may be temporarily affected but it cannot be permanently crushed by the action of any foreign nation. (Loud cheers.) I may here speak of the approaching abrogation of the fishery clauses of the Washington treaty. There is a feeling, a very considerable feeling, in the Maritime Provinces that the cancellation of the fishery clauses, will greatly affect them, and you hear some people in their despair and their apprehension talking very foolishly, I think, of going down on their knees to the United States and asking for a continuance of that treaty. Now, gentlemen, the moral of our past experience is this, that the fishing interests of the Maritime Provinces, though they may be temporarily affected if the Americans persist in their course, will not be so for long. (Hear, hear.) It may for a short time compel them to use middlemen in the sale of their fish, and that will be all, while we will have secured to us the exclusive right to fish in British American waters. (Applause.) No course is more suicidal; no course shows a more absolute want of common sense in any negotiations with so astute a nation as the people of the United States as to show anxiety. (Applause.) If we go down upon our knees and say we will be ruined unless we have reciprocity, and that without reciprocity annexation would follow, the Americans, who are a proud people and who believe they have a mission to govern this continent, will say, "Very well, the best way of making Canada a part of the United States is simply by refusing you what you ask; you therefore, cannot have it." (Applause.) I believe the course of my Government is the proper one. We say to the Americans, "We would be happy to continue our reciprocal relations; we would be happy to increase our commercial relations. We are willing to discuss the question of a Reciprocity Treaty on the most liberal terms consistent with our own interests. We know perfectly well that you will not do what is contrary to your own interests; you cannot expect us to do what is contrary to ours. Let us sit down and see if we can make an arrangement. If we can it is well; if we cannot, there is no harm done. You can take your course, we must take ours." (Hear, hear.) Already, gentlemen, in consequence of some unguarded and unwise utterances in St. John and the Maritime Provinces, the Americans have begun to hold back a little, to see what the result upon Canada will be. But, gentlemen. we know the unwisdom of such a course—not only the unwisdom; but the utter folly, because nothing done by the United States will force us to give up our allegiance to the Queen. (Loud cheers.) No matter what may be the action of the United States we will stand by our allegiance; we will not desert the country to which we are so deeply attached, and the institutions we revere. (Loud and continued applause.) Now, gentlemen, the government dragged on from 1854 to 1858. In 1858 we were defeated in the city of Toronto. At the time we were defeated we had a large majority in Parliament, but we were defeated upon the question of the seat of government. You may remember that after that unfortunate event in Montreal the seat of government went to Quebec, and then there was the alternate system, of having the seat of government for four years alternately at Quebec and Toronto. This was found to be ruinously expensive and greatly detrimental to the best interests of the province. But we could not settle upon any one place. Kingston, my constituency, had been the seat of government in 1841, Montreal in 1843. Quebec and Toronto had also been the seats of government. Ottawa was ambitious; Hamilton and London were ambitious; in fact by no possibility could we get Parliament to agree to any one place. Under the circumstances we did agree to get rid of this insufferable nuisance of moving between Quebec and Toronto every four years by leaving the selection of a new seat of government to her Majesty the Queen. Her Majesty—on such advice as was given her—and we gave no advice because we pledged ourselves not to do so—selected Ottawa ; and Ottawa, on the whole was a very good compromise. Mind you, this was before Confederation, and the capital was to be that of only Upper and Lower Canada. Ottawa was chosen for two reasons. In the first place there was a military reason. The Duke of Wellington had previously decided that Ottawa was a most important point from a military point of view, and had caused the Rideau canal to be built at a cost of a million pounds sterling, the idea being to connect Ottawa with Kingston, so that troops could get up by that route if the Americans had possession of the St. Lawrence. Military reasons then were in favour of it. Then, on the other hand, the city of Ottawa is on the River Ottawa, which divides Upper from Lower Canada. It is therefore a place where the two people could be considered to be on an even footing. At this moment we have at Ottawa a Lower Canadian Ottawa which is called Hull, and is a city of more than ten thousand inhabitants, as well as an Ottawa in the Province of Ontario. (Hear, hear.) We had left it to the Queen to choose a site, and we were bound in honour to sustain her decision. But in the ensuing session Mr. Piche, a Rouge member, moved that Ottawa was not a fit place, without giving any reason for his motion, and without proposing to ask her Majesty to reconsider her decision ; throwing it back, in fact, in her face in an insulting manner, without rhyme or reason. When that was carried against us we felt that our honour was concerned. We had asked the Queen to be the arbitrator, and we felt bound in honour to support that reference, although my own constituency was bitterly disappointed. I consequently felt myself bound to resign and all my colleagues did so too. It was the honourable course for honourable men. But we were not long out. (Laughter.) It was the most impudent thing—if I may use that expression—in the Liberal Opposition to take office at that time. There was a large majority against them in Parliament. It was a new Parliament, and the people had sent representatives to the House opposed to the policy of Mr. Brown. Still that gentleman took office, and he took it although Sir Edmund Head, acting with perfect constitutionality, told him that he must not expect to be granted a dissolution. "If you can give me good reasons for it I am open to those reasons ; but if you accept the obligation of forming a Government you are not to suppose as a matter of course that you are to have a dissolution." Mr. Brown formed his Government notwithstanding, and he concealed the effect of that statement of Sir Edmund Head from all but two or three of his leading colleagues. I know it, because two or three of those gentlemen, who were afterwards my colleagues, told me. The consequence was that Parliament took the bit in its teeth and said no, they had not the confidence of the majority, and they must go out. There was a vote of want of confidence and they did go out. They remained in office for two days and I do not think I can charge them with doing much mischief during those two days. (Laughter.) Then we came in, and continued with small majorities. Our majorities were not large as they are now-a-days. We had sometimes very small majorities. At last we were defeated on our militia bill. Now, gentlemen, you must remember that the relations between the United States and Canada were very much strained at that time. There was danger of war. Her Majesty's Government resolved that all the resources of the empire should be employed in our defence, and consulted as to what we should do and could do in our own defence. A commission was appointed to consider what Canada ought to do in the way of militia organization. I was chairman of that commission. When we prepared a measure and laid it before Parliament it was considered too thorough—too expensive. That was the ground, at all events, the Opposition took, and they defeated the bill on the second reading. We would not take the responsibility of a less efficient measure. We knew what our duties were to the Mother Country. We knew what our duties were to our own people, by protecting our own frontiers in case of war. We accepted the defeat of that measure, and the Government resigned accordingly. All that was then proposed to Parliament, then suggested in 1862, has since been carried out by the Parliament of Canada, because we have now got a militia system more thorough, more complete, with a larger and better organization. Even Mr. Mackenzie, during his term of office, assisted in completing the militia system which his whole party voted against in 1862. That organization is now so complete that I believe Canada will show as efficient a force for its population as any country in the world. (Hear, hear.) We have in command an officer of great experience and trained in the regular service, and I say also, though it is in his presence, that we have an efficient, earnest, and zealous Minister of Militia in the person of my friend Mr. Caron. (Cheers.) Then, gentlemen, a new government was formed under the Honourable John Sandford Macdonald which lasted until 1864, when we took office again, but held it only for a few months. Statesmen began to be appalled at the deadlock. In less than two years two Administrations had been forme l, one under Mr. John Sandfield Macdonald and the other under Sir Etienne Tache and myself. Both were defeated, and it seemed as if we were going to have anarchy again. Then a coalition took place between Mr. George Brown and myself. In order to avoid this anarchy, to restore peace, in order to the successful administration of affairs, we agreed, although we had been personally and politically hostile, to forget everything except the good of the country. (Cheers.) The coalition took place, which resulted in the confederation of the provinces. A question of some interest which you have seen discussed in the papers, has arisen as to what gentleman suggested, and to whom the merit of confederation belonged. Why, it was so obvious a proposition that a union of all the provinces would be much better than four scattered provinces, without power, without community of action, isolated, without community of trade—it was so obvious that a confederation was so infinitely superior that it suggested itself to everybody. So far as I can learn, the first suggestion was made by Mr. Joseph Howe, in Nova Scotia, years and years ago. In 1850 it was made the main plank in the platform of the British North American League, which met at Kingston. In 1858, as Mr. Morris in his able letter in this morning's *Mail* showed, the government of which I was a member, put it in the Governor-General's speech that steps would be taken to get the consent of her Majesty's Government to communicate with the sister provinces, regarding confederation.—(Cheers.)—and then in 1864, at the time of this deadlock, the question had been an old one. It was obvious to everyone that some such solution must be found for the difficulties then existing, but the proposition for the union of all the provinces, as Mr. Morris shows by this paper, which I myself read in Parliament, did not come from Mr. Brown. Mr. Brown and his whole party had been in favour of passing a resolution, and the elder gentlemen who are here may remember, passed a resolution that the legislative union between Upper and Lower Canada should be severed, and there should be a federal union, each province having its own legislature, and some joint authority to govern both. That was the proposition they originated in 1864. Mr. Brown said that by-and-bye the larger confederation might be undertaken, but that federation of the two provinces which had before been legislatively united, should be taken up first. We objected, but compromised afterwards upon this arrangement, that we should try what we could do to get the Lower Provinces to unite with us, and that the two questions should be considered together. If we could not get the larger federation we might take the smaller if we could agree upon the terms. Mr. Brown yielded. and then we went to Prince Edward Island. In Prince Edward Island, by a Providential combination of circumstances, representatives of the Maritime Provinces were to hold a meeting for the purpose of forming a federation of the three provinces, Nova Scotia, New Brunswick, and Prince Edward Island. They met, and we asked permission to be present and state our views. The whole government went down from Quebec to Prince Edward Island. We laid before the assembled representatives of the three Maritime Provinces our larger scheme, and they thought so much of it that they postponed the consideration of their scheme. We had subsequent meetings, and it culminated in the Quebec resolutions by which the larger scheme was adopted. Upon these resolutions Confederation was founded. This question of Confederation is a marked historical event, and the facts of it should be ascertained and known without misapprehension or misstatement of any kind.

In 1866, in consequence of this preliminary arrangement, a delegation from each province went to London, and sat there several months settling the terms of the British North America Act. Unfortunately we had not the assistance of Mr. Brown. He had withdrawn from the Government on a question respecting reciprocity, and at the expense of being tedious I will shortly state to you the difference. We found that there was no chance of getting a reciprocity treaty ; no chance of the Americans meeting us hand in hand in this question. In fact the Secretary of the Treasury of that date, the Finance Minister of the United States, had declared that treaties could not be made affecting charges upon the people by the action of the President and Senate only, but that it might be done by simultaneous legislation. That is to say, the United States might pass an Act putting certain duties upon Canadian products, or making them free. We could pass a similar Act in Canada, and the two Acts would have the effect of a treaty. We said: "We must try to get a renewal of this reciprocity arrangement in some way ;" if not by treaty, then let us try simultaneous legislation. Mr. Brown objected. and said that he would not be responsible for similtaneous legislation as Congress might at any time repeal their Act. We said that if we could not get a treaty why not try the legislation. Mr. Brown retired from the Government and I am very sorry that he did so. I think that he would have been of great value to us in England in settling the terms of the British North American Act. The unwisdom of his retirement was shown in the fact that we could neither get legislation nor treaty. Since Confederation we have, with the exception of five years, governed the country. The history of events since has been so recent that I need not take up your time in referring to all that we have done. From 1867 to 1873 I was at the head of the Administration. Then came our downfall, in consequence of the Pacific slander. But looking back upon that matter, I say that there was nothing in my condnct, or in that of my colleagues in the Administration, of which we have cause to be ashamed. (Cheers.) We had brought British Columbia into the union. In order to get her to join the Confederation Parliament promised to build a railway across the continent. We were bound to carry out that obligation. We were pledged to do it, and we have carried out the pledge. We took every step possible for the purpose. Parliament declared that the road should be built by a company and not by the direct act of the Government. Two companies were formed, one of which, having its headquarters in Toronto, was presided over by the present Minister of the Interior, and the other formed in Montreal was headed by Sir Hugh Allan. They competed for the advantage of building the road, and had both obtained charters. We endeavoured to get a union between the two companies, but circumstances prevented it, and the Government refused to give the contract either to Sir D. Macpherson or Sir Hugh Allan. A new company was formed of leading men in the leading provinces with Sir Hugh Allan as a leading capitalist as one of the corporation. If this company had succeeded we should have been much nearer to the completion of the railway than we are now. It was said that we had sold the charter to Sir Hugh Allan. We refused to give it to him, but formed a company of independent representatives, many of whom did not know Sir Hugh Allan and had never seen him. Sir Hugh Allan was put upon the company because he was a large capitalist. He was worth some millions, and as a Canadian was anxious to have the road built. Besides it was of very great importance to him to have a transcontinental road running to meet and supply with freight his magnificent fleet of steamers which were plying between Canada and England. But they found out that Sir Hugh, who was an old Conservative, had contributed largely in 1872 to the election fund. Well, he had a right to do so. Such things occur in England and in Canada, even in the county of Lennox, I am told. (Laughter.) Sir Hugh had a right to subscribe. In England it is well understood that the Carleton Club, which represents the Conservative party there, has a fund before every election, while the Reform party has a similar club which acts in the same manner. This money is not used in bribing the individual voter, but simply for the purpose of defraying the legitimate expenditure which you all know must be incurred in the purest constituency in order to carry on a contest efficiently. (Cheers.) We had no Carleton Club, and, therefore, Sir Hugh sent his contribution to me as the head of the party. I used it honestly, and can account for every farthing. (Cheers.) More than that ; although there were a series of controverted elections not one single farthing of the money placed in my hands was shown to have been appropriated for the purpose of bribery, (Cheers.) I have vouchers to show where the money went and to whom it went, and know it was honestly used for the purpose of assisting those who could not risk their small property in the expenses of an election contest. (Cheers.) But a confidential communication between Mr. Abbott and myself was stolen. The Opposition paid their money to bribe a man to steal papers from his employer. This, gentlemen, was the slander which for a moment upset the Government. The country taken by the cry, and reading all these exaggerated statements, naturally believed many of them, and we were defeated in 1874. At the next election, notwithstanding the attacks made upon me, the country declared in 1878 that the party which I led was worthy of guiding the destinies of the Dominion. (Cheers.) I will not say much on the demerits of the Government of Mr. Mackenzie. He is defeated, his party was defeated at the election in a most marvellous way, and we had a majority of between 70 and 80 in a Parliament of 208. God knows he had a hard time of it when he was there. (Laughter.) In the first place he had rather a fighting Opposition to contend with, as you may remember—(laughter)—and in the next place he was obliged to guard his rear, because men were firing into his back behind him. (Laughter.) He had to suffer what I never had to suffer, he had to suffer not only the attacks of his open foes, but the treachery of his own supposed supporters. (Hear, hear.) That Government was disastrous in every respect. Mr. Mackenzie did his work to the best of his ability. He worked hard and faithfully, and I think, personally, he worked honestly. (Hear, hear.) To be sure in some things, I think he winked pretty hard—(laughter)—at the action of some of his colleagues, but, personally, I have no reason to believe that he was implicated in the scandals of his five years' Administration. Some say respecting the steel rails he might, perhaps, have exercised his worldly wisdom, to say the least of it—(laughter)—but I do not desire to add, in any way by a single word of mine, to the position that Mr. Mackenzie has been placed in by his friends, " deserted in his utmost need by those his former bounty fed." But it must be admitted, gentlemen, that we were justified in stating, because the country has endorsed the opinion, that that Ministry did not deserve to last. With the best intentions Mr. Mackenzie was an unfortunate administrator. Look, gentlemen, at his vague and futile attempt to build the Canadian Pacific railway. (Hear, hear.) Remember the " magnificent water stretches." (Laughter.) Remember the St. Francis lock. A monument of folly of no earthly value to man, woman or child, bear, wolverine, or buffalo. (Laughter and cheers.) (A voice, " The Neebing hotel.") Oh, yes, there was the Neebing hotel. (Cheers.) That was a work of art—(laughter)—for its mingled beauty and utility, unequalled in the history of civilization. (Renewed laughter.) The power of æsthetic architecture could go no further—(loud laughter)—than in the Neebing hotel. However, like other great works of art it has been destroyed by some barbarians who have come since. (Laughter.) Then, gentlemen, if nothing else would have destroyed that Government the brilliant success of their finances would certainly do it. While we had a series of surplus money in our pockets to pay our debts and carry on the improvements of the country, by an unfortunate fate Providence decided against the Mackenzie Government, that they should have bad harvests and certain deficits. There were some attempts made to overcome these deficits, and the earnest and able exertions of the Finance Minister, Sir Richard Cartwright—(laughter)—were employed for the purpose of converting them into surpluses. At first he said, modestly, We are mere flies on the wheel, no more can a fly make a cart-wheel go round than we can change the course of events. However, he tried his hand, and I am sorry to say he did not succeed.

He increased the taxes a little, but he was not going in the right way or to the right extent. The *Globe* called him—and the *Globe* is a great Reform authority—we should always take the opinions of great Reform authorities as worthy of consideration—(laughter)—the *Globe* pronounced him a "mixer and muddler" of figures. (Laughter and cheers.) Certainly he mixed them, certainly he muddled them, but he did not produce the surplus. (Laughter.) I am inclined to think that if Mr. Mackenzie had thrown him over and made him a Jonah he might have saved his Government, but he was true to Sir Richard Cartwright, and Sir Richard Cartwright now is true to Mr. Blake. (Laughter.) We went to the country as an Opposition. We laid before the country not a new proposition as has been alleged, not a mere means of getting power, we laid before them and before Parliament, in three different sessions, resolutions affirming the necessity of adopting a National Policy and a re-adjustment of the tariff, which would not only convert the annual deficit into a surplus, but would incidentally encourage and develop all our great interests, manufacturing, mining, mineral or agricultural. It was said of us that we were not sincere, that when we came into power we would not carry out those resolutions, forgetting that it was the fixed policy of my party, which we had declared as far back as 1850, in the British North American League. When Sir Alexander Galt became Minister of Finance, in 1856, he declared that policy to be the policy of the Liberal-Conservative Government; and, gentlemen, we were only acting on the lines we had laid down years before when the opportune moment came, and when the call from the country came. When the exodus from the country was going on, when our skilled artizans and agriculturists were leaving for the States, we had no industries of our own, and were obliged to trust to foreign countries, England even in that respect being a foreign country. We were shut out from the United States, from which we were drawing most of our supplies, the goods coming from there being manufactured in many cases by the hands of Canadians in a foreign country. We were resolved that this should not exist any longer, and the first thing we did when we carried the elections in 1878 was to come to Parliament and lay before it the result of our labours. Gentlemen, that policy, I venture to say has been completely successful; it has prevented the exodus, the goods we were getting from foreign parts are now manufactured in our own country, and although it was only in 1879 they came into operation we have manufactories in all parts of the country to-day, and skilled workmen who but for that Act would be working in the United States. (Cheers.) These manufactures are still in their infancy, capital cannot be generated at once, but by degrees all that we want, all that our climate and soil will give us, can be manufactured in Canada. (Cheers.) You will remember we were told we were raising up a gigantic monopoly, that those cotton and woollen lords, these capitalists, would lord it over us, that they would accumulate enormous fortunes at the expense of the people. What has been the result? At this moment the manufacturers of cottons and woollens are suffering from over-production. Cotton and woollen goods have never been so cheap as they are to-day. We are suffering, not from want of anything, but from having too much. (Laughter.) We have more cotton than we can use. We shall soon have as many woollens as we can use. We are getting our goods cheap and making them in our own country instead of importing them from abroad. (Cheers.) You know that the price of articles is regulated by supply and demand. There was a rush into cotton manufacturing. Everybody thought money was to be made from cotton. The earlier companies had certainly divided large sums of money in the way of profits, and everybody who had a spare shilling put it into a cotton factory. The consequence was that unless everybody in Canada took to wearing three shirts instead of one—(laughter)—there would be no means of using all this cotton up. That was a temporary difficulty. But the people of Canada did not suffer. The manufacturers who had worked not wisely, but too well, had to work less and to change the character of the cottons they were turning out. They are doing this now; they are going into coloured cottons, bleached cottons and other varieties which formerly they did not touch, and the result is that the thing will right itself.

There may be lines in which work is short, but it must be remembered that the workingman in the United States is more short of work than the workingman in Canada—(hear, hear)—and that the workingman in England is shorter still—and that is a free trade country. (Applause.) While both England and the United States are suffering our people cannot hope to escape. (Hear, hear.) But the depression is temporary. These things right themselves. We have the machinery in our country; we have the customers in our country. We have also the customers for the produce of our farms; so that our farmers have their market here and are not compelled to send their produce to feed the producers of their manufactured goods in the United States. (Hear, hear.) I therefore say that the National Policy has not in one single particular been a failure. (Cheers.) And I nail my colours to the mast on that point. (Applause.) I am a National Policy man. Those who do not agree with me on that subject, though they may support me on others, will fail me on the point which is more essential and more important to the future prosperity of Canada than any subject that can be submitted to the legislature of a nation. (Cheers.) Well, gentlemen, we not only carried the National Policy but we had to take up the almost abandoned threads of the Pacific railway. You know what we have done. Instead of fiddling about the Neebing hotel or about Lake St. Francis we made a contract with a company of capitalists whom we knew would build the road. True we gave them liberal terms, but it was an enormous responsibility. (Hear, hear.) It was a responsibility from which many others have shrunk. It was a responsibility which very few men would have undertaken. (Hear, hear.) But we got hold of the right men, and we made a contract, under which the road was to have been completed by 1891. So earnest are these gentlemen in their work, so anxious to make it a great success, though not obliged to complete it till 1891, they will finish it by the spring of 1886. (Loud cheers.) In March, 1885, it is confidently expected the road will be running from Montreal to the waters of the Columbia river. (Cheers.) By the autumn the road will be running to the Pacific ocean; and by the spring of 1886 we may consider that we will have railway connection direct from Quebec in summer, and from Halifax in winter to the Pacific, over lines running through Canadian territory from one end to the other—(applause)—without touching a foreign country. Now, gentlemen, I have told you that whatever the Government of which I have been a member have proposed for the good of the country has been violently opposed. The Canadian Pacific Railway was no exception. We had the most virulent and, I may venture to say, the most senseless opposition. Faction could go no farther than the Opposition went on that occasion. (Hear, hear.) And now we are told that we are building the road too fast. We are told that we ought to have built a hundred miles a year instead of finishing it outright. (Laughter.) Yet the same public men who are making this complaint are charging the Department of the Interior with negligence because it has not surveyed all the country to the foot of the Rocky Mountains. (Laughter.) However, the road is built at this moment to Calgary, at which point it was thought land would not be sought for by settlers for some years. We had already, with the push which I believe we may attribute to ourselves as a Government, surveyed 65,000,000 of acres in the North-West for settlement. We thought that would surely be a sufficient area for settlement for some time to come. We therefore let out—because it was of great importance that we should initiate every kind of industry—ranches under lease, the capitalists who took them for the purpose of raising cattle and horses to hold them only until the settlers required them. That system is in operation and it is successful. We have arranged that if immigration goes in there the bullock must give way to the settler. But at this moment the settlers are rushing into Calgary. A town is growing there. The place is booming more than any other place along the line of the Pacific railway. It is a favorite spot for the immigrants—and yet they say you have built the road far too fast; you ought to have built but a hundred miles a year. (Cheers.) Moreover the road in going to the foot of the Rocky Mountains passes through one of the most magnificent coal countries in the world. There is no such coal area in the world as we have in the North-West. I forget how much coal was a ton at the home of Mr. Norquay, the Premier of Manitoba, whom I call upon you to greet—(loud cheering)—but I think it was $27. He will tell you what they wanted in that magnificent country was fuel. By building the Canadian Pacific railway we have found it. (Cheers.) At this moment Sir Alex. Galt is building a road from his mines in the heart of the coal country to the Canadian Pacific Railway, 110 miles long. This line will be built in a few months, and will take fuel along the whole of that line to Winnipeg. But more than that. It has been discovered that some of the most magnificent forests in the world are embedded in the recesses of the Rocky Mountains, which are pierced by the railway, so that while from Georgian Bay and Parry Sound in Ontario lumber will be carried to Port Arthur and supplied to the settlers in the eastern portion of the North-West, so from the Rocky Mountains will come lumber to supply all the wants of the people, and these two great sources of timber supply will meet in the centre, supplying the whole range of that country with a most needed want, lumber for house building, lumber for fencing, lumber for fuel and lumber for all purposes. In order to convey, in a very succinct form what has been already done, and the position of the C. P. R., I shall read you a paper coming from the best authority on that subject. I know, gentlemen, you are all interested in the future of that great country. That is the country where our sons and our grandsons will go. My own son has gone there already—(laughter)—and he has informed me by telegraph that he was favoured with a grandson there. (Laughter.) He must have thought that I was not very unpopular there, because he has christened him John A. (Renewed laughter.) Yes, gentlemen, that is the country of the future. Here we are shut out from the United States, and in that country there will be sufficient market for our eastern manufactures. For years and years the North-West must be an agricultural country. They must cultivate the soil and send eastward and westward to the Pacific ocean by the same railway the products of their farms, and the artizan of the older province of Ontario which is close to them, and the artizan of Quebec and of the Maritime Provinces will find there a certain market for all they can make. (Cheers.) If that country has only fair play, and its future is not destroyed by the malignant statements that have been poured upon it by the Opposition—(hear, hear)—there is a great future before it. It has great value and enormous fertility, and healthfulness and resources, and all that promises to make a great country. If these valuable resources were known and not denied, by our own people, that country would soon be settled by millions of inhabitants. (Cheers.) All that falsehood and malignity could form and disseminate has been used to destroy the future of that country. We have been told in Parliament and on the stumps that men had better go to Kansas, or Dakota, or anywhere, but to keep out of that country. We have to fight in England against the language of our statesmen and the statements of the Opposition press. (Cheers.) But, gentlemen, one of the deepest stabs of all came from Manitoba itself, from what is called the Farmers' Union, which protested against further immigration. Gentlemen, that is called a Farmers' Union, but the leaders of that agitation belonged not to the Conservative party. (Cheers.) For factious purposes, following the hints and suggestions given them from the east, they set to work and they deliberately and greatly contributed to ruin the immigration of last year, and if they continue the same course they may greatly impede, obstruct and postpone the settlement of that country. However, we must hope for the best, and that even the Grits will look to reason. (Laughter.) Let us hope that they will think more of their country and less of their party, and that they will not continue the ruinous, unpatriotic, suicidal course that they have pursued in the past by maligning and diminishing the value of that great country. Now, gentlemen, I shall read this short memorandum. "The Canadian Pacific Railway is rapidly approaching completion. Through trains will be running from Montreal to the Pacific ocean next autumn. The distance from Montreal to the Pacific ocean is 2,900 miles, or 430 miles less than from New York to San Francisco. From Montreal to Yokohama in Japan via C. P. R., the distance is 10,977 miles, or 1,013 miles shorter than via New York and San Francisco. When the C. P. R. has been extended eastward to the Maritime Provinces with a direct line to Louisburg, C. B., the ocean voyage from England to America may be accomplished easily in five days, and the railway journey from Louisburg to the Pacific ocean may be done in five days more. This will be ten days from London to the new city of Vancouver on the Pacific coast. The run across the Pacific to Yokohama may be made in fourteen days ; the whole trip will thus be made in 24 days from London to Yokohama, a saving in time of at least 20 days over the route *via* Gibraltar and the Suez canal. The English colony of Hong-Kong may be reached by the C. P. R. in less than 30 days from England, or 16 days less than by Gibraltar or the Suez canal. During all that time the traveller will never be out of the sound of the British drum, and may always have his eyes resting on the Union Jack." (Tremendous cheering.) Gentlemen, I have told you the opposition we had to contend with, and the opposition has been enormous. Among other things they opposed the building of the road to the north of Lake Superior. It was said that it would be going through a country fit for nothing. It would be enormously expensive, and would not pay for greasing the wheels of the locomotives. The Government of which I was a member said if that road was not built we shall have no Pacific railway at all. In the first place it would be a breach of contract with British Columbia, and in the next place it would fail altogether in the great objects which the older provinces had in going in and agreeing to pay $25,000,000 cash of the hard earnings of the people taken from the public treasury for the building of the road. What would have been the consequence if the road north of Lake Superior had been abandoned ? The Pacific railway would be simply a feeder to the American railways running to the south. What commerce from Canada, what of our products would go through the United States when burdened by a foreign tariff, foreign rates of freight, and the trouble and delay of the bonding system ? What freight would go from Old Canada to the North-West by such a route ? It was absolutely necessary that the road should be built. That road is completed all but seventy miles. It will be built by the time next session of Parliament ends. There is now a line building connecting the northern railway system with the Pacific which will give direct communication between Toronto and Callendar. By this branch the manufacturers of Western Ontario, of Toronto and Hamilton will be able to send their goods to the North-West through Canada at rates to be fixed by the Government, who have provided for a control of the freight charges. These are acts of which the Government believe they have every reason to be proud, and for which they consider they should retain the support of the majority of the people. (Cries of "So they will.") Among the various acts of the Administration with which I have been concerned not the least important was the Washington Treaty. It is no part of my business to defend that treaty as a whole, most of it affected Imperial interests, or the relations of England and the United States. I had the honour of being appointed an Imperial Ambassador to look after the interests of Canada, and I did the best I could for Canada. (Cheers.) I did not get all that I wanted or nearly all, but at all events we got a settlement of the question in dispute. For the time between the commencement of the operation of the treaty and the 1st of July next we have got five and a-half millions of money for allowing the Americans to fish in our waters. You remember what a fuss was made when I came back from Washington by the Opposition. Mr. Mackenzie said that he looked with loathing on the sacrifice of the territorial rights of Canada for the filthy lucre of the arbitration. I was bitterly attacked and was compared to a cross between Arnold and Judas Iscariot. (Laughter.) I did not feel that our honour was affected, and if it was, Mr. Mackenzie forgot it very soon, for when he came in he carried out the reference, and it was to his Government that the five millions and a half were awarded for the right of fishing in our waters. They did not refuse that money, but were very willing to take it. Not only that, but Mr. Albert Smith was made Sir Albert Smith because he had submitted to the great humiliation which caused Mr. Mackenzie so much loathing. Now what do we see ? We see in the Maritime Provinces some of our most extreme Grits, instead of feeling that the country has been humiliated by the treaty in which it was said I betrayed it, crying out for the renewal of the treaty, and charging the Government with want of energy in trying to get it renewed. It is no use now trying, because the Americans have resolved not to renew it. They have given us notice, and we shall have to submit. We shall, however, do all we can to increase our commercial relations with the United States, and if we can in the course of such negotiations obtain a renewal of the fishery clause on fair and equal terms, we shall spare no pains in doing so, but we are not going on our knees, which would be dishonourable and defeat our object, to ask the United States to be good enough to save us from ruin by making this arrangement. I am told that this building will be wanted ere long for a far more important matter than this meeting—(laughter)—and therefore I shall be obliged to bring my remarks to a close. There are some things which I would like to say, but which I shall have to defer till to-morrow. I will therefore now conclude what must have been a wearisome speech to you. (No, no.) Well, you will pardon me, because as an old man I have the right to be garrulous, and three hours is but a short time in which to review the political proceedings of forty years. I felt it was my duty to tell you in my imperfect way what we had done, what we had attempted, and what we intended to do. In connection with this unequalled demonstration I have to return you my heartfelt thanks. As long as memory holds its seat this reception will remain in my mind. My children will look upon it as the culminating event in their father's career. (Cheers.) Proud as I am of the honour conferred upon me by my Sovereign, when she placed the decoration with her own hand upon my breast as a recognition of my services, all must yield to the overwhelming expression of the approbation of the people of Ontario as represented by you on this occasion. My time cannot be long, but I can depart in peace with the consolation and comfort of feeling that the Conservative cause, that is the cause of the country, is safe in your hands, and in the hands of those who will be governed and influenced by you. I appeal to the young Conservatives of the country to put their shoulders to the wheel. We old men are disappearing from the stage, but we leave behind us young and vigorous men who will fight the battle as enthusiastically and successfully as we have done, although I shall not be here to see it. I shall rest my head upon the pillow to-night with the confidence that for long after I have gone the Conservative cause is safe ; the country is safe in the hands of men like these I have now the honour of addressing. (Loud and prolonged cheering.)

THE PROPOSED ASSOCIATION.

Mr. L. WIGLE, M.P., said—I do not take the stand for the purpose of making a speech, but to move a resolution. Before doing so I would say that I suppose this the largest, the most enlightened, the most influential convention that ever met in the Dominion of Canada. (Loud cheers.) We remember that in the latter part of September last there was a large demonstration given here to the Hon. O. Mowat, Premier of the province, and it was held during the time of the agricultural exhibition in this city, and I have no doubt that thousands who attended that convention would not have been there had it not been for the exhibition, but we have the proud satisfaction of knowing that out of the thousands who are here to-day not a single man of us came to a cattle show. (Prolonged cheering and much laughter.) I beg leave to move, first, That in the opinion of this convention it is desirable in the interest of the Liberal-Conservative party of the province, that a permanent provincial organization be formed. That a committee, composed of the Chairman, Messrs. Dalton McCarthy, M.P., Peter White, M.P., J. C. Patterson, M.P., Donald MacMaster, M.P., Arthur Williams, M.P., J. C. Rykert, M.P., Clarke Wallace, M.P., C. H. Mackintosh, M.P., H. Kranz, M.P., T. Farrow, M.P., T. White, M P., John Carnegie, M.P.P., A. P. Ross, M.P.P. (Cornwall), J. Kerr, M.P.P., J. H. Medcalf, M.P.P., C. O. Ermatinger, M.P.P., D. Creighton, M.P.P.,

Alfred Boultbee, Thomas Cowan, C. W. Bunting, J. A. Macdonnell, Capt. Gaskin (Kingston), John A. Mackenzie, T. W. Crothers, W. A. McCulla, Col. Tisdale, R. Pringle, and the mover and seconder, be and is hereby appointed for the purpose of preparing a constitution and rules for the association; the committee to report on the re-assembling of this convention to-morrow morning.

Mr. DEACON, Q.C., seconded the motion, which was adopted unanimously.

THE RESOLUTIONS.

Mr. HAGGART—I beg to move, seconded by Mr. Kranz, that a committee be appointed to prepare resolutions expressing the opinion of this meeting in reference to the National Policy and the benefits that have accrued to the province through its adoption, also with reference to the policy of the Government regarding the Canadian Pacific Railway, and that the committee be composed of Hon. G. W. Allan, Hon. J. B. Plumb, Hon. John O'Donohoe, Messrs. O'Brien, M.P.P., Creighton, M.P., R. Hay, M.P., Burnham, M.P., T. White, M.P., Kilvert, M.P., Hilliard, M.P., Hesson, M.P., D. McMillan, M.P., Bergin, M.P., T. Robertson, M.P., McCarthy, M.P., S. White, M.P.P., A. Williams, M.P., Carnegie, M.P.P., Ferguson, M.P., Ermatinger, M.P.P., Clarke, M.P.P., Clancy, M.P.P., J. J. Hawkins, Brantford; J. H. Fraser, London; Adam Brown, Hamilton; Andrew McCormack, London; A. R. Boswell (Mayor) Toronto; Samuel Keefer, Brockville; W. P. R. Street, London; Francis Clemow, Ottawa; Thomas Long, Collingwood; Robert Brough, Gananoque; J. S. McQuaig, Picton; John McIntyre, Kingston; James Hamilton, Peel; N. A. Coste, Amherstburg, and the mover.

THE BRUCE BANNER.

Mr. ALLEN, President of the North Bruce Liberal-Conservative Association, on behalf of the ladies of North Bruce, said :—I have the honour of presenting this banner to Sir John Macdonald. You will observe, Sir John, that you enjoy not only the kindly feelings and the affection of the gentlemen, but also of the ladies. (Cheers.)

SIR JOHN MACDONALD.—Mr. Allen and gentlemen, I accept this gift with the greatest pride and satisfaction. Coming as it does from the ladies, I as a handsome young man—(laughter)—am especially gratified. It is a testimony to my good looks. (Renewed laughter.) It is also a testimony to the soundness of the political principles of the ladies of North Bruce. (Hear, hear.) I shall not only take it to Ottawa with pride, but when I visit my friends in the constituencies I shall take it with me, and I shall say to the Conservative ladies everywhere, "Go thou and do likewise." (Loud laughter and cheers.)

THE CONSTITUENCIES.

Mr. BOULTBEE moved that presidents of associations report as to the state of political matters in their constituencies. Carried.

Cheers were then given for the Queen, Sir John, Sir Hector Langevin, and Sir Leonard Tilley, and the convention adjourned until Thursday at ten o'clock.

SECOND DAY.

The Liberal-Conservative Convention re-assembled in the Grand Opera House at ten o'clock Thursday morning, Mr. Meredith, M.P.P., in the chair. There was again a large attendance of the delegates, the theatre being crowded.

The Chairman opened the proceedings, calling upon the Hon. Alex. Morris to open the meeting.

HON. ALEXANDER MORRIS, on coming forward, was received with enthusiastic cheers. He said :—I do not intend to occupy your time for any lengthened period to-day, but I am glad to have the opportunity of expressing the satisfaction with which I witnessed yesterday such a representative gathering as was here assembled, and the equal of which I believe has never before been held in the history of the Province of Ontario. To those who have been fighting the battles of their party and their country for some twenty-three years, as I have done, it was refreshing to find that among that audience there was so large a number of the youth of the country, of the men who are going to take our places, when like our venerable chieftain we find, as he may find, that the burden on our shoulders is greater than we can bear. I trust, however, that under Providence, Sir John may long be spared to guide the destinies of the country, even as Palmerston and Beaconsfield were spared in England, and as Gladstone, although he does not belong to our political side, is spared to carry on Imperial affairs. I trust that it may be many a day before Sir John finds himself compelled to withdraw from the control of the affairs of the Dominion, for which he has done so much. I think you recognize the necessity of having what we have never had before—a thorough organization of the party in this province. If our party are to continue in the proud position they now hold in the Dominion Parliament, if they are to obtain control of the interests of the public in the Local Legislature of Ontario, they must understand that this result can only be secured by steady, honest work and thorough organization. I am glad to see young men's Conservative associations springing up in Toronto, Hamilton, and other places, because we must depend upon the young men through their energy and power in the coming contests before us, and we should do everything we can to encourage them to come forward and take an active part in politics. Owing to the good will of the people of Toronto, who took me up five years ago, and thrice elected me to represent them, and once, when in competition with the present Premier of Ontario, it has been my good fortune to do battle in the Legislature for the party, beside my friend, your chairman. I owe that position not alone to Conservatives, for I am proud to say that while the Conservative party stood by me I had the generous support of men who differed politically from me—men of the Reform faith, who gave me their support. I desire only to say this, that in the leader of the Conservatives in the Legislature of Ontario you have a man of whom any party might well be proud. (Cheers.) I have sat alongside him for five years, and know his ability and talents. A young man placed in a critical position, he has risen with the responsibility placed upon him. There is no measure submitted to that Legislature in which he does not take part, or no measure framed by the Government which he does not examine and criticise. He is now recognized as one of the first Parliamentarians in the country. He has won the respect and esteem of our people in Ontario of both sides of politics, and I hesitate not to say that if Providence spares him he will be found equal to any position to which he may be called ; and I have not the slightest doubt that when the roll-call of eminent men is made hereafter you will find in the record of the future history of this country as one of the ablest Conservatives of Ontario, my friend, Mr. Meredith, your chairman. (Cheers.) I trust that when you leave this hall you will go to your homes with the determination to work for what your influence and proportion in the province entitle you— the support of the majority of the representatives of the Ontario Legislature for your party leaders. Next election you will rise in your strength and place our chairman in the position of premier of the premier province of the Dominion. (Cheers.) Let us have then, our provincial association, let us have thorough organization, and let us assist the local organizations without interfering with their right of action. May all of you remember that the Empire and Canada expect every man to do his duty. (Cheers.)

The CHAIRMAN said :—We have here to-day with us a gentleman well known from one end of the Dominion to the other. He once occupied a prominent position in the political life of Quebec for many years, and is now the colleague of our Chieftain in the greater councils of the nation. I refer to the Hon. Mr. Chapleau. (Cheers.) Although indisposed, he has consented to address to you a few words, and I am sure you will enjoy a treat. (Cheers.)

Hon. J. A. Chapleau, who was greeted with loud cheers, said :—Mr. Chairman and gentlemen,—As the chairman has said to you, I am not in very good health, and having to perform a pleasing duty this evening I am afraid I would be trespassing upon your time and would make you pass a very bad four or five minutes if I attempted to address you this morning. My stock of English is pretty small—(laughter and " No, no,")—and if I was to unbundle this morning I do not know what I could say this evening. There is only one thing I can say, and it is this. I was in Montreal the other day, and as I passed near a group of young Grits they were talking about this convention, and I overheard them say, among other things, that it was useless for Sir John to go to Ontario, as there were no more Conservatives there. (Laughter.) Well, gentlemen, I think you have disappointed these young people by this convention, and will again by the demonstration to-night—the continuation of this convention—and I believe in 1887 they will see that there are more Conservatives in Ontario. (Cheers.) Gentleman, you have been honouring our chieftain, our old leader, a man who is so intimately connected with the history of this country. You should be proud of your leader, and your chief must be proud of you. (Cheers.) You have fought great battles, and you are ready to begin over again. Surely when the time comes you will be ready. No matter when the time comes. It is by such meetings, it is by such aggregation of the forces of a great party, representing the strength, the life, the future, of the country—(cheers.)

Sir John Macdonald entered at this stage, and was received with enthusiastic demonstrations of respect, the whole convention rising and cheering again and again.

Mr. Chapleau, continuing, said—I was saying, gentlemen, that with these meetings, these congregations of party, you know how to appreciate each other, you make friends, and you gain knowledge of what strength you can rely upon when the hour of battle comes. I am sure that the consequence of this convention will be—what every good patriot must expect—the triumph of the Conservative cause in the future. (Cheers.) Gentlemen, I told you I am not able to make you a speech. I came here to tell you that our friends of Lower Canada, those who like myself have been for the last twenty years connected with all the political events of the Province of Quebec, in the great struggle of the country for its independence in wealth, and its greatness among the other nations, have been one with you in supporting your leaders. You may rely upon us for the future struggle. Let the Grits and the Rouges say what they like, the party in Lower Canada is and will be united in support of the great cause of Conservatism. (Cheers.) It was with pleasure, with a deep affection that I have for my leader that I came here to-day. (Cheers.) Gentlemen, remain as you are, true to the country, because you are the country, and true to your leaders, and we of the Province of Quebec will sing also the same note which was sounded before, and that note is but of triumph. (Cheers.) We Conservatives are not accustomed to be on the losing side We love power too much, we appreciate the virtue of qualities ; will we allow our enemies to say we only believe in quantities ? We reserve for ourselves and for history to say of what quality we are. (Cheers.) I hope I shall be able this evening to address those who will partake of the banquet, but I have exhausted really my stock of English. (Laughter and " No, no," " Speak in French.") It would take too long. I hope that we will all be spared by Providence for the future grand days. I hope, if God gives me health, which I require, to be able to continue the work which I began more than twenty years ago. In 1859 I was on the hustings, defending one of the colleagues of our very honoured leader, I mean Mr. Morin, and since that time I have been devoted to my friends, because I believe in friendship as being one of the elements in true politics—true to my friends, true to my party and true to my country. (Loud cheers.)

THE MANITOBAN TRIBUTE.

The Chairman—The time has now arrived when the address from the Conservatives of Manitoba will be presented by Hon. Mr. Norquay, Premier of the Province. (Applause.)

The Manitoba delegation, on coming forward, was loudly cheered. It was composed of Hon. J. Norquay, Mr. Speaker Murray, Dr. Harrison, M.P.P.; Mr. George McPhillips, D.L.S., president of the Winnipeg Conservative Association; Mr. Amos Rowe, proprietor of the Winnipeg *Times*; Mr. N. F. Hagel, and Mr. J. S. Aikens.

After the Manitoba Premier had introduced the deputation to Sir John, Mr. Norquay said—I am delegated by the Conservatives of Manitoba to present to you this address on the occasion of this great gathering :—

To the Right Honourable Sir John Alexander Macdonald, Knight Grand Cross of the Most Honourable Order of the Bath, Doctor of Civil Law, Doctor of Laws, one of Her Majesty's Counsel learned in the law, and a member of Her Majesty's Privy Council for Canada, &c.

RIGHT HONOURABLE SIR :—On this the fortieth anniversary of your entry into public life we, the Conservatives of Manitoba, beg to tender to you our sincere congratulation as the great and wise statesman who has moulded the destinies of Canada during the last forty years.

Out of the disjointed provinces and colonies of British America, under your enlightened statesmanship the Dominion of Canada has been formed, and we recognize the ability and wisdom that were required to allay sectional feelings and promote the spirit of harmony that now exists among the provinces of the Union.

The test of seventeen years of practical experience demonstrates the wisdom and statesmanship of the framers of Confederation, and the distribution of power between the Federal and Provincial Legislatures, as provided in the British North America Act, is calculated to furnish the best and the most liberal means of self-government. (Cheers.)

As one of the results of Confederation and the important status that Canada has attained under your illustrious leadership, we would mention that commercial treaties have been formed with foreign nations, by which her trade has been materially increased and an impetus given to the industries of the country. (Cheers.)

In all branches of the public service we are glad to mention that legislation in keeping with the progress of events, such as the improvement of the criminal laws, the promotion of public instruction, the extension of the municipal system, and other measures of progress has always received attention at your hands.

The freedom, liberality and soundness of our institutions have secured us immunity from those agitations that have shaken kingdoms and empires elsewhere to their centres, and the maintenance of law and order in the country has been remarkable, notwithstanding the employment of large numbers of a class inclined to set law at defiance.

We congratulate you on the success that has attended the many measures of utility and progress inaugurated and carried out by you during your long career as a public man, and now that that great enterprise, the Canada Pacific railway, which has engaged your attention so largely, is approaching completion, we trust that a merciful Providence may not only spare your life to see its consummation, and also an outlet from this country by Hudson's Bay secured, but may grant you health to witness the beneficent results to Canada of the far-reaching statesmanship that conceived and carried to a successful issue this great undertaking. (Loud applause.)

Permit us to convey, through you, to Lady Macdonald our feelings of respect and admiration for the many estimable qualities of heart and head which have endeared her to all with whom she has come in contact, and to express the hope that she may long be spared to brighten your fireside, and to lighten the arduous duties devolving upon you in the high and important sphere of life you occupy. (Prolonged cheering.)

We extend to you an invitation, and trust that you may ere long visit the North-West to see for yourself the magnificent heritage acquired by Canada, and witness the marvellous development that is taking place in this part of the Dominion. (Cheers.)

        (Signed),   JAS. MULHOLLAND, Chairman.
Winnipeg, Dec. 9th, 1884.   ALEX. McQUEEN, Secretary.

(The address was beautifully engrossed on parchment, and enclosed in a case covered with blue plush, and bearing an appropriate inscription on a silver shield).

MR. NORQUAY—I also received this communication yesterday, Sir John, from the Liberal-Conservative Association of Portage la Prairie, then in session :—

"The Liberal Conservative Association of Portage la Prairie, now in session, request you to extend to the Right Hon. Sir John A. Macdonald, at the reception, their heartiest congratulations on this the anniversary of his fortieth year in public life. They fully appreciate his great services to our Dominion in the past, and earnestly hope that he may be long spared to administer her affairs. (Cheers.) God save the Queen.

            J. McWENNY, Chairman.
            J. M. ROBINSON, Secretary.

THE NORTH-WEST SPEAKS.

The delegation from Assiniboia, consisting of Mr. Wm. White, member for Regina in the North-West Council; Mr. N. F. Davin, Major Bell, and Mr. V. Foy, were next introduced.

MR. WHITE, addressing Sir John Macdonald, said,—I have been delegated by the Liberal-Conservatives of Regina and neighbourhood to present to you the following address :—

To the Right Honourable Sir John A. Macdonald, G.C.B., Premier of the Dominion of Canada.

We, the Liberal-Conservatives of the town and district of Regina in meeting assembled, desire to congratulate you upon this the fortieth anniversary of your entrance into public life.

When we look back to the time when you commenced your public career, and compare the condition and population of the country which now composes the Dominion of Canada with its present condition and population, we have as Canadians reason to be proud of our country's advancement, and we recognize the fact that the present exalted position of the Dominion is in a great measure due to your untiring energy and to the masterly statesmanship which has characterized your actions in the various high offices of State which you occupied and adorned.

Without enumerating the various reforms and measures tending to the development and prosperity of the Dominion at large, which you have inaugurated and carried through, we, as citizens of the Canadian North-West, feel that to your patriotic efforts is mainly due the opening up and settlement of what was only a few years ago known as "The Great Lone Land." The district of Assiniboia which was but as yesterday the haunt of the Buffalo and the hunting ground of the Indian, is now, owing to the rapid construction of that great national highway, the Canadian Pacific railway, the home of sixty-five thousand industrious and thriving settlers.

We congratulate you upon the distinguished honour which our Most Gracious Sovereign has lately conferred upon you. We recognize it as a tribute to your eminent services as a statesman and leader of public opinion in the Dominion.

In conclusion, we desire to express the hope that you may long be spared to occupy your present high position, that the success which has attended your brilliant career in the past may continue, and that for many years to come you may control the political destinies of our country.

(Signed),   JAS. H. BENSON, Chair.ian.
A. R. McGIRR, Secretary.

THE PREMIER'S REPLY.

SIR JOHN MACDONALD, in reply, said :—Mr. Norquay, Mr. White, and gentlemen, it is peculiarly gratifying to me to receive these addresses from the North-West. I take a great pride in the North-West. I take a great pride in the Province of Manitoba, because the Administration of which I was a member at the time, in some degree, may be considered as the creator of that country. (Cheers.) Immediately after Confederation we set to work to endeavour to get possession for Canada, for the white man, for the English, for the Irish, Scotch, and Frenchman, for the German, for the European, who would come to visit our shores, and settle in our land to redeem the North-West from being a wilderness—or, as it has been called in the last address—"the haunt of the buffalo and the red man." We succeeded in getting possession of it for a very moderate sum, and it has been my gratification and pride to see it rapidly develop itself, to see it the resort of the young men of Ontario, and of the other provinces, and to see it peopled by our fellow subjects from the Old Country. (Hear, hear.) In the settlement of the North-West everything before our time was in a state of infancy—in a state of embryo. At first, not only the Government of which I was a member before 1873, but Mr. Mackenzie's Government had to deal with the problem, yet unsolved in a great measure, and I am here to state that I must give due credit to Mr. Mackenzie's Government for the earnestness of their intention to do the best they could, according to their judgment, for the settlement of that country. (Laughter and cheers.) They made some mistakes, and no doubt we have made some mistakes, but we have earnestly tried to learn by experience how best to promote the settlement and the development of that great expanse of territory. (Cheers.) In the first place, when we came in again, in 1878, we adopted a liberal land policy. (Cheers.) We offered great inducements to the settlers to go there and make it their own. (Cheers.) We studied with some care and attention the system that had been in successful operation in the United States, and our land policy was based in principal on them, but we liberalized their system in very many important instances. (Loud cheers.) I shall not trouble you, gentlemen, with a discussion of affairs in the North-West, because you all know what our policy has been. I shall not trouble this audience by entering at length into the land policy, or the immigration policy connected with the North-West, because everyone is no doubt impatient to hear the other speakers who will address you to-day. But I will say that we have tried to the best of our knowledge, with all earnestness, with all honesty, to advance the interests of that country. In our ideas as to the best means of settling that country we are supported by the voice of the Parliament of Canada. Confident of the approbation of the people of the Dominion we have ventured—boldly ventured— to charge them with the expenditure of large sums of money in the construction of the great transcontinental railway. (Cheers.) We were charged by those opposed to us with having a wild and reckless policy in agreeing to pay twenty-five millions as a loan on the road nearly completed. But we knew the responsibilities we were assuming. We know of what immense consequence it was to the best interests of the whole

Dominion to have that great enterprise completed as speedily as possible. We boldly ventured to charge the people with the payments of these large sums, confident that we would be more than repaid by the development of that country, and by the large addition to the wealth, strength and recources of the Dominion through the instrumentality of that great work. (Cheers.) It is true, gentlemen, that you, the older people of Canada—the older provinces of Canada—have charged yourselves with the expenditure of twenty-five millions in building that road, but I venture to tell you, as we told Parliament, that that country will repay every dollar of it and that not one single sixpence of that large sum will fall upon you or your children, because the lands of the North-West reserved for the purpose will recoup and repay every farthing. (Cheers.) At the same time I will state on behalf of the Government and Parliament that we are in no very great hurry to get that money back again. We would rather see the immediate settlement of the country, the occupation of the free homesteads, and the encouragement of immigration into the North-West, than be severe and harsh and demand the money back again. It will eventually come back, principal and interest, and we are rich, generous and powerful enough to wait. Gentlemen from Manitoba, I thank you very much for this too flattering address. It is peculiarly pleasant to me that it should be presented by the Hon. Mr. Norquay, the first man in Manitoba, the Prime Minister of that great province—great already, although yet only in its infancy. It is a great pleasure to have it come from a man of such known influence, a man born in that country, and whose sole energies are directed to the development of that country. (Cheers.) I am proud also to receive an address from the capital of the North-West, from Regina. I was attacked, and those who acted with me were attacked, for the selection of Regina as the capital. Experience has shown it is the centre of one of the most beautiful and fertile tracts in that beautiful and fertile country. Its future is assured. It is in the richest portion of the North-West, from an agricultural point of view. It is on the line of the C.P.R., and every one can reach it from all parts of the Dominion with railway speed. I am also obliged to the gentlemen from Portage la Prairie. The address expresses the hope that I may visit the place when I go to the North-West. It will be my particular pride to do so and I shall take the opportunity as soon as I can go there without too much rattling of my old bones, when I can go from Montreal to Vancouver and traverse the whole distance by the Canadian Pacific Railway. (Cheers.) A line which will join all the provinces by an iron band which will never be broken. (Cheers.) I have also to thank you, Mr. Norquay, for the kind expressions used to Lady Macdonald. She has been my helpmate in the best sense of the word, and if at my time of life I am in good health and strength I owe it all to her wifely devotion and womanly care and affection for me. (Three cheers were here given for Lady Macdonald.) I hope you will convey to all those you represent when you have an opportunity of speaking to them my most sincere and cordial thanks for the kind expressions contained in the address. (Cheers.)

HON. MR. NORQUAY'S ADDRESS.

Hon. Mr. Norquay was then called upon by the meeting. He was received by loud and prolonged cheering. He said—Mr. Chairman and gentleman, I feel I am exceedingly fortunate in being present with you to assist in tendering to our venerable chieftain this grand tribute of respect which has been the object of your gathering here yesterday and to-day. Although Manitoba has only had an existence of fourteen years, yet her public men have already learned to appreciate the qualities of the eminent statesman who, during the last forty years, has moulded the destinies of Canada. It did not take them long to judge the relative merits of the two parties who claimed their support. (Cheers.) As a representative of the old settlers of that province I may fairly say that all whom I have the honour of representing join with me in offering our allegiance and tendering our support for the purpose of continuing that party in power which has done so much for Manitoba. In Manitoba we are very closely allied to the older provinces as our population is mostly composed of citizens who have left the older provinces in order to better their condition. Whether they have succeeded or not it is for them to say. At all events we find very few of them wanting to come back to Ontario or Quebec. The Province of Manitoba holds out to intended settlers many natural advantages, and it is building up institutions on the model of those found in the older settled parts of the continent. We can hold out fair inducements to parties who find themselves hampered or restricted by the circumstances of the Eastern Provinces. We have the broad and fertile plains of Manitoba and the North-West to be peopled. We consider them a great factor yet to be in the development of the Dominion of Canada. (Applause.) We consider the acquisition of the North-West as one of the greatest facts accomplished by Canada for her future. (Cheers.) The institutions established there are much the same as your own, inasmuch as they were inaugurated by your own brethren, your own friends, who, having left you here, and having enjoyed those institutions in the older provinces have transplanted them there, that they may make their new homes as nearly like the old ones as possible. (Cheers.) I may say to you that it will gladden the hearts of the Conservatives of Manitoba when they hear of this great demonstration held not only for the purpose of honouring our chieftain, but of recording the many glorious deeds in statesmanship which are attributable to him. It will be one of the pleasing features of my return to tell them how united the Conservatives of Ontario are in the support of their leader, who is so highly esteemed and so much thought of by the Conservatives of Manitoba. (Loud cheering.)

THE CONSERVATIVE UNION.

Mr. McCarthy—I beg to present the report of the committee appointed to draft the constitution of the Liberal-Conservative Union. I will explain briefly the objects of the association. It is to be of a provincial character. We have in most of the ridings, and we ought to have in all the ridings, local organizations for the purpose of doing battle when the proper time comes. But we have felt the want, in some contests which have recently taken place, of that which our opponents have, and that is a provincial organization which enables them to work in a contest, and particularly at bye-elections. (Cheers.) Now the proposed organization is to be composed of a certain number, and we have fixed the number at fifty. It is not in any way to interfere—and this is a cardinal point in regard to it—with the local concerns of any particular riding. But it is intended to assist and promote the election of any Conservative candidate who may be selected in the riding. It is more especially for the purpose—not at election times, but at times when all is quiet—of seeing that the party is organized throughout the whole province. (Hear, hear.) It is not intended to interfere in any way with the policy of the party. That is a matter which properly belongs to the leaders of the party and to the representatives in the different bodies to which they are elected. It is simply an organization for the purpose of endeavouring to keep us in proper form so that we will not be found wanting on the day of battle. (Cheers.)

The report was read and adopted.

ONTARIO FRENCH CANADIANS.

The Chairman—While we are waiting for further resolutions, we will hear one of the French-Canadian representatives in the Local Legislature. (Cheers.)

Mr. Robillard, who was received with cheers—I certainly feel proud to have the honour of being called upon at such a large meeting. I am only afraid that I cannot do justice to the occasion, for my stock of English is rather small. As you are aware, I am, as I announced myself in the Legislature, a French-Bleu, living in Ontario. (Laughter.) My announcement at that time created some consternation, as you may well understand, because there was only seventy-seven English-speaking members to keep me—a full-grown Frenchman—in good health, and my friend, Mr. Sol. White, who is half a Frenchman, in check. (Laughter.) But you need not be afraid of French domination. (Hear, hear, and laughter.) In my county one-fifth of the population is French. I have lived there since I was two years o'd ; they know me ; yet they elected me because they knew that I am what I tell you I claim only to be—a Canadian. (Cheers.) I do not come before you as a French Canadian—(applause)—but as a Canadian. (Cheers.) Much has been said in certain quarters against the French-Canadians ; but let me tell you that the more you know us the better you will like us. (Cheers.) We already number 102,000 in Ontario, and I really believe we are so peaceable that most of you do not know we are among you. (Cheers and laughter.) But, sir, the great mass of French-Canadians are Conservative. We are so by our institutions, we are so by our religion. The Province therefore need not be afraid of us. (Applause.) We will rather be a source of strength than a source of weakness to Ontario. (Cheers.) I thank you once more for your kindness in calling upon me. I am glad to see this organization formed. I hope it will see to the assessment rolls so that we will have no more Apjohns—applejohns I call them—(laughter)—to rob the electors of their votes—(cheers) ; so that all men will be able to vote according to their consciences without any interference from the pressing machines which Reform ingenuity have invented. (Applause.)

MR. SOLOMON WHITE, M.P.P., was then called upon. He expressed the great pleasure it gave him to see such a great assemblage of Conservatives. There was no doubt that the occasion was a grand one. The gentleman who moved the appointment of the chairman told them that the occasion required a grand chairman. (Cheers.) He hoped the young men would stand at the back of their chairman and see that he was carried triumphantly to that position which his merits entitled him to. (Cheers.) He thought that they need not be alarmed at the prospect of French domination. If they did have it the domination would be of that kind that would be satisfactory to them, and would be in the interests of the Conservatives of Ontario. He had counselled the French-Canadians in his constituency to stand by the phalanx of Conservatives in the Province of Quebec. They in Quebec had stood by their right honourable leader in time of need. They had stood by him in times of adversity and at other times. They in Quebec were true Conservatives, and would stand by their leader as long as he was able to guide them. The French were Conservative in their institutions, in their instincts and meant to continue so.

MR. J. J. HAWKINS expressed the gratification he felt at the great demonstration in honour of Sir John Macdonald. He was only expressing the opinion of all Conservatives when he said that Sir John was now a link, a bond, a golden bond, binding them closer than ever to that glorious Empire of which they formed so important a part. (Cheers.) He wished to add his little meed of praise to what had been said of the manner in which the leader of the Local Opposition (Mr. Meredith) had conducted the campaign against those in power in Ontario. He believed that under Mr. Meredith's able leadership the Conservative party was destined at the next general election to secure a magnificent triumph. (Cheers.) He said, that because at the last general election they succeeded in carrying seventeen constituencies which had been in the possession of the Grit party since Confederation, and had it not been for over-confidence they would have swept the constituencies. (Hear, hear.) He recognized the necessity for such an organization as they were forming, and believed they would be able to carry not only the next Local election, but the next Dominion election.

DRAFT OF RESOLUTIONS.

MR. JOHN HAGGART, M.P., presented the draft of resolutions as adopted by the Striking Committee.

The CHAIRMAN said that some five or six resolutions had been prepared, and these it was proposed to submit to the convention in the afternoon.

ELECTING THE OFFICERS.

Mr. McCarthy, M.P., said :—As the last business to come before us, after having formed the Liberal-Conservative Union of Ontario, our duty is to appoint the officers. First, the president; second, the vice-president, and third, fifty members composing the Executive Committee. I therefore beg to move that the following gentlemen compose the officers and executive committee of the Union :— President, Right Hon. Sir John Macdonald—(cheers); Vice-President, Mr. W. R. Meredith—(cheers); members of the Executive Committee—Hon. Frank Smith, Edward Gurney (Toronto); John Haggart, M.P.; D. Creighton, M.P.P.; Thos. Long (Collingwood); A. R. Boswell, Mayor of Toronto; R. R. Pringle (Cobourg); E. F. Clarke (Toronto); S. R. Hesson, M P.; John A. Mackenzie (Sarnia); A. McNeill, M.P.; F. Clancy, M.P.P.; Dalton McCarthy, M.P.; Dr Sullivan (Kingston); J. W. Carruthers, (St. Thomas); T. Cowan (Galt); Col. T. Tisdale (Simcoe); N C. Wallace, M.P.; J. J. Foy, Q.C. (Toronto); H. E. Clarke, M.P.P.; F. E. Kilvert, M.P.; Dr. Bergin, M.P.; C. H. Macintosh, M.P.; J. C. Rykert, M.P.; J. C. Patterson, M.P.; J. J. Hawkins (Brantford); Frank Madill (Beaverton); J. A. Macdonell, D. R. Murphy (Trenton); Hon. A. Morris, M.P.P.; L. Wigle, M.P.; Peter White, M.P.; T. Coghlin, M.P.; Major Gray, M.P.P.; James Anderson (Georgina); Hon. G. C. McKindsey, A. Robertson, M.P.; John Carnegie, M.P.P.; A. Boultbee (Toronto); John Muir (Hamilton); W. P. Atkinson (Parkdale); P. Baskerville, M.P.P.; John Shaw (Yorkville); A. Shaw (Walkerton); L. McCallum, M.P., R. Henry (Brantford); W. P. R. Street (London); A. F. Wood, M.P.P.; J. H. Fraser (London); G. T. Blackstock (Toronto).

We have endeavoured to distribute the representation fairly over the Province, but of course you will understand that there will have to be a certain number within the immediate neighbourhood of Toronto so that when unimportant matters come up a quorum may be obtained. When important business is to be transacted we hope to have the attendance of members from all parts of the Province. The chairman wishes me to state that this committee will exist until September next, when according to the rules a general meeting will be held and a new committee appointed, and so on from September to September. (Hear, hear.)

Mr. White, M.P.P. (Essex), seconded the resolution, which was adopted unanimously.

The convention then adjourned to meet again at one o'colock.

(AFTER RECESS.)

THE BOUNDARY QUESTION.

Mr. G. T. Blackstock then moved the second resolution as follows :—" That we express our satisfaction that the question as to the boundary of the Province has been finally determined by the decision of the Judicial Committee of the Privy Council, and the speedy settlement of the dispute by the Privy Council within the period of seven or eight months from the time the case was submitted is the clearest and best indication of the wisdom and patriotism of Mr. Meredith as leader of the Opposition in the Legislative Assembly, in persistently and consistently advocating that the matter should be referred to that tribunal as originally proposed and insisted on by Sir John Macdonald so long ago as 1872; and we regard with the scorn it merits the unwarranted attempt of Mr. Mowat's Administration to claim the credit for the result of a policy which they had all along opposed, and accepted only to escape the grave consequences brought about by their reckless agitation and wilful delay." He expressed his pleasure at having this opportunity of meeting so large a gathering of provincial Conservatives. He might say he attended as a representative Conservative young man, and in that capacity could protest against the union invited by the Grits between themselves and the youth of the country. What could the youth of the country hope from the Grit party who had at various times advocated disruption of the Empire and annexation ? (Cheers.) The present demonstration would in years to come be looked back to as a memorable event in the history of the country, and it would be said that the Conservatives of those days knew how to appreciate the ability of a statesman who combined the talents of a Beaconsfie'd and a Gladstone. He went on to say that if the Conservatives were true to their cause they would see in future the leaders of the party in Ontario should receive as loyal a support as their leaders in the Dominion. They had made the great mistake of supposing that provincial issues were of little importance, so long as they had the power in Federal matters. But the power in Ontario was often a key to power at Ottawa, and he asked them to see to it, that they in future gave an energetic support to the party leaders in the Province. He besought the young men not to be led away by the false cry of Ontario's rights as enunciated by by the Grits. (Cheers.)

MR. JOHN MILLER (Pickering) seconded the resolution, which was carried.

THE ALLEGED CONSPIRACY.

Mr. N. A. COSTE, of South Essex, moved, "That the charges made by the members of the Local Administration on the floor of the Legislative Assembly against the members of the Government of Canada, in direct terms, and by inuendo against the members of the Opposition in that Assembly, of complicity in the so-called attempt to bribe some of the members of that House, without any evidence to support it, was a grave offence against the amenities and common decencies of public life ; that the result of the investigation before the commissioners appointed to take evidence on the subject is admittedly a complete exoneration of the members of the Dominion Cabinet and of the Local Opposition ; and that the sworn testimony of the Ministers themselves established the fact that a conspiracy to entrap the Opposition and others into an attempt to bribe certain 'members of that Assembly was entered into by the Mowat Administration, to serve a party purpose, regardless of the honour and dignity of the House." He wished he had a more savoury subject to deal with. (Laughter.) However, as he happened to come from a county represented by one of the informers employed by the Mowat Government, he supposed he must speak to the resolution, if only to say that the county was ashamed of itself for having sent to the Legislature a man who could be induced to become a vile informer. (Hear, hear.) The bribery case was one which reflected much discredit upon the Mowat Government. It was prepared with the sole purpose of injuring the Conservative party, but he hoped it would recoil upon the heads of the men who got it up. Mr. Mowat and his colleagues, of course, hoped that the affair would hurt more particularly the leader of the Opposition ; but they dared not come out openly and attack that gentleman with reference to it. (Hear, hear.) On the contrary, they came out against the Ministers at Ottawa ; when Mr. Mowat rose in his place in the House and made that infamous charge against Dominion Ministers, he well knew that he had no grounds for it. (Applause.) This was a disgraceful circumstance. But equally disgraceful was the guise in which Mr. Mowat posed before the people of Ontario. He called himself, above all things, a Christian politician. The Bible, as everybody knew, instructed us how to pray that we be not led into temptation, yet this man, who called himself a Christian, was privy to the leading of others into temptation, and meanly boasted of his cleverness in that regard. (Cheers.) He (Mr. Coste) believed that no man, except one who had used the word Christian for the purpose of making political capital out of religion, would be so sly and sneaking as to do the work with which Mowat's name is now irreparably connected. (Cheers.) Nor was there much true morality in men who put the Sabbath day to the vile purpose for which Mr. Mowat and his followers used it. It was on a Sunday that they hatched this conspiracy. (Hear, hear.) Three times on a Sunday did the member from Essex go to the Walker House begging to be bribed. (Hear, hear.) It was on the Sabbath that the Local Government met at Mr. Mowat's house to complete the conspiracy. It was on a Sunday that the County-Crown Attorney went to work to prepare his indictment. (Hear, hear.) Throughout the whole affair, the Sunday was desecrated. One of the first principles of Christianity was sacrificed in the attempt to decoy opponents into an offence. Truth was sacrificed by the agents of Mr. Mowat who sought for bribes. The decencies of private life were outraged, and that precept which honourable men obeyed, teaching as it did that opponents should be fought honourably and not stabbed behind the back, had been departed from. (Cheers.)

Mr. N. CURRIE—I second the resolution.—Carried.

THE NATIONAL POLICY.

Mr. McKECHNIE, of Dundas, moved, "That this convention, on behalf of the Conservative party of Ontario, endorses the National Policy, which the country declared for in 1878 and again in 1882, being convinced, from the plain and manifest results that have followed the application of the tariff since 1879, that it is the policy best calculated to promote the welfare of a young community (more especially of one lying alongside a great protectionist nation like the United States), and to secure its interests against destruction from the slaughtering of foreign goods in seasons of temporary depression; and that we call upon Parliament to maintain this policy intact until such times as the Americans, who rejected our reciprocity proposals in 1874 think fit to offer the free interchange of those natural products which by law the Government of Canada have now the power to admit free on reciprocal conditions." He was sorry the duty of moving this resolution had not fallen to better hands. He might say, though, that he was a thorough believer in the National Policy. He had something to do with it long before it was taken by any political party, and he was thoroughly convinced that it was correct, although some little depression might now exist, for depression existed the world over. Our temporary trouble was nothing to what it would be if we had no National Policy. (Hear, hear.) In many vital respects the National Policy had benefited; but it had done so particularly as regarded the variety and number of the industries which it had introduced. It had helped Canada to take a place among the nations. It had placed us ahead of those countries whose statesmen were just finding out that the political economy of the writers of the old school was not all it was alleged to be. He declared that if it had not been for the introduction of a protective policy, a host of industries that had sprung up since its introduction, could never have existed. It was a policy which affected the whole country, and would eventually result in the placing of Canada among the foremost manufacturing nations of the world. We were merely following in the wake of the most prosperous nation of the world. The manufacturing industries of the United States, and even Great Britain, had been built up by a protective policy; and in Great Britain at present, after many years of free trade, they had discovered that it was a failure, and no doubt at the next election in the old country, the question of protection or free trade would be one of vital issues.

At this point SIR LEONARD TILLEY entered the room and was received with loud cheering.

Mr. McKECHNIE said he was glad to hear the applause with which Sir Leonard was greeted. The speaker contrasted the reception accorded to deputations of manufacturers by Sir Richard Cartwright with the reception they received at the hands of Sir Leonard Tilley. The former told them to go home, mind their business better, and be more economical. Sir Leonard listened to their representations, thought about what he had heard, and gave the country the policy which had done so much good and would do more. What he wished to say, in conclusion, was that a reversal of this great policy would be ruin to Canada. The only argument in favour of such a reversal was the statement that the market was over-stocked. Certainly the necessities of the country, in some lines, had been more than overtaken. But that would right itself. The consumption would soon be equal to the production. Then, of course, the argument for a reversal of the policy would be gone. (Hear,

hear.) The speaker hoped that the Government would do even more in the way of protection than it had done. The iron and other industries needed more protection. If the present policy of protection were abandoned, he asked, what would become of our manufacturing industries? Free trade was very pretty as a theory. So was the millennium. But the world was not prepared for either at the present time.

Mr. McKechnie was loudly applauded in the course of his remarks.

MR. JOHN E. DOYLE, of Essex, seconded the motion—I am a practical farmer. Since the National Policy has been in force I have been materially benefitted by it. I live in Essex. It is a frontier county, and to-day, I am happy to say, it is a prosperous county. (Cheers.) Previous to the carrying of the National Policy, we, though shut out from the American market, were the victims of the competition of the Americans who had our market. (Hear, hear.) But that is all changed now, thanks to the National Policy. It is true that there is a sligh depression, but we have a bountiful harvest. We have two bushels of wheat where we had only one before. (Hear, hear.) The advantages, other than the natural advantages we possess, are attributable to the National Policy, and to the man who said to our neighbours, "You shall not enjoy the privileges of our market unless you give us equal privileges in yours." (Applause.) Long may that great man live to defend our rights. (Cheers.)

MR. ROBERT BROUGH, Gananoque.—I am the oldest protectionist but the youngest Conservative in this hall. For thirty long years I fought in the Reform ranks, and though I stand on this platform I am still a true Reformer, because I believe in reforming what requires to be reformed as sincerely as I believe in conserving what is good. (Cheers.) Years ago I told our South Leeds Reform Convention that the Reform party must adopt protection. But they would not take the advice—those old Reformers are as a matter of fact the worst kind of Conservatives. (Loud Applause.) But we had a protection association in South Leeds thirty years ago; and we actually went to the expense of sending to Glasgow to get out a gentleman by the name of Abraham Duncan to go through the province and teach the principle. (Hear, hear.) So when my friends who are still in the old Reform party say I left that party I reply I was always a Reformer and a protectionist, and I am both now. (Cheers.) I hope this party will stick together. I am but a new member of it. At the time of the Pacific scandal, I must acknowledge that I was not with the Conservative party. I know that with many others I was misled. But I am not disappointed altogether with the conduct of the country on that occasion. The fact that when grave charges were made Canadians rose to condemn, though mistakenly, the statesmen implicated, shows that at heart Canada is sound. (Applause.) However, I have lived to learn that I was mistaken. I rejoice now to join in this greeting to Sir John. I adhere to his great principles, and I believe that those who would unsettle this country by talking of annexation and independence are merely preparing the way to a career which will end unwept, unhonoured and unsung. (Cheers.)

THE CANADIAN PACIFIC RAILWAY.

MR. THOMAS COWAN, of Galt, then moved the following resolution:—"That this convention heartily approves of the energetic construction of the Canadian Pacific Railway, now approaching completion, believing that the country will greatly benefit by that vast undertaking, not only politically, but materially, beyond all present calculation; that it will lead to an immediate development of the North-West and of British Columbia, in the prosperity of which the older provinces must share, and that it will complete without further delay the great fabric of Confederation, and place Canada in a position as regards natural wealth and extent of territory second to that of no other country in the world." He said:—I did not know until a moment or two ago that I would be called upon to move such an important resolution as this in reference to the Canadian Pacific Railway. The construction of this railway is one of the main planks, if not the main plank, of the platform of the Conservative party as I understand it. Like my esteemed friend from Gananoque, and my esteemed friend the Finance Minister—all old Reformers, and they tell me they are the worst Tories in the land—I am with you heart and soul. So long as the Dominion Government and the Conservative party stand true to the Canadian National Policy, and to the scheme of a Canadian national highway extending from the Atlantic to the Pacific, so long, I say, as these are the planks in your platform you will have hundreds, nay, thousands, of the old Reformers with you. (Cheers.) I say here advisedly that every true Canadian who has national feeling and national blood running through his veins will in support of this policy bury party politics and stand by you and the Dominion Government. (Cheers.) I am not here to make a speech. (Go on.) In carrying out the national policy of welding the whole of our provinces into one great country we are only realizing to-day what the old Reformers saw in the vista of the future. We are realizing what Lord Durham predicted in the early days of reform, when he said he looked forward to a time when the whole of British North America would be one. Are we not one to-day? (Cheers.) Baldwin, Lafontaine, and Rolph all looked forward to this event with prophetic eye. D'Arcy McGee and the late George Brown, when sitting at the convention at Charlottetown, saw this in the future. But what would be the use of the realization of these dreams if you had not men of Canadian ideas, of determination and energy, of faith and hope, and confidence in the resources of this country, to push it forward? If you had left it in the hands of the so-called Reformers it would still be in dreamland, and a thing of poetic imagination. (Laughter.) In the hands of my friend, the Finance Minister, it is neither a dream nor a poetic fiction nor a romance, but a fact, and before 1886 has done its days the whole Government will be able to take the cars at Halifax and proceed on a triumphal trip to the Pacific shore. (Cheers.) Although I have voted against my old chieftain in the early days of my life, my earnest wish is that the grand old man may live to see the day that he can take the cars at the Atlantic coast and go on a triumphal procession to the Pacific terminus. Talk of the conquests of the heroes of early days, men who have laid everything waste before them and trampled ankle deep in their brethren's gore, none of their victories are so glorious as this triumph of peace achieved in this land by four or five millions of people under the guidance of the Conservative Government. "Peace hath her conquests more glorious than those of war." (Cheers.) I ask what policy had the Opposition in reference to these national objects. Where is it? Echo answers, Where? (Laughter.) As Sir John Macdonald said in regard to these questions, he had nailed his colors to the very top of the mast, and by this would stand or fall. What is the policy of the Opposition? What is it on the trade question? Incidental protection to protectionists and free trade to economists who have read Adam Smith's "Wealth of Nations." No duty on coal if a man happens to burn a great deal of it, and a high duty if he is a farmer and happens to burn wood. (Laughter.) The Grits were as wise as serpents but not as harmless as doves. The so-called Reform party has absolutely no platform or policy. They have incidental protection, free trade, revenue tariff, and everything and nothing. In regard to the Pacific railway, the next plank in our platform, what is and has been their policy? Their scheme was one of postponement. They said that it would not do to build a railway along the barren regions of Lake Superior. But when there was some likelihood of there being delay in the construction of this section they said we must have a road around Lake Superior. Then next, they said postpone the building of the line through British Columbia. Whether they would build it in five years or five hundred years no one knew. They would not have the line built through the huge projection of the American desert, or what is now known as the fertile belt of the Saskatchewan. So, in every part of the scheme their policy has been one of delay and of procrastination. Instead of opening up our own territory, developing our own commerce, and securing the trade of the North-West for our own cities, they wished to divert it to Milwaukee, Chicago or St. Paul, away from Toronto or Montreal. (Cheers.) Our policy is essentially a Canadian one. I thoroughly believe that every one of the Grits may bow down and

worship their policy without violating a single command of
it is unlike anything in the heavens above or the earth benea
the earth. (Laughter.) To-day the leader of the Opposition
his sentences are, cannot evolve out of his brain one single
which he is prepared to stand. (Cheers.) I am only too gl
the two grand essential principles which you have adopted.
of the Imperial Act binding us together. But we are one by
Policy and by virtue of the national highway linking us toge
and iron. We are one nationally, one politically, and one co

Mr. MOBERLEY, of Collingwood, seconded the resolutic
political parties were agreed that they should do all possible
which they purchased from the Hudson Bay Co. Up to th
they differed as to the means by which a population shoul
country. Mr. Mackenzie's policy was to build a line up t
French river, connecting with the Northern Pacific railwa;
and making use of 1,000 miles of that line to make conne
territories of Canada. He asked whether that was a polic;
posed by any man holding the reins of power. He compa
Macdonald's policy, which saved the country from dissolutic
it would not have been many years before they would have l
showed that during the late civil war in the United States th
followed in the construction of the Central Pacific railway,
for the purpose of binding the Pacific slope close to the older
railway the chances were many that it would not have ri
Union. Canada was in a similar position, and could not l
North-West without such a railway. By Sir John Macdona
was going to be welded together.

The resolution was put and adopted.

FRONTENAC'S SPLENDID TRIBU1

The CHAIRMAN—There is a deputa...on of gentlemen he
Frontenac, and they wish to interview Sir John. (Laughter

The deputation, consisting of Messrs. Henry Wilmot, M
T. J. Walker, William Stokes, McNab, C. M. Spooner, H. 1
Walkem, secretary of the Association, advanced to the front
the deputation bearing a large and beautiful silver epergne, a
present.

Mr. WILMOT said—Sir John, on behalf of the Conservat
County of Frontenac, I present this small tribute of respect
of your long services. We wish you long life to enjoy it.
occupy the highest seat in the realm, and after this earthly
that you may fill a mansion above, not built with hands. (L

THE PREMIER RETURNS THANK

SIR JOHN MACDONALD said—Mr. Wilmot, and gentleme
and gratification your handsome present from the County of
years I lived in the county town of Frontenac, and for many
in Parliament, in the good old days when the City of Kings
borough. (Cheers and laughter.) I think I used to kno
living in Frontenac. Although Kingston has temporarily go
constitutional position there is still hope of its returning to s
Conservatism, which means, I think, the same thing—(renev
ever has to change and assume this condition of mind it wil
doing so by the persuasion of the surrounding county. (C
years and years, almost as long as I can look back, has bee

stituency. It returned Sir Henry Smith, my friend and colleague, for many years; it returned Sheriff Ferguson and many other distinguished Conservatives, and its present representative is the Hon. George Kirkpatrick, the worthy and respected Speaker of the House of Commons. (Cheers.) Therefore I have particular pleasure and pride in receiving this gift—a testimonial which shows that I am not forgotten by my old friends and old clients, (Laughter.) They were clients of mine, gentlemen, and it would seem that my bills were moderate, and that I left them some money, or they could not give me this testimonial to-day. (Much laughter.) I shall have great pride in showing this testimonial to those who honour me with a visit at Ottawa, and when I am removed to the place which my good friend wishes me to occupy by and bye—(laughter)—I shall hand it down to my children, who, when they look at it, will remember with pride that it comes from the good old Conservative County of Frontenac. (Loud and prolonged cheering.)

FIDELITY TO THE EMPIRE.

Mr. DEACON, Q.C. (Renfrew), moved the following resolution:—"That we have read with astonishment and disapprobation the speeches of certain leading men of the so-called Reform party, in which a severance of the connection of this country with Great Britain is boldly advocated; that we oppose all such attempts to disturb our present most satisfactory relations with Great Britain as being mischievous and uncalled for, and that we here reiterate our adhesion to the British Crown and to British institutions, under which this country has made great and enduring progress." In the course of an eloquent address, in which he condemned those who decried British connection, he said it was well that the Conservative party should leave no room for doubt as to the position it took. (Cheers.) If the rot had begun in the other party, let care be taken that not a speck of it be found even on Conservative skirts. (Cheers.) What should we have to gain by being independent? By being nominally independent, we should be dependent, but by being nominally dependent, we are really independent. (Loud cheers.) We are the freest people in the world. (Cheers.) We are relieved by our position in not electing a chief magistrate from the turmoil, excitement, disturbance of business, and every other evil attending a great election, as we have seen recently on the other side of the line. (Cheers.) A gentleman is sent from England as our Governor, and we are as free as any country under the sun. (Cheers.) We may make laws not in harmony with the policy of the Imperial Government, and yet we may not be disturbed. (Cheers.) We are, therefore, completely free and completely independent. (Renewed cheering.) I do not desire to trespass upon your attention any further, but simply to say that I am sure this resolution will meet with your entire approbation. I have therefore pleasure in moving its adoption. (Applause.)

At this stage Lady Macdonald, accompanied by Lady Macpherson, entered one of the private boxes. She was recognized by the audience, which rose and cheered enthusiastically for some moments. Lady Macdonald graciously bowed her acknowledgments.

Mr. ROBILLARD, M.P.P., said he felt proud as a French-Canadian to be asked to second the motion. He was proud to say that his compatriots in this province were peaceable and intelligent enough—seven-eighths of them—to be Conservatives. (Cheers and laughter.) He was not going to be led into making another speech, but he would just say that as a whole the French-Canadians were proud to be living under the British flag—(loud cheers)—and as one of his countrymen—well known to them—Sir George Étienne Cartier, once said, "The last gun that will be fired in British North America to defend the British flag will be fired by a French-Canadian." (Loud cheers.) He felt proud at being asked to second the motion.

The resolution was unanimously adopted amid tremendous applause.

APPROVING THE GOVERNMENT POLICY.

Mr. MORGAN (Middlesex) moved the next resolution as follows:—"That we approve of the general policy of the Dominion Government in encouraging railway development; in maintaining the efficiency of our canal system; in prosecuting all necessary public works tending to facilitate trade and commerce; in exempting from taxation tea, coffee, and other necessaries of life not produced here; in reducing the rate of interest payable on the public debt; in keeping the expenditure within the revenue, so as to maintain public credit, and in furthering by every lawful means the material welfare of the people."

Mr. F. MADILL (Beaverton) seconded the motion.

The resolution was adopted unanimously.

THE FINANCE MINISTER.

The CHAIRMAN—I have now the pleasure of introducing the Minister of Finance. (Loud cheers.)

SIR LEONARD TILLEY—Mr. Chairman and gentlemen:—This is a deeply interesting occasion. (Cheers.) It is interesting to me personally, because of the cordial welcome you have given me; but it is doubly pleasurable and interesting because I have witnessed what must delight the heart of every public man, namely, a due and proper acknowledgment of a public service of forty years' duration. (Cheers.) As a public man, let me say I have always deeply regretted the abuse that is poured out on the heads of public men, especially those of the Liberal-Conservative party. (Hear, hear.) Though abuse is the tribute paid by envy to worth, and though we always find the sticks and stones at the foot of the tree which bears the best fruit— (hear, hear)—still this constant abuse and misrepresentation of men who have devoted themselves to the best of their abilities to the service of the country keeps out of public life able and valuable men who would be otherwise disposed to give the country the benefit of their talent and their labour. (Cheers.) Such demonstrations as this, however, indicate that abuse is not the only reward a conscientious public servant will receive. (Applause.) They show that the majority in the Dominion of Canada recognize faithful services. (Cheers.) My friend, Mr. Cowan, who has just preceded me, is always acceptable on the platform. (Hear, hear.) When I first heard him some three or four years ago I said that if ever I had a contest in St. John again and he could spare the time he would have to come down and help me. (Laughter and applause.) But he refers to a fact which renders it desirable that I should make a few remarks with reference to my early political career, and with reference to the party with which I have been identified. In New Brunswick, before Confederation, I was identified with the Liberal party. We took up and carried through the Legislature such measures of reform as we considered necessary. When we had carried them the further question of the union of the Maritime Provinces arose. Just then our friends from Ontario and Quebec came down to Prince Edward Island and proposed a larger union, and we were led to conclude from the evidence before us that it might be to our interest to come into this larger union. We therefore delayed any action with reference to the smaller union, and subsequently agreed to come in with you and make the then scattered provinces a great country, with national aspirations. (Applause.) When that question was settled Sir John Macdonald, who was then entrusted with the organization of the Government, sent for me with others from the Maritime Provinces. I came and saw him. I recollect very well the differences that had to be harmonized and the different interests that had to be dealt with. It was then proposed to have a coalition Government—a Government that would lay aside all old issues and take hold of the questions which the union would bring up. Our chieftain asked some of the leading men of Ontario to enter into his Government, and I remember that they asked Mr. Archibald and myself to come up here and confer with them and their friends on political matters. We came, and while here were closeted for two hours with Mr. George Brown. He said : "You were with the Reform party in the past ; let us have a Reform party now. Refuse to enter a Government with the Conservative leaders." I said, "We have settled all former questions ; we have buried past issues. The only parties in New Brunswick now are Unionists and Anti-unionists, our elections in New Brunswick were fought out on that line, the union having been agreed upon we must make this union a success. Well, I entered the Government. We laid aside old issues—(cheers) —with a determination to make this great country what it is destined to be—(applause)—and what with the assistance of Sir John Macdonald it is becoming. (Cheers.) Well, I as a Liberal, with other Liberals from Ontario and Nova Scotia, joined with the Conservatives or Tories of Ontario and Quebec, and I must say I have never found any lack of true liberality on the part of our chieftain. I do not hesitate to say that the experience of the twelve years I have been associated with him is that a more liberal minded man does not live in Canada. Politicians—not statesmen—will sometimes attempt to make capital out of sectional issues.— local issues ; but whenever anything of that kind has arisen Sir John Macdonald has put his foot down upon it. (Cheers.) When any attempt has been made to do what was found to be unjust to the smaller provinces Sir John has always frowned it down. (Cheers.) As a proof of this I may point out that from 1867 to 1872 many of the men who came into Parliament from those Provinces opposed to Sir John A. Macdonald's government, subsequently declared that they would support his Administration because they found it more liberal and fairminded towards the smaller provinces than the men who were in Opposition. (Applause.) It was the same with regard to creeds. While he would permit no injustice to communities he has been careful that no denomination should meet with oppression. Justice to all has been his principle. (Cheers.) Is it a question of nationality? He has succeeded by his fairness in securing the support of an overwhelming majority of the representatives of the French population of Quebec. (Applause.) I do not hesitate to say that he has done justice to even the smallest provinces. You all know right well that he has been charged in Ontario with neglecting the interests of Ontario, because he has meted out justice to the other provinces. As I say, a politician may take advantage of these local issues, but not a true statesman. He must at times even risk his popularity in his own province, when he has to act for the interests of the whole country. (Cheers.) Then is it to be wondered at that I have felt it to be a pleasure and privilege to stand by him and give him any assistance I could in the furtherance of his broad, liberal and progressive measures, in the interests of the country and of the great masses of the people. Before proceeding with the few remarks which I propose making with reference to the policy of the Government, I desire to say something about a matter personal to myself. I have read in the newspapers that Mr. Tilley, in 1879, all at once became a protectionist, that I was a free trader down to 1879, and suddenly developed into a protectionist. Let me here tell you a little bit of history. I was first nominated in 1850. I have not had, like Sir John, forty years of public service, but have had nearly thirty-five years since I was first elected. (Cheers.) I have sat either in the Local or Dominion Parliaments for twenty-seven sessions, and I think I can say what few men living can say to-day, that I have been so far in accord with public sentiment that during nearly the whole of that time I have been a Minister in Parliament. I was first nominated when absent in Boston, and much against my personal wishes, by a number of manufacturers who met in St. John, to choose candidates for that city and county favourable to protection. (Cheers.) In the first session we sat there the Government of the day did not have the responsibility of introducing a tariff, as they did a few years after. A committee of thirteen, one from each constituency, was appointed to prepare a series of resolutions for submission to the House. Well, our representatives from St. John were elected in favour of protection, and we carried through by a majority vote of the Legislature, a more protective tariff than is on the statute book of the Dominion to-day. In 1854 we accepted the reciprocity treaty between the United States and the different provinces, including New Brunswick. We made concessions because our American neighbors made concessions to us. We say to them still, the moment you take down one rail of the fence we will do the same. In 1867, when we came into Parliament, we arranged a tariff with the view of making it as harmonious as possible for the different provinces. But, as our chieftain said, it was the policy of Canada as far back as 1850 to increase the tariff on articles which could be made in the country. What was the answer I made as Finance Minister to the deputations which waited upon me in 1873? I said that there were reasons why we should not disturb the tariff as it stood then, but when Parliament met again the Government would be prepared to do justice to the different interests of the country. It was no new policy with me. As early as 1850 I felt that although we were small provinces, if we were to have any vitality we must get it through protection. This has, therefore, been my conviction for more than thirty-five years. (Cheers.) I know that there are a large number to speak to-day, and I shall therefore condense what I have to say in as few words as possible, so that you can take away with you a few answers to the unfounded charges and assertions which have been made in reference to the policy and conduct of the Government in the administration of affairs under the National Policy. Sir Richard Cartwright was at Montreal recently and delivered an address there, and he commenced his remarks by telling the audience that he would tell them the truth. (Laughter.) I hope it is not necessary for me to make such a declaration to this audience. (Cheers.) I will present to you some statements and you can go home and take the records, the Public Accounts, and Trade and Navigation Returns, and study them for yourselves, and if you do not find my statements correct, brand me as a man whose statements cannot be relied on, and do not listen to me any more for the future; but if you find my statements correct it will strengthen your confidence and enable you to meet our opponents and answer the assertions they make, and triumphantly carry into future elections the principles adopted in 1878 and confirmed in 1882. Well, what did Sir Richard Cartwright say? He said that the population of Canada had been driven out of the country by the increased taxation under the national policy, and by the taxation rendered necessary by the extravagance of the Government. Now, let us just deal with this briefly. He says the population is drifting out of the country. It is the easiest thing in the world for a gentleman to sit down and make statements, and make calculations from these statements. But if those statements are known to be unreliable, he might pile up a column of calculations 100 feet high and they would not amount to anything, because the foundation is false. (Hear, hear.) We know he started upon a false basis. He relied upon statements, with regard to the exodus, made by interested officials in the United States. He could not plead ignorance on the subject, because the Minister of Agriculture in his place in Parliament showed by the most undoubted evidence that these statements were fallacious. But still he brought them up nearly two years afterwards in order to base upon them an attack upon the Government and upon its policy. He was speaking in Montreal the other day, where in 1878 there might have been seen the words "To Let" upon many doors and in many windows. There are now but few places unoccupied, many in addition having been erected during the last year or two, several of them magnificent residences, as well as many built for the mechanic and artisan. (Cheers.) And he said, while giving these doleful accounts of the exodus of the country :—"It is true you are an enterprising community, and the remarks I make will not perhaps apply to Montreal." (Laughter.) It would not do to say so of Montreal to an audience of his own supporters even. But throughout the Dominion, he might say, you will find so-and-so. I suppose if he had been speaking here he would have excepted Toronto, and I know of other towns that have been built up and that have increased in population of which he would have made the same exception had he been speaking there. These statements we know are erroneous. But what is the fact? Has it decreased our population? You know that in the cities we have municipal organizations able to take the statistics, and by them we know it is not the case. Speaking in the presence of the representatives of the city of Ottawa I may say that I saw it stated that the increase in the population of that city was 4,000 during the last year. In Toronto I find a large increase. I never come up here without seeing much building going on, residences for good workingmen, and palaces for your merchants and professional men, and magnificent structures being erected for your commercial transactions. The decrease is not here. But we know that there has been a large influx of people during the last few years, and some are beginning to cry out that we are bringing in too many immigrants. Sir Richard Cartwright is saying that we are not bringing them in, or if we are bringing them in, that they are only passing through, and then he is counting them as part of his exodus. (Laughter.) These statements do not agree. We know there has been an increase in the population. Sir Richard Cartwright may take up some school statistics. I can quite understand that the National Policy may affect the attendance at schools. I should be sorry if it had, but what is the tendency? The probability is that children of thirteen or fourteen years of age, or perhaps younger, that would otherwise have been at school, are taken away from the schools. Why; Because they have tempting wages given them. That might be one reason why, in some localities, the school attendance might be smaller than before. It cannot be that there is a decrease in the population. Above two hundred thousand have been brought in and settled in the country during the last two years. The population that has been retained in the country must have placed it in a better position that it would have been in without that population. Take up the census returns of 1871 and of 1881, and we have some important facts, but what we wanted to find out was the increase from 1878 to 1884. Well, we have got that to some extent from a report of gentlemen employed to get information for the Government, and this we propose to submit to Parliament. In May last the Government felt that this matter was of such importance, not in order to meet the charges made against the Government, but in order to meet the damaging statements that are made by our opponents, which go into foreign countries and into Old England, with reference to Canada, that we should have reliable data regarding the effect of this policy. The Government, therefore, decided to spend a small sum of money in employing gentlemen to obtain information with regard to the progress made by the country from 1878 to 1884—the effect of the National Policy, the increase in the number of hands employed, the increase in the amount of wages paid, the value of the products of Canada, and the increase in the capital employed. I have this day received from one of the gentlemen employed, who is now in Toronto, some information, and it covers about one half of the manufactures of the Dominion. We will have it more complete when Parliament meets in order that it may be criticised generally, and that the effects of this policy since 1878 may be seen. The number of hands employed in 1878 was 26,764. The wages paid in 1878 amounted to $7,729,010; the value of the products in that year was $32,554,900, and the amount of the capital employed was in that year $24,353,500. Now, the gentlemen who collected this information visited 670 factories, 440 being old established ones, and 230 of them having been started since 1878. They have ascertained the increased number of hands employed, the wages paid to the employees, the increased quantity of products, and the result of their labour. Then they have taken the statistics of the old 440 and the new 230 and they have given us this statement. The number of hands employed over and above the number employed in 1878 is 23,914, and that covers only about half the industries. (Loud cheers.) The increase in the amount of wages paid is $7,594,650. The increase in the value of the products is $38,771,700; and the capital invested since then is $19,714,000. Taking this as a report of half the industries inspected down to the present time, let us see what the total increase will be on the basis I have given you as a result of the introduction of the N. P. The number of hands employed over and above the number employed in 1878 will be 47,828, wages paid $15,189,000, increase of manufactures $77,543,000—(cheers) —and increased capital invested $39,428,000. (Cheers.) Gentlemen, when we consider what has been done in the short period of five years—you can hardly call it five years, as the new tariff only came into force in March, 1879—it is most marvellous. Machinery has been set up, capital introduced, buildings erected and these enormous increases have taken place which I have stated. (Cheers.) These 47,000 operatives represent one hundred thousand inhabitants, that is, by including the wives and children of these artisans. We know what the change is which has been brought about. Take any town to-day where there are manufacturing industries and compare its position with what it was in 1878—(hear, hear)—when the labouring men of Canada were asking the Minister of Public Works to give them bread, or else employment. (Cheers.) This is not the position of affairs to-day; and when we consider these facts, I ask you, is it possible that there has been a decrease in our population, as some would have us believe, or an increase in work? We know we have it on undoubted authority that there has been an increase in our population, an increase so great that there are men in the Dominion to-day—perhaps not far from where I am now—who are beginning to complain regarding the immigrants coming to this country. I do not question their right to do so, but I will say this for the Government, that it has been our aim to encourage the immigration of agricultural labourers and domestic servants, and if on examination we find more artisans coming in than we can find labour for, we will discourage such immigration and confine ourselves to encouraging the immigration of those two other classes of which I have spoken. (Cheers.) I merely mention this fact to show that while on the one hand our opponents are complaining that the people are leaving the country, another class are complaining that we are bringing in more immigrants than the country requires. So much for the question of population. I hold it has been increased, and I think I have given you evidence of it. What has that increase done? I was delighted to hear a farmer on this platform to-day express his conviction on the subject. He did it with an earnestness that must have led you to believe what he stated—that in the N.P. the farmer had got his full share of the benefit. (Cheers.) Sir Richard Cartwright said, the other day, that the imposition of this tariff had increased the cost of the necessaries of life to the consumer, and therefore this policy was of no benefit to them. Well, I think my good friend, Mr. Carling, very recently showed that on many articles there has been a very considerable decrease in price since 1878. Take woollen goods, take cotton, sugar, all kinds of leather manufactures, boots and shoes, everything of the kind, and there is no increase. The competition has been sharp, those men who were represented to be the bloated aristocrats of Canada, were to roll up their wealth by millions, and take it out of the poor man's pocket, but we don't hear that now. No, gentlemen, these men are not making enormous fortunes, and so far as the Government is concerned, we don't want them to make more than a fair living profit out of their investment—(hear, hear)—but we do desire that they should give employment to as many as they can find work for. (Cheers.) As an instance of the competition which exists, let me mention that this morning, as I walked down here, a gentleman said to me, "We have pretty sharp times now; competition is so great that we are not making so much profit as formerly." Under it the people are now getting their supplies in the Dominion as cheap, or cheaper, than they did under the policy of 1878. Those hundred thousand people who have employment now, which could not be had in 1878, are occupying houses then unoccupied. (Hear, hear.) Many of them have obtained land of their own, and have erected substantial dwellings on them; the men in business have one hundred thousand customers more than in 1878, and the farmer who comes to market knows he comes to a place where he can dispose of his produce. Why, we were told we humbugged the farmers; that they did not receive a cent more for their wheat than they did when there was no tariff in their favour. The N. P. has increased the price of wheat to the miller, and they have to pay more for it in Manitoba and the North-West than they have across the line; and in saying that they have not sufficient protection against American flour, it is a declaration that the farmers are reaping a benefit now they did not enjoy before. (Hear, hear.) Under these circumstances it may become a question whether we should not take into consideration the present position of the miller. So I might refer to many other products of the farm, fruit raising, butter making, etc. Go and ask any housekeeper if their expenditure has increased since 1878. The answer will be that the increase is mainly in the price of the products of the farm. I am not surprised to find that this policy is not in the interests of the farmer alone, it is in the interests of the manufacturer, the lawyer, the doctor, and the artisan. (Cheers.) It is in the interest of Canada, because no country can be happy and prosperous where the masses of the people do not receive a fair day's pay for a fair day's work. (Applause.) It is true that our manufacturing interests are depressed to some extent just now. It is true we are feeling the depression which exists in the old world. It is true that our own manufacturers, in addition to competition among themselves, have a keen competition from outside, and it is also true that there is less work or distress in Canada to-day than in any other part of the world. It is true that the manufacturers outside are paying into the treasury in order to get their products into the country—that they are giving larger discounts by ten per cent. But let me say when, forty years ago, our chieftain entered into public life this question of protection was not of so much importance as it is at present. Then we in the Maritime Provinces were just shipping timber to England and dried fish to the West Indies; while you in Upper Canada were exporting potash. (Laughter.) Forty years ago the arrival of the first consignment of Canadian wheat on the other side was considered a marvel. (Hear, hear.) Would you be content to remain simply as you were then—the hewers of wood and the catchers of fish—honourable though those occupations were? Would you be content to remain at that, while the country at your side is prospering, because it has a variety of industries? (Applause.) If, should you have remained like this, one industry failed, where were you? If to-day one industry fails, you have others which keep things moving. (Applause.) But I must not dwell too long upon this policy. (Cries of "Go on, go on.") Sir Richard Cartwright talked in his speech about the taxation and the extravagant expenditure of the Government. Why, when in England last summer, Canadian papers came to me containing the declarations of some leaders of the Opposition on this point, which, unless you knew the facts, you would regard as unanswerable. They were to the effect that since 1879 the expenditure had increased from $24,000,000 to $30,000,000, and that in the face of a declaration of mine when speaking to my constituents in 1878 that $22,500,000 was sufficient to run the country. Now, there are two pretty bold statements here; there is besides a suppression of the truth, which I take it is as bad as a direct lie. (Applause.) It is not true that I said in 1878 that $22,500,000 would be sufficient at this time or any subsequent time to meet the expenses of the country. What I did say was, that if the Government of Sir John Macdonald had been in power, it would have expended, on an average, not more than $22,500,000 from 1874 to 1878. (Hear, hear.) But as to the expenditure of $30,000,000 now; there is a justification for that. What are the facts? Increases of expenditure have become necessary since then, and they have not cost the people a cent. Take, for instance, the Post-office Department. The expenditure of that department has increased, but though it has increased, the improvements effected have brought into the treasury more money than was expended in giving increased accommodation to the people. (Applause.) I would ask you this: Suppose the Postmaster-General came to you and said, "I am asked for increased postal accommodation in the North-West and in Manitoba, for the men who are in the wilderness portions of Ontario, of Quebec, of Nova Scotia, or of New Brunswick. I can give this accommodation without costing a penny; the revenue I will obtain from it will pay for it." Would you say, give the accommodation? I do not think there is a man, even in the Opposition, who would say, no. (Hear, hear.) But if, in giving this accommodation, the expenditure is increased—though the revenue covers it—they shout from platform to platform that the expenditure is increasing and that we are extravagant. Is that honest? (Cries of "No, no.") What are the facts? In 1874 down to 1879 the Government of that day had but a small portion of the Government system of railways completed. The Intercolonial railway was not completed for some years after they had come into power. You know it costs more to run a line of 700 miles than it does one of 300. What have we done ? We have gone on adding to our mileage, finishing the Canadian Pacific railway, purchased the Riviere du Loup section of the Grand Trunk, purchased from Nova Scotia eighty miles of railway, were running the Windsor branch, and a complete system of P. E. I. railways, and had of course increased the expenditure largely by this increased mileage. But had the increased mileage really cost us a dollar ? No ; for it has enabled the Government by good management to change a deficit on the Intercolonial railway into a small surplus. (Cheers.) Is it fair or honest to say then that the increased expenditure has increased your taxation ? And so with the assistance given to the harbour of Quebec. We exacted from the Commissioners, a majority of whom were appointed by the Government, that they should get back from the harbour dues enough to meet their harbour accommodation. Advances were made to the harbour commission of Montreal, but they paid interest for the money ; but in all these cases only the increased expenditure was taken into account by the Opposition. No credit given. In the North West the Government has spent large sums of money in the management of sale of lands and placing immigrants, but the returns from the sales of the land were enough to pay for the service. Nevertheless the increased cost is charged against us, without the facts being given showing why the cost was incurred. I shall proceed to show you that while the expenditure has increased we have not increased the taxation. I shall not commence at 1873, because our opponents will say that we brought in Prince Edward Island with a large subsidy, and assumed the debts of Ontario and Quebec, which increased the charges. I will take the years 1874 to 1879, which were free from these exceptional circumstances. Although they increased the taxation by a change of tariff, they did not collect enough money to meet their expenditure. I ask you, is it not fair when comparing the extravagance of one Government against another, that if they did not pay their debts and did not tax the people enough to pay them, their deficiency should be added to their whole expenditure ? If a municipality increased its liability in its expenditures in a certain year, and did not assess the taxpayers sufficiently to meet the obligation, the assessment of that year could scarcely be taken as the evidence of the economy of their administration. I have prepared a statement of the expenditures from 1874 to 1879, and it shows that the necessary taxation to meet them for these five years was $4.88 per head on every man, woman, and child in the country. If we make the same calculation for the years from 1879 to 1884, we find the expenditure required a taxation of $4.81 per head or seven cents per head less than during the previous period from 1874 to 1879. (Cheers.) If the period from 1879 to 1884 be taken, and the past year was an exceptional year, three millions having been paid out on public works, the rate of taxation required to meet the expenditure for those five years was $4.86 or two cents less than in the five years from 1874 to 1879. These facts cannot be gainsaid. It was a terrible business, our opponents say, to take away from the people this money in the shape of a surplus which was not necessary. You know that last year we had not a very large surplus. I should not be surprised if when Parliament meets the Opposition instead of attacking us for taking so much money out of your pockets attack us for not having a large surplus. What are the facts in reference to this surplus ? From 1874 to 1879 the expenditure on public works by the late Government was over thirty-three millions, charged to capital account. They not only increased the debt to this amount, but increased it to the extent of the deficit. What was the result to the taxpayer ? The amount of interest paid per head in 1874 was $1.31½. When they went out they had increased the amount of interest $1,300,000 a year, and the amount of interest paid by the people rose 25 cents per head additional during their Administration, making the total $1.56 per head. Now let me tell you the other side. You know the Government took hold of the Canadian Pacific railway with vigour. We took hold of the sections that were to be built by the Government, and hurried them on rapidly. As a consequence of the vigorous course of the Government since 1879 we have spent $35,000,000 in the completion of the sections that were commenced by Mr. Mackenzie at the head of Lake Superior, in Manitoba, in British Columbia, and subsidy to the Canadian Pacific railway. We paid $35,000,000 from July 1st, 1879, to July 1st, 1884. We spent $12,000,000, chargeable to capital account, in the deepening and enlargement of the canals since that time. We spent nearly $7,000,000 in finishing the Intercolonial railway, and providing increased accommodation and advantages at the termini, the whole amounting to 54,000,000. Well, what is our position with reference to the interest to-day ? While the interest was increased 25c. per head of the population during the former period ; by the surplus, contributed at a time when you did not feel it, by the increased issue of notes by the Dominion, giving the people the benefit of the increased circulation, the interest on our debt and securities was reduced out of proportion to the general fall of interest on the money market—(cheers)—we have been able, notwithstanding that we have spent $54,000,000 chargeable to capital account, to reduce the net interest per head less than it was in 1879, when we came into power. (Cheers.) Now I ask if this is not some evidence of the good management of our chieftain's Administration, and whether he is not entitled to some credit ? (Cheers.) While we have been going on building this railway which it was said would ruin the country, we are paying less interest per head of the population than in 1879. (Cheers.) The prices of goods have not been increased to the consumer, and the taxation is two cents less per head. You paid more, but you have had compensation in the saving of ten cents per head interest, and here you are to-day with less taxation to meet expenditure and less interest to pay per head. (Cheers.) There have been some comments with reference to the loan I made in England when I was there last summer, and it was stated in some of the Opposition papers that I made it on the same terms as Sir Richard Cartwright made his loans from 1874 to 1878. Well, I obtained it at a little higher rate per £100, but I only paid three and a half per cent. instead of four per cent. interest. To give some idea of what that is to the country I had a calculation made by the Auditor-General. I said to the Auditor-General, supposing we take one-half per cent. a year on our debentures floated last summer, put it into a sinking fund, and re-invest it every six months as the interest comes in, how long will it take to pay off that debt ? The answer he gave me was 55½ years. So the difference between the loan we floated last summer and the loans of Sir Richard Cartwright between 1874 and 1878 would in 55½ years pay that debt off. (Cheers.) I want you to carry this in your mind, that when the Canadian Pacific railway is completed, and it is said it will be completed next autumn, the amount of interest the people of Canada will have to pay net will not exceed the amount which was being per head paid when we came into power in 1879. I have merely grouped together these statements. ("Go on.") The fact is that in the interest of the country it is necessary that these things should be known. We, as public men, are abused. Do you feel that it is in our interest to be abused. (Laughter.) With all Sir John's ability, and it is great; with all his tact, and with all his genius, I doubt whether he would have had as large a place in your affections to-day if it had not been that he has been maligned. (Cheers.) It is unfortunate that the young men of the country, and people abroad, should get the idea that the public men of Canada are scoundrels and villains. It is to be regretted that the late presidential contest in the United States was not one between parties with clearly defined platforms, but that the contest was one of personal abuse. But there is one thing in which we can follow our neighbours' example to advantage. Of no man there, whether he was of the party of Mr. St. John, or of Ben Butler, or of Mr. Blaine, or of Mr. Cleveland, was it read that he abused his country. (Loud cheers.) What have we seen here during the last year or two ? A Canadian was travelling to the West in a car lately with a gentleman who came out to visit Canada with the British Association. The Canadian said to the English gentleman : "Well, what do you think of Canada ?" " Well," was the reply, " I am very agreeably surprised." "Excuse me, but you English people," said the Canadian, " do not, as a rule, know a great deal about Canada, and, therefore, we can quite understand it." "But it is not that," the Englishman said. "We know much more of Canada of late years than formerly, but we have read in the Manchester papers and in the Scotch papers extracts from the Canadian papers running down your country." (Cries of "The *Globe*.") Yes, the *Globe* was one of the papers copied from, and he spoke of it. (Cheers.) He said, "When we see such statements coming from your own papers, is it not natural that we should place reliance upon them?" And then the agents of the American railways in England and in Germany all take up these statements and put them before the people who are thinking of emigrating, and point out what kind of a country Canada is. Therefore, let me say that I had hoped when I entered this Dominion of Canada that all the party and personal issues of the past would have been buried, and that all parties would have united in discussing great principles and national questions, and have raised the political arena above what it had been in the past. I had hoped so. But let me say it appears to me to be with the Opposition a question of rule or ruin, they seem regardless of the effect their statements may have on their country abroad or at home if they can only strike a blow at our chieftain, his Government, or his party. (Cheers.) I for one think I can claim that during my whole public career I have endeavoured, as far as possible, to avoid personal encounters, or say aught that would or could hurt the feelings of my political opponents. (Hear, hear.) I desire always to follow that course, and I think it is in the true interests of the country to do so unless one is driven to hit back. Why, gentlemen, it would be unnatural to expect, however great his forbearance is, that our chieftain should not at times cast back on his slanderers something to make them feel that he can give blow for blow. (Cheers.) But they complain just as bitterly as the gentleman who had a ferocious dog which a neighbour killed. The dog would often growl and bark at him as he passed the house, but he took no notice of it, until one day the dog bit him in the calf of the leg. (Laughter.) He thereupon made up his mind to be even with the dog, and putting a long spike into his walking cane, the next time the dog attacked him he put the cane and spike down its throat and from the effects the dog died. The owner came in a furious rage to know why the dog had been killed. "Is he dead?" asked the neighbour. "Yes, he is," replied the owner. "Well, that was his fault not mine." (Laughter.) "But," said the owner, "did you ever know a gentleman carry a weapon like that?" "Well, I carried it because your dog attacked me in such a way that I was determined he should not do it again without feeling something." (Laughter.) "But why did you not take the other end of the cane?" said the owner. "Why did not your dog come at me with the other end?" (Roars of laughter.) It is the best policy to stand to your principles and present your case in a calm and dignified manner. (Cheers.) I think as a rule the Liberal-Conservative party are not open to the censure to be laid at the doors of our opponents with reference to personal abuse. I trust we shall long continue as we are—(cheers)—standing on a defined and broad platform. (Renewed cheering.) Let us defend honourably our policy and principles. We believe that they are in the interests of the country, and believing that, we have "nailed them to the mast," as our chieftain said yesterday. (Cheers.) There they stand, if the ship goes down, down we go with them. (Cheers.) I have all along felt that nothing can occur, which will change the intelligent verdict of the people of Canada on the N. P. (Cheers.) We believe it will grow in their hearts, in their affections, and in their confidence. (Cheers.) More than that, I believe that our party is the truly liberal and progressive party, and if our chieftain and his subordinates were swept away to-day there are men still with you on this platform and in Canada possessed of ample ability and energy to sail the ship into a safe harbour. (Cheers.) That growing feeling with reference to Canada and Canadians in the mother land will increase in strength and volume, and our increased population, wealth, and importance will cause us to stand higher and higher in her estimation, and in addition we will command, as we are commanding to-day, the respect of our American neighbours. There is some anxiety in the Maritime Provinces with respect to the negotiations now going on between the government of the United States and the West Indies. I am not in a position to state what we shall do, but I will say this to those provinces, to all the provinces, indeed, that as Sir John Macdonald has been equal to every occasion in the past, he will be found sufficient for every occasion in the future. (Loud cheers.) You can safely trust the matter to his judgment and sound wisdom, and I do not hesitate to say that whatever is done will be done in the interests of Canada, done in a manner that will reflect the highest credit on him. (Loud and prolonged applause, in the midst of which the hon. gentleman resumed his seat.)

THE FRENCH LEADERS.

The CHAIRMAN then introduced Sir Hector Langevin to the meeting.

SIR HECTOR LANGEVIN, on rising, was received with a burst of applause, he said:—Mr. Chairman and gentlemen, I feel a delicacy in addressing you this afternoon, not being a member of the convention, although I am an elector of Ontario. (Cheers.) When saying that I am an elector of Ontario before such a gathering as this, composed entirely of Liberal-Conservatives, I am guilty of no breach of confidence if I add that whenever I have voted my vote has been a Liberal-Conservative one. (Cheers.) But, gentlemen, I feel that though I cannot address you with the same fluency in the English language as have those who have preceded me, nevertheless you will understand better my broken English than you might French, if I spoke it. (Laughter and cheers.) I suppose, gentlemen, I must postpone my French speech to another period, when the influx of French-Canadians to the eastern portion of Ontario, the influx of French-Canadians on the north shore of Lake Superior, where already several thousands are to be found, when the increased French population in Essex and other western counties has been felt, and your public men will have learned to speak French as we speak English, then we shall be able to come here on an equal footing with them and address you in our mother language, as we now address you in English. (Laughter and cheers.) Nevertheless, gentlemen, let me tell you that if we in the east do not speak the English language as you do, if our religion is different to yours, if our blood is not yours, if our history before the conquest of this country is different to yours, our feelings to-day are the same as yours. (Cheers.) We pride ourselves upon being British subjects. (Applause.) We intend to enjoy all the advantages that the constitution of this and the Mother Country confer upon us. We intend to work in harmony with you, as in the past, and to follow, as of old, the great chieftain whom you are to-day honouring. (Cheers.) Let me tell you this:—A million and a half of French-Canadians in Quebec speak to-day through my mouth, and through the mouths of my colleagues, telling you that, though not present in the body, their hearts are with you in the honouring of Sir John Macdonald, who is our chief as well as yours. (Cheers.) He certainly does not speak our language; he is not of our religion; he comes from another province; but he is as heartily beloved by us as he can be by you, and when he comes among us he is as cordially cheered as when he is among you. And why do we support him? Why, if it were possible, would we be glad and proud to support him for forty years more? It is because he is imbued with Conservative principles. It is because his measures are patriotic. It is because he is so determined to be just to all that he would rather suffer a temporary wave of unpopularity than do that which is not absolutely fair. (Hear, hear.) We claim him as one of ourselves, just as you have claimed Sir George Cartier. (Cheers.) I do not intend to make a speech, but simply to offer a few remarks. I thought that as I had the honour of being the leader of my province that I should tell you that that province is at the back of Sir John as much as the Province of Ontario is. The Province of Quebec, through its representatives, has supported Sir John for the last thirty years. We have been through fire with him. For my own part, since I entered Parliament in 1857, I have never swerved in my allegiance to him. I followed him through good and bad fortune, and whenever he required my services he had them. It was my duty to do this because one should be faithful and loyal to his chief. If we want to go to war we must obey the general. The general is surrounded by officers who communicate his orders.

But if the rank and file take the lead and direct movements the army is sure to be defeated. Thank God this has not been the case amongst us. We have seen Sir John fight the good battle under the first Minister of the day, Sir George Cartier, and afterwards Sir John became leader of the Government and Sir George was his right-hand man. That example I have always intended to follow and have followed it up to now, and Sir John has evidence that up to the last moment we have always followed him. (Cheers.) Before I take my seat allow me to congratulate you on this demonstration. It is a credit to the whole Conservative party and to the Province of Ontario. I doubt very much whether in any other part of the world such an intellectual audience could be brought together in so short a time and from so many distant places. If you keep up your organization and follow the instructions which will be given you I am sure that by the next elections you will bring to the support of Sir John from your province and we will send back from Quebec the large majority we had at the last Parliament. (Cheers.)

Sir D. L. MACPHERSON, who was next called upon, was received with loud cheers. He said that he would have made a few remarks in reference to the affairs in the North-West, and the administration of which he had the charge, had not his chieftain said all that was necessary. Sir John had told them of the great progress in the work of surveying and preparing the country for settlers which had been made. He had told them that 65,000,000 acres of land had been surveyed in Manitoba and the North-West Territories. He would explain what this meant. It meant the subdivision of 65,000,000 acres into farms of 160 acres each. One-fourth of this great area was open for free settlement. He thought that the result made known was one of which every Canadian had reason to be proud. We had acquired an immense inheritance in the North-West. We had not locked it up, but had opened it to the world at large, and had called upon industrious men from every country to take up a home amongst us without enquiring as to their origin or faith. We only asked them to bring strong hands and strong wills and redeem the country from what it had been too long, a mere hunting-ground. All that was required was the labour of the tiller of the soil to make the country the most prosperous under the sun. He congratulated those present and the country upon the Convention, upon that gathering of intelligent men assembled there to honour their chief, the patriot statesman of Canada. He had seen a great many assemblies in his life, but had never seen one which had so impressed him as that had done. Representatives from all parts of the country had come to it, and no man in this country had ever obtained such a tribute to his ability and patriotism as Sir John had been given. He had received that tribute because he deserved it. (Cheers.) The intelligent men he saw before him would never pay such an honour to one who had not deserved it. Those present at the Convention had expressed their delight at the honour and distinction conferred upon Sir John by his Queen and the leading statesmen of both parties in Britain. No such honour had ever been paid in England to a Canadian before. It was gratifying to see that the universal opinion was that it was to the interests of the country that the party led by Sir John should remain in power. (Cheers.) We had the Prime Minister of Manitoba declaring this morning that the intelligent men of that province—men most of whom had gone from these provinces—did not hesitate long as to which of the parties of the older provinces they would cast their lot in with. They cast their lot in with the Liberal-Conservative party. Sir Leonard Tilley spoke representing New Brunswick, and you know that he is followed by a majority of representatives of that province in parliament. He is their leader, and I need not tell you that he is a truly worthy leader in every sense of the word. Following him came Sir Hector Langevin, the leader of the party from his province, and who, out of a representation of 65, stands up, one of fifty, in support of his leader. (Cheers.) I think it is a proud position not only for the leader of the administration and of the party to occupy, but it is a gratifying position, and a proud position for every man who is here present, and for every member of the Liberal-Conservative party throughout the Dominion. (Cheers.) The matter of organization has been receiving your attention. Upon the firmness of your organization will depend the fate of the Liberal-Conservative party at the next election. Seeing those who are assembled on this occasion I cannot doubt they will see that their organization is made thorough, and that they will have every member of their party go to the polls. If they do there can be no question as to the result. And let me remind you that the party opposed to you are an unscrupulous party, and I am sorry to say they are an unpatriotic party. (Hear, hear.) Their efforts have been directed to retarding and keeping back and injuring the North-West, by saying what is calculated to prevent men of capital and men seeking homes from going to that country. We know the efforts they have made in Manitoba, stimulated from Ontario, and there is no denying that they have done much mischief. Their efforts have been successful to some extent in injuring that country, and this is almost the only instance in which I have known them to have attained much of a party success. (Cheers and laughter.) It is for evil, unfortunately, but the effect is only temporary, I am certain, in its character, because the attractions of the country are such as to induce all those desiring to make new homes for themselves to go there. (Cheers.)

Hon. A. P. CARON was called for, and on rising was loudly cheered. He said: Really I feel that it is due to your very great kindness that I should be called upon to say a few words to-day. In fact, after the very great speeches which you have already heard, it seems to me that it is almost impossible for me to add anything to what has been stated by those who have spoken. But, Mr. Chairman, if you will permit me, I beg through you to express to the committee who have organized this great demonstration my sincere thanks as a Conservative coming from the east for the great success which has been achieved. Mr. Chairman, although I am a good many miles from the city of Quebec, I feel so much at home among you that I feel almost tempted, just merely for the sake of diversion, to address you in French. (Laughter.) I feel that a great reason why we, coming from the Province of Quebec and meeting Ontario Conservatives, feel at home is that we are of a great political family, whose destinies are controlled absolutely by the great leader whom we acknowledge. (Cheers.) The leader of the Province of Quebec, Sir Hector Langevin, has told you that a great majority of those elected to represent constituencies of that province have always given their confidence to Sir John Macdonald. I remember well long before I entered public life that when Sir John Macdonald's name was mentioned among the people of Quebec—those people belonging to a different race, and belonging to a different church, but belonging to the same great political party which recognizes him as its great chieftain—it was always associated with the name of another statesman, a compatriot of mine—Sir George Cartier—(cheers)—who aided Sir John Macdonald in working out the great measures which have made the Dominion the Dominion it is to-day. (Cheers.) We all remember when the provinces composing the Dominion of Canada were divided. We remember when those provinces were not only separated by distances, but were divided by differences of tariffs, and differences of currency, until the time came when men like Sir George Cartier and Sir John Macdonald, helped by their associates in public life, met together and concluded that the future of this country depended upon its becoming a united country. And if Sir John Macdonald succeeded in making of Confederation as great a success as Confederation has become, I believe that in reading the history of our political party that nobody will deny that Sir George Cartier and the Conservatives of Quebec gave them help, and not only gave them help, but contributed as much as any person in this Dominion in carrying out his great measure. And, sir, I can tell you that, great and successful as has been his demonstration, when Sir John Macdonald, our loved and revered leader, comes down to the Province of Quebec, I leave it to him to say whether the same amount of enthusiasm is not shown by his French-Canadian supporters. (Cheers.) Why is it so? It is because men like Sir John Macdonald and Sir George Cartier have completely wiped out those differences of races, of nationalities, of religions. (Cheers.) Like you in Ontario, we in Quebec regret to find in our midst men ready to decry their country. We like you, have read articles in the press written by men dissatisfied at home, because they cannot control the Government or command the confidence of the people. (Cheers.) Mr. Chairman, let me tell you that we in Quebec have been following your efforts; we have been watching the energetic manner in which you have been keeping up the Liberal-Conservative flag in the local politics of your own province—(cheers)—and, sir, let me tell you that from my own province to-day comes up a representative in my friend, Hon. Mr. Blanchet, to show the intimacy existing between the Conservatives of Quebec and Ontario. (Cheers.) Let me return my sincere thanks for your kindness in inviting me to address a few words to this gathering. In conclusion I have only to say, let us obey our leader, let us take our orders from those who have the right to give them, and if we follow that rule in the future the great victories which have led Sir John Macdonald to occupy his present exalted position as Premier of the Dominion will still be ours. (Cheers.) Unless we are a united party it will be impossible for us in the future to contend against the elements which are in antagonism to us, and unless we remain united we cannot expect to achieve success. (Cheers.)

The CHAIRMAN—It is said that we are under French domination,—but I do not think you are terrified by seeing French-Canadians on the platform—(laughter)— nor do I think it will hurt you to hear some of those whom our opponents malign. I have great pleasure in introducing to you a member of the Provincial Government of Quebec—Mr. Blanchet.

HON. MR. BLANCHET, who was received with cheers, expressed the pleasure it afforded him to be present to do honour to the leader of the Conservative party. He felt that it was a great honour to be selected by his chief, the Prime Minister of Quebec, to attend, and attending he brought with him the feelings of devotion which all Liberal-Conservatives entertained towards the great chief. (Cheers.) He was happy to say that the good cause was flourishing in Quebec. The last battle fought there was fought in his own county of Beauce. If that had been fought on purely political grounds there would have been a Conservative majority of 1,200. But it was fought rather on personal issues, and the Conservative majority was 313. That did not look much like a Reform reaction. If it was a reaction it was not a reaction which the Conservatives need regret, for a majority of 313 was not to be despised. (Hear, hear.) Quebec, he could say, was proud of Sir John, and was well satisfied with the manner in which the affairs of the country were being managed. (Cheers, cries of "Tom White" and "Mr. Bowell.")

The CHAIRMAN—It is now after five o'clock, and we have promised to conclude here at five in order that the hall may be otherwise occupied. Under the circumstances I am afraid we cannot call upon other speakers.

THANKS TO MR. MANNING.

MR. A. BOULTBEE, who was warmly applauded, said he thought that they would all agree with him that this was the grandest demonstration their party, or any other party, had ever had in this province. (Cheers.) With all the enthusiasm which existed and all the disposition shown to come there, however, they could not have had such a demonstration without the use of that building. There was not another hall in the city which would hold such a crowd, and even it had been insufficient to accommodate all who presented themselves. It would, therefore, not be a graceful thing to part without passing a cordial vote of thanks to Mr. Manning, who had lent the use of his building for two days free of any charge. He moved that the cordial vote of the convention be tendered to Mr. Manning for his kindness. (Cheers.)

SIR JOHN MACDONALD said—I rise with great pleasure to second the motion which has been made by my friend Mr. Boultbee. It has been an act of great kindness and generosity on the part of Mr. Manning to have given us the use of this building for two days gratis, and to sacrifice the profits which he might legitimately have received had it been otherwise occupied. It is an act which I feel as a personal courtesy. It is a piece of kindness like many others which I have been accustomed to receive from Mr. Manning. He has been a good friend of mine, and I have been intimately connected with him in many subjects and places. (Cheers.)

A standing vote of thanks, and three cheers were then given to Mr. Manning.

THANKS TO THE CHAIRMAN.

SIR JOHN MACDONALD—I beg to move that the cordial thanks of this meeting be tendered our chairman—the leader of the Liberal-Conservative Opposition in Ontario, who I hope will ere long be the Liberal-Conservative Premier of Ontario—(cheers)—for his conduct in the chair. (Cheers.) When I say I hope I will soon have the opportunity of greeting Mr. Meredith as the leader of a Liberal-Conservative Government I do not merely speak from the lips. (Hear, hear.) All I can do to hasten that happy event, all the influence I can exert will be exerted to bring about that change, which I am convinced is so desirable in the interests of Ontario, and which will redound so much to the advantage of this great province. (Cheers.) I hope that ere long there will be a Liberal-Conservative Government in Ontario. (Cheers.) I know that a few years ago I would have been charged with great impropriety in making such a statement. I should have been told that there should be no entangling alliance between the Ontario and Dominion Governments. But as the present Minister of the Interior said we must fight fire with fire. Mr. Mowat some time ago used that expression when there was something like a dispute as to how certain elections were carried. We find that the Government of Ontario is being employed in the interests of the Grit Opposition in the Federal Parliament. Therefore I call upon all my friends in the Conservative party to rally round my friend, the leader of the party in Ontario, just as warmly and enthusiastically and energetically as they would in my behalf and that of the Dominion Government. (Cheers.)

A VOICE—What about the Scott Act? (Laughter.)

SIR JOHN replied by drinking a glass of water amid loud laughter. He then said—"I move that the thanks of this meeting be given to Mr. Meredith for his able conduct in the chair at the sittings of this convention."

HON. MR. PLUMB seconded the motion. He thought that those present at the convention would take away the recollection of having participated in one of the most glorious demonstrations which had ever been held in the Dominion of Canada. He believed that the result would be that each delegate would go home determined to carry out all the principles of organization impressed upon him by the central department, determined to do his duty better and more vigorously, and with the consciousness that in doing so he would be acting in the best interests of the country. He seconded the motion with the best wishes that they would soon see the chairman at the head of the Ontario Government, where he should have been at the close of the last election. (Cheers.) He believed that it was owing to the Ontario Conservatives not being sufficiently sanguine that Mr. Meredith was not in power now. (Cheers.)

THE MAYOR put the motion, which was carried with immense enthusiasm.

THE CHAIRMAN'S REPLY.

MR. MEREDITH, on rising, was received with prolonged applause. He said—Mr. Mayor and gentlemen, I am sure that no word of thanks from you to me is necessary on the occasion, but rather my thanks are due to you for the honour done me by being present on this occasion, and presiding temporarily over this assembly. Mr. Mayor and gentlemen, I think this gathering has demonstrated one or two things we should bear in mind. It has demonstrated, notwithstanding the malignity of the attacks made on the right hon. gentleman who was the chosen head of the Conservative party, and who has for many years led it to victory, that he still holds a warm place in the affections of the Conservative party and of the people. (Cheers.) I think it has also demonstrated this, that the great heart of the Conservative party represents the feeling of the people of this province—(cheers)—because I did not believe there could have been gathered together in so short a time from all sections of the people, in every walk of life, such an assembly as this, evincing such an enthusiasm as it has. (Loud cheers.) Assembled under these conditions it represents the feeling of the province, and, as has been well said, it has been the grandest demonstration of any political party ever held in the history of this country. (Cheers.) So far as the observations addressed to myself are concerned, I have to thank the mover and seconder for their kind words, and you, gentlemen, for the cordial way they have been received. (Cheers.) Ever since I have had the honour of occupying a seat in the Legislature of this Province or taking a part in the discussions which arose there, it has been my fortune to sit in the cool shades of Opposition. (Laughter.) But, although that has been so, I am always ready and willing to take any position in furtherance of the interests of the Conservative party. (Loud cheers.) I am not—and I think that is a matter we should bear in mind here—I am not a Conservative simply because it is the party with whom my associations have been in the past. I am a Liberal-Conservative because I believe the future interests of this great Dominion are bound up in the success of that party. (Prolonged cheers.) And although our numbers in the Legislature are small, we are a band representing more than one-half of the votes of the people of this Province and battling for their rights. (Applause.) We have been maligned, scorned, and charged with being traitors. I have on every platform hurled back on those who made them these accusations, and I say here to you now, if it be treason to the interests of Ontario that I should be willing to respect the rights of the other provinces of the Dominion, to respect the rights of those Frenchmen—though they are French they are our brethren in the great work of building up this Dominion—(cheers)—if that be treason then I plead guilty to the charge. (Loud cheers.) It has been well said on the platform here to-day I am a son of Ontario, born within its limits, but I owe an allegiance to this great Dominion, of which Ontario is only a part. (Cheers.) I fully recognize the greatness and prominence of my native province in this Confederation, I recognize that she is first in wealth, first in population, and great in intelligence and education—(cheers)—but I say that she ought to be generous in her treatment of the other provinces of this Dominion—(hear, hear,)—and it is only by means such as these that we can build up this great nation we are attempting to build up on the northern half of the North American continent. (Loud cheers.) We are engaged in a great and glorious work, and I say to you to-day, Go on with this work notwithstanding those who traduce you and yours, and if it be not in these times that you receive your reward, those who come after you will say you have done your duty, done something to advance the interests of our common country. (Loud cheers.) I appeal to the young men of this country. As has been well said by Mr. Blackstock, they have no part or interest with the Reform party, and I ask them to cast in their lot with the Conservative party and join our union. There is no telling what can be accomplished if its energies are directed aright. No man who has attended here and has heard the representatives from the North-West, Quebec, and the other provinces, but must have felt his heart swell with just pride, and no man who calls himself a Canadian need be ashamed to go anywhere where the sun shines and putting his hand on his heart declare, "I am a Canadian." (Loud cheers.) Let me say in conclusion, let us inscribe on the banner of the Conservative party that this union must and shall be preserved intact and inviolate. (Loud cheers.) Let that be inscribed high up on the banner of the Conservative party, let us go on in our work, and in accomplishing it we shall deserve the thanks of posterity. (Loud and prolonged applause.)

Three hearty cheers were given for the Queen and Sir John Macdonald, after which the Convention adjourned.

THE BANQUET.

To the Right Honourable Sir John A. Macdonald, M.P., P.C., LL.D., D.C.L., G.C.B.:

The Banquet given in the pavilion of the Horticultural Gardens on the evening of the close of the convention, in the number and enthusiasm of those assembled, and the heartiness of the reception accorded the distinguished guest of the evening, was unequalled in the history of political demonstrations in Canada. The largest hall in the city had been secured, but long before the first day of the convention it became evident that it could not possibly accommodate the thousands who were desirous of doing honour to the man who more than any other is to be credited with building up the Dominion. Thanks to the excellent arrangements of the committee and to the well directed enterprise of the caterers the banquet was in every way a great and most gratifying success. Great care had been taken in the decoration of the building, and the results were in every respect satisfactory. Behind the spacious platform the wall was hung with Union Jacks. The ceiling was festooned with evergreens. The coats-of-arms of the provinces were displayed in front of the galleries. The building was emblazoned with inscriptions bearing testimony to the patriotism and loyalty of the party and to the labours and successes of its leader. The following are the inscriptions:—OUR QUEEN, GOD BLESS HER; OUR VETERAN SIR JOHN—HIS NAME IS DEAR TO THE PEOPLE AND IS WRITTEN IN HISTORY; PRO REGE ET PATRIA—WITH THE PARTY, BY THE PARTY, BUT FOR THE COUNTRY; WHAT NEED WE ANY SPUR BUT OUR OWN CAUSE; YE'VE NO SEEN THE LAST O' MY BONNETS AND ME; THE DOMINION, ONE AND INDIVISIBLE; LOYALTY TO THE EMPIRE, THE DOMINION, AND THE PROVINCE; A BRAVER PLACE IN OUR LOVE HATH NO MAN THAN THYSELF; THE PROMOTION OF AGRICULTURE; OUR SHIPPING INDUSTRIES AND OCEAN FLEET; OUR ARTISANS AND WORKINGMEN; THE SUCCESSORS OF PITT AND FOX COMBINE TO DO HIM HONOUR; THE DEVELOPMENT OF OUR INDUSTRIES; THE NATIONAL POLICY AND FAIR TRADE; OUR CANALS AND GRAND TRUNK RAILWAY; OUR GREAT ATLANTIC AND PACIFIC RAILWAY;

"NOUGHT SHALL MAKE US RUE
IF CANADA TO HERSELF DO PROVE BUT TRUE;

AND OFT' WE THOUGHT HIM SINKING, BUT OFT' AGAIN HE ROSE; TAKE HIM FOR ALL IN ALL WE SHALL NOT LOOK UPON HIS LIKE AGAIN; HONNEUR SOIT A QUI HONNEUR EST DU; ADVANCEMENT OF OUR COMMERCE; OUR FISHERIES; THE BUILDING UP OF OUR DOMINION; THE QUEEN CITY WELCOMES THE QUEEN'S HONOURED SERVANT; WE WELCOME THEE AFTER FORTY YEARS, 1844—1878—1882—1884; ONTARIO HAILS THE CHIEFTAIN; THE CONSERVATION OF THE RIGHTS OF THE DOMINION AND THE PROVINCES AS ASSURED BY THE CONSTITUTION AND SUBJECT TO IT.

The tables which covered the entire ground floor of the pavilion and the conservatory, were laid out in splendid style. Those on the platform were adorned with lilies and rare flowers. Everything was carefully arranged down to the minutest details. The *menu* provided was excellent.

About eight o'clock the guests began to arrive, and in a short time the seats at the tables were all filled. The arrival of Sir John Macdonald, accompanied by a number of distinguished gentlemen, was the signal for a burst of applause. The platform was occupied by the members of the Dominion Parliament and the Local Legislature. At the front table facing the vast audience were seated the most distinguished guests, at the centre of the table sat Mayor Boswell in the capacity of chairman. On his right were Sir John Macdonald, Sir Alexander Campbell, Hon. A. Caron, Hon. J. A. Chapleau, Sir Narcisse Belleau, Hon. Alex. Morris, Hon. J. Norquay, Hon. Frank Smith, Hon. John Costigan, Mr. Alex. Murray, Speaker of the Manitoba Legislature, and Dr. Harrison, M.P.P., of Manitoba. On the left of the chairman, the following gentlemen were seated:—Sir Leonard Tilley, Sir Hector Langevin, Sir David Macpherson, Hon. John Caring, Mr. Wm. Meredith, Hon. George Allen, and Hon. Wm. Cayley. Throughout the banquet not one hitch occurred in the arrangements. After the repast had been commenced the ladies began to arrive and fill the upper galleries. A portion of the first gallery was reserved for the delegates so that those who could not be accommodated at the tables could have an opportunity to hear the speeches. Before nine o'clock the gallery was packed by a brilliant gathering. There were a very large number of ladies present as spectators. On the arrival of Lady Macdonald the entire audience rose and cheered her enthusiastically.

The chair was ably filled by A. R. Boswell, Esq., Mayor of Toronto, and J. D. Henderson, Esq., officiated as secretary.

After full justice had been done to the *menu* the Chairman stated that the most interesting part of the proceedings had arrived, and called upon the secretary to read the following letters and telegrams:—

"*To the Chairman of the Banquet to the Right Hon. Sir John Macdonald, G.C.B.,*

"FORT QU'APPELLE, N.W.T., Dec. 17.—The inhabitants of Fort Qu'Appelle desire to join with you in doing honour to Canada's greatest statesman. Congratulate him for us. We trust that he may be long spared to Canada. On behalf of the inhabitants of Fort Qu'Appelle. T. W. JACKSON."

"*To F. W. Barwick, Toronto:*

"END OF TRACK, B.C., Dec. 18.—May I ask you to convey my exceeding regret that I cannot join the vast assembly of grateful and admiring Canadians who meet in Toronto to honour your distinguished guest. Every thoughtful Canadian recognizes the far seeing wisdom and boldness of action displayed by that right honourable gentleman, who has guided the destiny of Canada from, one might say, its childhood days as a small British colony to its present proud position and vast proportions as the Dominion of Canada, exemplifying, as it does, British rule in its most beneficial and attractive form, where the greatest good to the greatest number, and each for all, and all for each is consistently aimed at, imbued in its growing manhood with that unwavering loyalty to the empire which forms so marked a characteristic of our much beloved Premier. One master-stroke of that statesman like policy—the early construction of a Canadian inter-oceanic railway—approaches rapidly to completion. Ten days ago, let me tell you, the first crossing of the Columbia river was effected, and ere this reaches you the iron horse will be eleven miles further west, and it is now beyond a doubt that a junction will be effected with construction under Onderdonk from the Pacific early in October next, and then our Canadian Grand Old Man will have his fondest dream of glorious achievement for his country realized; and amidst the intermingled plaudits of his loving and admiring countrymen he will be able to pass —not with the wings of an angel looking down upon his work, but in his earthly form in a Pullman car—over one of the finest roads in the world, from the Atlantic to the Pacific on the soil of his dear country, viewing as he travels the marvellous fields he has opened up for the development of agricultural, mineral, forest, fishery, manufacturing, and commercial wealth too wonderful to describe, in which happy and prosperous homes can be found for the over-crowded populations of the Motherland and Europe, as well as richly profitable investment for the accumulated capital of Britain and other older countries for ages to come, and contemplating the magic effect he has wrought by thus binding every section of our country with an iron band of mutual interest and sentiment, and further establishing, as far as human foresight can tell, the future centre of Imperial power in British America. This rapid completion of our national highway will be forever a monument to our great statesman's memory, the "Organized Hypocrisy" to the contrary notwithstanding. Friends here join in congratulations on restored health and recent honours conferred by the Queen on our patriotic chieftain.

"GEORGE T. ORTON."

From HON. J. J. ROSS, the Premier of Quebec :—" To my great regret I am deprived the pleasure of attending the banquet in honour of Sir John Macdonald. Sir John, by his fidelity to his friends, his broad, non-sectional and statesmanlike policy, has endeared himself to all classes of the people, and I would be most happy to join you in doing honour to the veteran chief. One of my colleagues in the Governmen will certainly be present."

From HON. A. W. MCLELAN, Minister of Marine and Fisheries :—" I exceedingly regret that I cannot attend the banquet on the eighteenth, to be given by the Liberal-Conservative party of Ontario to Right Hon. Sir John Macdonald, whose long and faithful services to party, country, and Queen entitle him to honours from all."

From HON. A. A. C. LARIVIERE, Minister of Agriculture, Manitoba :—" I deeply regret being unable to be present at banquet to be tendered Right Hon. Sir John Macdonald. Though absent I heartily join with those present in the expression of admiration and recognition of the brilliant and patriotic career of our leading Canadian statesman, and trust he will long be spared to serve this Dominion of ours."

From Mr. D. H. WILSON, Manitoba :—" I regret very much that I am unable to be present at the banquet to be tendered to the Right Hcn. Sir John Macdonald to-day. Kindly convey my congratulations to Canada's greatest statesman and the party whom he has so ably led, on the occasion of this anniversary. I would also express the hope that he may be spared many years to direct the destinies of the Federal compact in the consummation and preservation of which he has played so important a part."

From the HON. C. P. BROWN, Winnipeg :—" I regret exceedingly my inability to be present to do honour to Canada's greatest statesman on the occasion of his fortieth anniversary in public life. Mr. Norquay, who will be with you, will tell you how generally this regret is shared by others here, who, like myself are unable to be present, and also how hearty is the acknowledgment in this part of the Dominion of the eminent services rendered the nation by the gentleman you are so justly honouring."

From HON. J. B. PLUMB :—" In consequence of the lamented death of my brother-in-law, the venerable Bishop of Niagara, which occurred this morning, I deeply regret that I shall be unable to join with our Conservative friends in attending the great banquet to be given to the Right Hon. Sir John Macdonald, G.C.B., to-morrow evening, and to fulfil on that occasion the pleasing and welcome duty with which the committee of arrangements have honoured me."

Among the many expressions of good will was one from the Government House, Toronto, reading as follows :—" The Right Hon. Sir John Macdonald, G.C.B., with a thousand congratulations from an old friend. Dec. 18, 1884. This was accompanied by a magnificent floral offering.

After full justice had been done to the elaborate *menu*,

The CHAIRMAN said :—The first toast on the list to-night is the toast that is first on every list where good loyal Conservatives have met together at a social gathering like the present. (Cheers.) Our gracious Queen has paid many compliments to our country, and nothing more need be said to draw forth the applause of all present when her name is mentioned, but perhaps it would not be improper for me to suggest that in the reception of this toast we might give one cheer more because our gracious Sovereign has conferred honours upon him whom we also delight to honour. (Renewed cheers.)

The toast was drank with great enthusiasm, the band playing "God Save the Queen."

The CHAIRMAN—Gentlemen the next toast concerns the Queen's representatives in this country. We are called upon to drink the health of "The Governor-General and Lieutenant-Governor." (Cheers.) We have now for Governor-General a nobleman who has not been long in this country, but for the short time he has been here I may say, as has often been said before on similar occasions, that he has won golden opinions for himself. We have had the pleasure of seeing Lord Lansdowne and his accomplished Countess in the City of Toronto on more than one occasion, and we rejoice to find that we have a Governor-General who is desirous of making himself acquainted with our country, and with all its institutions. But connected with this toast there is also that of the health of the Lieutenant-Governor of the Province of Ontario. Gentlemen, I think I need not say anything to an audience composed of Ontario men about the Lieutenant-Governor of this Province. (Cheers.) But it occurs to me that it must be a very pleasing thought to our distinguished guest to-night when he reflects that every Lieutenant-Governor in the Dominion—the Lieutenant-Governors of Ontario, of Quebec, New Brunswick, Nova Scotia, Prince Edward Island, Manitoba, Assiniboia, and British Columbia—all owe their positions to the right hon. gentleman who sits beside me, and amongst those I am sure there are none who can rank higher in our esteem than the Honourable John Beverley Robinson, whom we know so well. (Loud cheers.) He comes from a good old stock—(cheers)—and he is a good and true Liberal-Conservative, and while we say that we must not forget that although he is placed in a position rather different from that which we would wish to see him occupying in one sense of the word, yet nobody can say that he has not been a thoroughly constitutional governor. And I cannot ask you to join me in drinking this toast without making a reference to the lady who now with him occupies Government House. (Cheers.) Government house at Toronto is noted for the fact that its doors are open to all strangers who visit Toronto. There, hospitality is the order of the day, and if I am not touching on dangerous ground I will express the wish, that if it were possible for our present Lieutenant-Governor to be appointed for a second term we would hail the appointment with all our hearts. (Prolonged cheering.) Band—"For he is a jolly good fellow."

THE ARMY AND NAVY.

The CHAIRMAN—The next toast on the list is "The Army and Navy, and Volunteers." It is not necessary for me at all to dwell on this toast, but I will just say this, that while a portion of the British army is engaged in active warfare in the East it is a pleasure for us to know that Canada is taking a part in that conflict, and it is a double pleasure for me, as Mayor of the City of Toronto, to be able to tell you that the Canadian contingent is commanded by Lieut.-Col. Denison, lately an Alderman of this city. (Cheers.) I do not think it will do any harm for me to say, too, that Lieut.-Col. Denison is a good Liberal-Conservative. (Cheers.) We have with us to-night the Minister of Militia, the Hon. Mr. Caron, who will do us the favour of responding to this toast. I might say something about the navy of Great Britain, but I will not take up your time, for I know you do not want to hear speeches from the chairman, but rather from the gentlemen who are to respond.

Band—"British Grenadiers' March."

HON. MR. CARON'S SPEECH.

HON. MR. CARON, Minister of Militia, was received with loud cheers. He said: —In any country where flies the British flag it is always a pleasure to respond to the toast which you have just proposed, to the army, navy and militia force. On this occasion, from the position which I occupy in the Government of my country, and, besides, as a French-Canadian Minister of Militia, I take particular pleasure in rising to respond to the toast which has just been proposed, because in doing so I feel that I may be permitted to say that I am speaking in behalf of two races who happily live together. (Loud cheers.) On this northern portion of the American continent, and of two races who count among the cherished traditions of their history the well-tried valour of their army, and the examples given by their soldiers of the possession of every possible virtue that can make a soldier useful to his country. (Cheers.) We know it by reading the history of our own country. We know that on the old historic battle-fields of Canada, France and Britain fought many a hard battle, but to-day what do we find? We see a united people—united under the old flag of Great Britain—French, English, and every other nationality acknowledging and revering it as the flag of our common country. (Loud cheers.) Mr. Chairman, it is a curious fact, but it is a historical fact. It was only seventeen years after this country had passed from under one flag to another when my ancestors, French-Canadians, who with you to-day form one people all over this great Dominion—it was only seventeen years after the cession of this country that they were called upon to show their loyalty to their new king and their new flag ; and you know—it is a fact, which can be read in the pages of our Canadian history—that Lower Canada, the French Canada of history, rallied under the leadership of men whose influences controlled public opinion—as the influence of men control public opinion to-day in Ontario and Quebec, men like the chieftain we follow—(cheers)—following their leaders they rallied round their new king and their new flag ; and history again says that the French-Canadians contributed a very great share towards keeping this colony to great Britain. (Loud cheers.) Mr. Chairman, we from Quebec, we old Conservatives who believe in the traditions which have been handed down from that olden period—we see to-day, at the call of duty, the Canadian voyageurs, those who are the descendants of the pioneers of civilization on this continent, the inheritors of their qualities and peculiarities, leaving their homes, and crossing the seas, they went to the help of the British soldiers (cheers) and under the leadership of Lord Wolseley they are going across seas and deserts to the relief of that great and brave soldier, General Gordon. (Loud cheers.) Mr. Chairman, when I address the brilliant assemblage around this festive board, when I am called upon to respond to the toast of the army, navy and militia force of Canada, I am glad to be able to say, as Minister of Militia, that the Canadian militia force is one of which every Canadian may justly feel proud. (Cheers.) I have told you the traditions of the past, and I can show you that, whenever the call of duty was sounded, whenever the militia force was called upon to do its duty by its flag and its Queen, the militia force of Canada always responded to that call. (Loud cheers.) Again, relying on history, I say that in Chateauguay and Queenston Heights you had proof of that fact—proof that when the call was made the force did its duty right well, and that Canada has no reason to complain of its militia force. (Loud cheers.) Permit me in a few words to tell you that the militia force of Canada is going through a process of organization, of formation which, taking into consideration the wants and requirements of the country, taking into consideration the amount of money which is voted by the Parliament of Canada, I believe must be satisfactory to the people of Canada. (Loud cheers.) My illustrious predecessor in 1868, Sir George Etienne Cartier—(loud and repeated cheers)—first started the organization which was represented by " A " and " B " batteries. This was for the purpose of giving to the artillery the training which is required to make a soldier—that training without which, indeed, it is perfectly useless to attempt to organize anything like a force ; and since that time, following the lead of my illustrious predecessor, I have organized the cavalry and infantry schools so that now each branch of the service can receive the instruction which is required for each particular branch of the service. (Cheers.) I may tell you further that the previous Government established the Royal Military College at Kingston, and the cadets who are turned out from this college have taken their places in England side by side (if examination tests can be relied on) in the scientific course—in the engineers and the artillery—with cadets who are turned out from the

English colleges. (Loud cheers.) As to the navy of England, it would be useless for me to go over the immortal record which every one of you knows so well. (Cheers.) Let me simply say that the navy of England is the bulwark of her power, and its record is such that every nation recognizes her as being the greatest naval power of the world. (Cheers.) But you must not suppose that because I speak of the army and navy and the militia that they confine their admiration to military deeds —that they have not a great feeling of admiration for those whose laurels are won on other fields—for glory which is acquired otherwise than by deeds of arms on land or sea. (Loud cheers.) Mr. Chairman, and you, Sir John, let me tell you that when you returned from England, bringing back that Grand Cross of the Bath-- (loud and repeated cheers)—with which our gracious Sovereign has invested you— (renewed cheering)—which she herself has placed on your breast—let me tell you that there is no class in Canada who were prouder of your proud success than the militia force of Canada. (Loud cheers.) We felt that the veteran of forty years, who had fought and won so many battles, could well bring back on such an anniversary a new decoration. And I say more—and I am speaking now as Minister of Militia—I say I believe if our revered leader had directed the great talents he has displayed as a tactician—and on that point I will leave it to the Grits to decide whether he has been a success or not—(laughter and cheers)— to military and naval pursuits I am perfectly certain that he might have commanded a large army and won many a battle as well as he has commanded the grand old Conservative army—(loud cheers)—and won its many victories—(renewed cheers)—an army which, under his distinguished leadership, has never lost a battle, but has always come back triumphantly when the people had a chance to understand why it was that he was attacked—I say that, when they understood that, he has always been brought back as the successful leader who controlled the destinies of this country. (Loud cheers.) Mr. Chairman, on his alighting from the car which brought him from New York to Ottawa, I was proud and glad to hear the right hon. gentleman state that in England the feeling was spreading that Canada was no longer a drag upon the Empire, and that we were looked upon in England as capable of being of some use to the Empire. Will you permit me, sir, in a very few words to state what in my own mind I believe to be true, and what will in a very short time be proved by events. I believe that Canada has done a great deal for the Empire in undertaking and vigorously prosecuting that great work, the building of the Canadian Pacific Railway. (Cheers.) Mr. Chairman, if we can be assured, and I believe we can, that England is getting through the Canadian Pacific Railway the shortest military route to its colonies in China, and the shortest possible route that can be traced on paper, I believe we point to a work for the completion of which Canada is entitled to be regarded with greater interest in the Mother Country. The distance from Montreal to the Pacific terminus by this route is 2,900 miles. Troops can be conveyed through by special train over this distance in four days, and not more than twenty-four hours will be required to go from Halifax to Montreal, so that five days, or five and one-half days at the outside, would be sufficient time to transport men from Halifax to Vancouver. Artillery, ordnance, and stores when carried in freight cars, would require from seven and a half to eight days to go from Halifax to the Pacific coast. By the use of fast Atlantic steamships between Liverpool and Halifax, and such steamships on the Pacific as the Canadian Pacific Railway are now planning for the transport trade on that ocean, infantry with the usual arms and accoutrements, may be transported from Liverpool to Yokohama in less than 27 days ; and to Hong Kong in less than 30 days, and three days' additional time would suffice for the transport of any materials of war. As far as I can make out the time which is now required over the old route is about 40 days. Let me apologize to you, Mr. Chairman, for having detained you so long, and let me return you my sincere thanks for your very great kindness in listening to me as you have done ; but before sitting down let me congratulate you, the Liberal-Conservatives of Ontario, upon the great success which has crowned your efforts in getting up this banquet, and (addressing the Premier) let me congratulate you, Sir John, upon being the recipient of this grand ovation. Although your merit is great I know that nothing can be more pleasing to you than this grand display of the loyalty of the Conservative party.

THE TOAST OF THE EVENING.

The CHAIRMAN—Gentlemen, I hope your glasses are all charged, and that you are all ready to drink the toast of the evening, which I am now to propose. Before proceeding, however, I want to make an apology on behalf of the Committee of Management, who regret exceedingly that we have not had sufficient accommodation to give a seat to every man who desired to come here to-night to do honour to the Right Honourable Sir John Macdonald. It is true that Toronto is making great progress in her public buildings and other improvements, but I am afraid our rate of progress is still behind that of the ever growing and ever widening feeling of respect and veneration which is everywhere evinced for our honoured chieftain. (Cheers.) I am not going to give you to-night a historical sketch of the life of Sir John Macdonald. It would be out of place for me to do so, because his career is pretty well known to most of those whom I am addressing. There is just one point which I want to touch upon in proposing this toast. I do not know whether or not you are aware of the fact, but I have heard it said that Sir John, when he first entered public life, had a platform, and one plank in that platform was an assurance given to his constituents, the free and independent electors of the City of Kingston, that if he was elected he would build a plank a road from Kingston to Gananoque. (Laughter.) Sir John will correct me if I am not right in this statement, but I am quite sure if that is true, that he little thought in those days he was going to be the means of building a road, not a plank road, but an iron road, from the Atlantic to the Pacific. (Cheers.) The grandson of a gentleman who has passed away from our midst, a gentleman who was one of Sir John Macdonald's old political associates —I mean the late Mr. Draper, who for a long time was Chief Justice of our courts in this country, and under whom I think Sir John first took office—has sent me this interesting paper, which, with your permission, I will read. It relates to a period when Mr. Draper was at the head of the Government, in 1846, and Sir John Macdonald had entered Parliament in 1844. The letter was written by Mr. Draper to the then Governor-General of Canada, Lord Cathcart, and in it he says:—"In reference to the situation of Commissioner of Crown Lands, Mr. Draper humbly submits that a man of activity of mind and familiar with business details is imperatively required in this department. Mr. Draper would think it of great advantage to the country if Mr. John A. Macdonald, the member for Kingston, would undertake that office." (Cheers.) That was written a long time ago when Sir John was young in Parliament, but it shows the opinion that was held of him even then by the head of the Government of the day. As further evidence of the esteem which he then commanded in public life, the Governor-General of that time writes in reference to this recommendation, "The Governor-General has formed a high opinion of Mr. John A. Macdonald, and his appointment to office in the administration would afford him much satisfaction." (Cheers.) Gentlemen, Sir John has been a successful man in politics in this country, and I believe I am correct in saying that one of the secrets which has made him the successful man he is to-day is that from the time he entered Parliament, and perhaps from the time he was able to understand and speak the English language, he has been loyal to the Crown of Great Britain—(cheers)—and I do hope and trust that our distinguished guest may live long, and that he will take every opportunity to discountenance and frown down any sentiment of independence or annexation. (Cheers.) It is related of Sir John that when he was about to leave Canada on his recent trip to England he replied to a newspaper interviewer, who asked him if it was true that he was going to England to be made a lord, "Yes, and my title is to be 'Lord To-morrow.'" (Laughter.) Well, I am not sure that this is not a good title. I will tell you why. Sir John is always looking out for to-morrow. He never allows to-morrow to look out for itself, but he takes time by the forelock. He is here to-day, and he has told us why it is advisable to take time by the forelock in order to carry our party to victory at the coming elections. (Cheers.) We were grieved indeed when we heard that it was illness that was taking Sir John home to England, and we rejoice that he returns to us with good health. We welcome him back to Canada, and this great gathering to-night of over 1,000 men, with the large number of Ontario's fair daughters whom we see in the galleries, will show him how he is regarded by the people of Canada. (Cheers.) I will only say one word more, and that is that, as a Minister, he has dispensed the enormous patronage of the Crown for half an ordinary lifetime, and to-day his most bitter political opponent is unable to charge him with personal dishonesty. (Cheers.) By his admirable social qualities he has secured the esteem of all classes and creeds, and races, and while he can count his personal enemies upon his fingers, his personal friends are as numerous as the sands upon the seashore. I ask you, gentlemen, to drink, "The health of the guest of the evening, the Right Honourable Sir John Macdonald."

The toast was received by the vast gathering with round after round of applause, the band playing "See the Conquering Hero Comes."

SIR JOHN MACDONALD on rising to respond was received with a storm of enthusiasm, again and again renewed—the immense gathering rising to their feet and cheering the veteran statesman for several minutes. After the enthusiasm which his rising evoked had subsided he said :—Mr. Mayor and gentlemen, I can scarcely express the emotions I feel at this great, this enthusiastic, this sympathetic reception. If, in the course of my political life, I have had sorrows, if I have found many unpleasantnesses, many griefs—aye, many woes almost—during the course of my long political career, I receive my compensation to-night. It is a great, a sufficient reward for me, for all I have undertaken, for all I have done, for all I have suffered—(loud cheers)—to find myself after forty years of long service, having of course like other men with the best intentions made mistakes—having had great shortcomings, great failings—to find myself greeted by an assembly like this—I say I feel rewarded for all that has taken place. I find myself accompanied by all that should accompany old age—"honour, love, obedience, troops of friends." (Cheers.) For the rest of my life this meeting, this culmination of the convention of to-day will dwell in my mind as the last and greatest compliment, the last and crowning honour. (Cheers and cries of "No, no.") When Voltaire, after being absent from France, from his love of liberty—for with all his faults and errors he was a lover of liberty, and was banished from France for a while—when he returned in his extreme old age and was met by a gathering of the classes of the society which drove him away, he said : "You smother me with roses," and he died from the caresses of his countrymen. I am perhaps made of sterner stuff, and not so old a man ; but it seems to me the people of Ontario are half resolved to kill me with kindness and if I had died to-day, I might say, like Othello : "If it were now to die, 'twere now to be most happy, for I fear my soul hath her content so absolute that not another *honour* like to this succeeds in unknown fate." But, Mr. Mayor and gentlemen, I am in no hurry to die. (Cheers.) Though I am the most accommodating of mortals, I have no desire to meet the wishes of my extreme Grit friends, and to make an early vacancy by my departure to another world. When I returned from England in 1881, after having successfully accomplished what I believe to be the greatest feat of my life—the signature and execution of the contract by which the construction of the Canadian Pacific railway was ensured—I was met at Montreal by my friends and I ventured to prophesy that old as I was then, three years ago, that road would be built perhaps not in my time, but that I would look down at all events upon the successful completion of that great undertaking with which I, and the Government of which I was a member, had so much to do in initiating and carrying forward. (Cheers.) Some of my kind friends who were opposed to me happened to doubt whether the aspect in the next world would be downward or upward. (Laughter.) I might be looking up, they said—(renewed laughter)—but I find myself now with a good prospect of that road being finished, and I am neither looking up nor down, but level-headed man as I am, seeing the trains on that road rushing across the continent in *propria persona*, and not in spirit. (Loud cheers.) And having succeeded so far, I may perhaps, finding that my wishes have been more than anticipated, make another prophecy that as you are now celebrating the fortieth year of my political life, I might perhaps have to ask you Conservatives of the Province of Ontario to pay me the same honour when I shall have been fifty years in political life. (Loud and repeated cheers.) I have no doubt that the Liberal-Conservative party will, ten years hence, be as strong, as vigorous, as staunch, and as true as it is to-day; and if there be any failure in their greeting, their enthusiasm, their support of me ten years hence, it will be my fault and not theirs. Mr. Mayor, you have alluded to the honours which have been conferred on me lately. I am proud of those honours. (Cheers.) I wear my blushing honours thick upon me—(laughter and cheers)—and it is a gratification to me, and it must be a gratification to you, and to all Canadians, that I—not from my own merits, but as the representative of this great Dominion—was honoured so far as to have this order—an unexampled honour so far as the colonies are concerned—conferred on me, without any previous intimation, certainly without any previous solicitation, and that the star that shines on my breast and the ribbon which adorns my shoulder, were placed on my person by the hand of my beloved Queen. (Loud and repeated cheers.) And I envy not the feelings of those men who, blinded by political passion, will, although subjects of her Majesty, although called upon to support not only her Majesty, but the monarchical institutions which form the basis —she being the Crown—of the great edifice—I say, I envy not them their feelings, when, through mere political opposition, they sneer at me and at the honour conferred on me, and therein sneer at the act of their Sovereign. (Hear, hear, and cheers.) I should have supposed that my political opponents would have recognized that although I might be opposed to them in political principles, and in my political course, I was in England the Prime Minister of Canada—I was in England, worthily or unworthily, the exponent of the feelings and the principles of the majority of the Canadian people; that the honour conferred on me was conferred on Canada, as well on those opposed to me as those who are my supporters; and that they would have been proud to see that Canada, which formerly was considered by eminent British statesmen rather as a source of worry and weakness to the British Crown, was now recognized by her Majesty and her administration, by such a man as Mr. Gladstone, the leader of a Reform Government—(cheers)— that the honour conferred on me was conferred on the people of Canada and was in itself a recognition that Canada was no longer a source of weakness and danger, but of strength and a support and a comfort to the Crown of England. (Loud cheers.) Mr. Chairman, solicited honours are supposed not to be of great value. It is my pride, and my honest pride, that whatever honours I have received, be they from the Crown or from the people, have been given voluntarily, and without solicitation on my part. The first honour I received from the Crown was that of the second-class of the Bath. It was given to me at Ottawa, and until it was put into my hand by Lord Monck I was not aware that such a distinction was to be bestowed upon me. Subsequently I received the honour of being appointed a member of the Privy Council in England, the first instance in which such a distinction was conferred upon a colonial Minister. I had been for years previously a member of the Privy Council of Canada, but the honour of being a Privy Councillor of England, entitled, according to the theory of the British constitution, to sit in council on the destinies of the whole Empire, was conferred upon me without my knowledge or my solicitation, and the first intimation of it was given to me by a letter from England through the common post. In 1865, I had another great honour conferred upon me in England, conferred upon me altogether as being a representative man and representing the Dominion of Canada. In 1865, I got the Blue Ribbon of the University of Oxford, that grand, old Conservative institution where education and science and religion all go hand in hand with Conservative principles. (Cheers.) It was, Lord knows, not from any scientific or other attainments of mine that I received this honour. (Laughter.) I had no scholarship to boast of, because I was educated, or rather uneducated, in Canada long before there was a college or university in what is now the Province of Ontario, but it was conferred upon me distinctly upon the ground that I was a leading Canadian, and senior of the delegation then in England to advocate Canadian rights. My three colleagues on that delegation were Sir Alexander Galt, Sir George E. Cartier, and the Hon. George Brown. It was conferred upon me distinctly as being the senior of the four, and I value it greatly, as an honour not only to myself but to the whole Dominion. So, gentlemen, is this honour that was conferred upon me the other day. I have told you that it was altogether unexpected on my part. I was going in to keep an appointment with the Colonial Secretary, the Earl of Derby, when a letter was placed in my hands from Mr. Gladstone in these words " Dear Sir, in acknowledgment of long and distinguished services her Majesty has been graciously pleased to authorize me to offer to you the Grand Cross of the Bath." (Cheers.) Then, Sir, I felt indeed a glow of pride in my bosom. I felt that at last in my person it was recognized in England that long and faithful colonial services are equal in the estimation of our beloved Sovereign and Her Government with long and faithful Imperial services. (Cheers.) And there is no going back in England when a step has once been deliberately taken, as this was, of giving this exceptional decoration to a colonist, so we may expect that hereafter similar recognitions may be obtained by colonial statesmen for long and faithful services. This will be an additional inducement to the young men of our country to enter political life, when they know that their services will be observed, and that they will be equally entitled to distinction for eminent public services performed, whether in a colony or at the seat of Government in the metropolitan city of London. Mr. Mayor and gentlemen, I have said that this grand demonstration has been a sufficient compensation to me for the abuse that has been poured upon me—for all the calumny and the malignant, persistent attacks that have been made upon me ever since I entered public life. Why I should be selected as the particular mark of the enemy I do not know, except that I have perhaps in my own mind the vanity to believe that my enemies consider me as their most formidable opponent; that it is a compliment paid to the success with which, whether by ability or good fortune, I have led the Conservative party, and that they think that by putting me down, by destroying me in the estimation of the people of Canada, they will achieve a great political triumph. But the success of this meeting to-night, and of the meeting yesterday, and of a similar meeting which, if I live, I shall attend on my birthday at Montreal, will prove to those who are so basely endeavouring to belittle me in the eyes of the people how great is their failure, and how firm is the union of my friends of the Conservative party. (Cheers.) I believe that the most obtuse, the most malignant Grit, in the world, must feel and must know, after the demonstration of yesterday and to-day, that like the viper, he is after all, only gnawing at a file. (Cheers.) But I have been abused in days past by the press of the Reform party with great success. For some years I was attacked because I preferred to risk the loss of my popularity in Upper Canada rather than be in any way a party to a severance between Upper and Lower Canada. Many of the older men here will remember how I was abused by the *Globe*, under the able and energetic management of the Hon. Geo. Brown, how I was traduced, how, to render me unpopular—and for a time I was unpopular—in my own province, because the people were taught to believe that I was untrue to that province, and to my religion, that I was under French domination and sold to the French priesthood. For this I was bitterly attacked by my Upper Canadian political opponents. But I knew that when the whole subject was considered, the country would acknowledge that I was right in sacrificing everything to the great principle of keeping inviolate the union between Upper and Lower Canada. My twin brother, Sir Geo. E. Cartier, actuated by the same principle and the same feeling, had to undergo in his province opposition from the Rouge party, which was just as malignant as the opposition which I met with in the western portions of Canada. I was told that I was a traitor to my religion, and he was told that he was a French Orangeman. But the whirligig of time has brought around its own revenges, and those very same men who were insulting the Catholics years ago, and who attacked me so fiercely because I supported the passage of the Separate School bill—when I had the testimony and support of so good a man as the late Egerton Ryerson, then at the head of the educational system, a Methodist clergyman, and therefore a staunch Protestant—are now only too ready to do the bidding of the Catholic hierarchy to-day. When, under the administration of the late John Sandfield Macdonald, the Catholic Separate School bill was introduced by the Hon. R. W. Scott, of Ottawa, then a good Conservative, I, being then in opposition, supported that bill, and with the assistance of those of my friends whom I could induce to vote for it we carried it, because Sandfield Macdonald could not have carried it alone. But there were two men, distinguished men, Ontario men, who from their conscientious feelings as Protestants could not vote for that bill, and those two men were the Hon. Oliver Mowat, and the Hon. Alexander Mackenzie. How different is the case to-day! (Laughter.) I do not think, at this moment, that there is anything that my very good friend, and staunch supporter in the National Policy, Archbishop Lynch, will ask from those gentlemen who would not then allow him to have a Catholic Separate school in his diocese, nothing he can ask from the Hon. Oliver Mowat that he will not get from him. But the whirligig of time, as I have said, brings around its own revenges. And the gentlemen who then made me the mark of calumny and abuse because I wanted to do justice to the Catholic hierarchy now go farther than I did then, and would attack me, I dare say, for not going far enough now. Gentlemen, I am not, in an after-dinner speech, going to enter into a long and wearisome detail of political matters. You have heard enough of that yesterday and this morning, and you are reading men, well acquainted with the political history of Canada. Therefore, I shall only allude to one or two points, some of them of personal interest to myself, and some of interest to the whole Dominion. I am sensitive—hardened politician as I am—to any attack on my personal honour, and during my absence in England a paragraph appeared in some of the newspaper press belonging to the Opposition, and I have no hesitation in saying at once that it was dictated, if not written, by the Hon. David Mills—(hisses)—who ventured to state that I had betrayed Lord Lorne; that in my explanations respecting the retirement or removal of Lieut.-Governor Letellier, I had allowed him to be attacked, and that he deeply resented that attack. Nothing could be more false, nothing could be more silly than that statement, when I tell you that communications between the Governor-General and his advisers, his sworn counsellors, are confidential, and that no communication can be made by any Minister, even in his own defence, unless with the sanction of the Governor-General. And when I had to make my explanation of that matter in order that there might be made no mistake, the statement which I was allowed to make to Parliament by Lord Lorne was carefully prepared by himself; and when I went down to Parliament I read the paper written by himself as the only statement I was authorized to make to Parliament. True, there was a discussion—there were statements made by Independent members over whom I had no control, and I could not enter into a discussion on the subject because I was limited to the paper I had read to the House; and after these irresponsible statements I read again the statement I was alone authorized to make to Parliament. But do you suppose that if I had acted improperly, perfidiously, and dishonourably towards Lord Lorne that he would have been to me the friend he has been since he went to England? Gentlemen, when the Conservatives of the Empire Club in England conferred on me the honour of a banquet they wrote to Lord Lorne, then in the north of Scotland, asking him if he would attend and preside, and he wrote that it would be both a pleasure and an honour to do so. (Loud cheers.) He came all the way down from Argyleshire and presided at that assemblage of noblemen and gentlemen; and the all too flattering remarks which he made with respect to my charac'er and conduct have already been published. (Loud cheers.) That was a great gratification to me, because, at the time he was making that speech, at the time he was unconsciously defending my honour by praising me as a statesman, as a man worthy of the honours which I believe he knew, though I did not, were going to be conferred upon me—I had that same day read this attack on me—this unfounded calumny that I had betrayed, that I had been disloyal to the representative of my Sovereign, whose honour I had sworn to defend. (Loud cheers.) There is another statement which affects myself, and although it is of old date, yet I cannot afford at my age to allow any suspicions to rest on my good name, which might injure my colleagues, my friends, or my party; and as this matter has lately been brought up I feel bound to interrupt the proceedings of the evening by referring to it for a short time. It has been stated that I intrigued against my leader, Sir Allan Macnab; that I pushed him off the stool; that I usurped his place. There is no charge more false, more foul; and at this table there is a gentleman who was then a colleague of mine—I refer to my revered and respected friend, the Hon. William Cayley. (Loud cheers.) A coalition was formed at the instance greatly, and with the support and assistance of Sir Francis Hincks, who was leader of the Reform party and head of a Reform Government, who had been pushed off his stool by the Grits—deserted by some of his followers, just as Mr. Mackenzie at a later date was pushed out of his place by the same party. He resisted that attempt, and he brought to the support of the Government and to the support of the Conservative party, that great body of Baldwin Reformers who united with us then and have been true Conservatives ever since. (Loud cheers) But it was done after great hesitation on their part. At that time Sir Allan Macnab was looked upon as head of the old Tory party, and he had been held since 1837 as particularly obnoxious to the Reform party. We made a coalition, and the Hon. John Ross, son-in-law of Mr. Baldwin, became a member of our Government with Mr. Baldwin's consent. There was Mr. Spence, another Reformer, and Sir Francis Hincks while he was in Parliament acted in support of the Government. But when he was called away by his Sovereign who recognized his merits and gave him a colonial appointment as governor in one of the West India islands, the Reform party became frightened, and though true and loyal, and desirous of supporting us they said, "How can we go back to our constituents and say we are supporters of the old Tory, Sir Allan Macnab." Mr. John Ross resigned rather than remain in the same Government with Sir Allan Macnab. We resisted, for we could not have continued without the united support of the Liberal-Conservatives and the Baldwin Reformers, and when Mr. Ross resigned we would have broken up if it had not been for my exertions. In order to sustain the Government I went to another political friend of mine, the present Mr. Justice Morrison, then holding one of the most profitable offices in the country—the registrarship of Toronto, and I asked him, and implored him, in order to sustain the Government, to give up that office and assume the place abandoned by the Hon. John Ross. I succeeded, and we went on for some time, until at last in caucus the Liberal supporters of the Government signed a round robin to the Hon. Robert Spence, representing that they would withdraw their support. Mr. Spence and Mr. Morrison then resigned; the Government was broken up; we could not help it, for we no longer controlled a majority in Parliament. The Government having been broken up Sir Allan Macnab was asked by the Governor-General to form another administration, but he stated that he could not do so, that there was not a sufficient number of Upper and Lower Canadian gentlemen faithful to the Government to carry it on, and then Sir Etienne Tache was sent for and formed a new government. Those who were Conservative and those who were Baldwin Reformers were not going to hand over the Government of the country—when we really had a majority of the country—to the extreme Grits. Sir Etienne Tache formed a new Government, of which Sir George Cartier and I became members, and, in 1856, we formed the Government which lasted with but a short intermission until Confederation. So, gentlemen, I tell you that I fought for the Government of Sir Allan Macnab to the last moment ; and it was only when the ship went to pieces, when every man had to seize a plank to get ashore, it was in order to save our party, that myself and others assisted Sir Etienne Tache in forming another Government, and after successfully meeting the attacks of the extreme Grits, we formed another Administration to carry on fully the affairs of the country. I was true to my friend and colleague, Sir Allan Macnab ; anxious to forward his interests, political and personal. After these events I did everything I could do to get him elected to the Legislative Council of Canada, and through my influence, in a great measure, he was elevated, at nearly the end of his career to the high position of Speaker of the Legislative Council, and I think he died holding that office. (Loud cheers.) It is a long story, but I felt that it was due to you, due to myself and colleagues, due to those who have served under me and those who will hereafter serve under me, that I should tell you the facts, so that you may see that I was true and loyal to my leaders. (Loud cheers.) It has also been a matter of pride with me that as a general rule I have been able, when circumstances of one kind or other have deprived me of my colleagues, to care for my wounded birds. (Loud cheers.) We were in the cold shades of Opposition for five years but we did not despair ; we lost not heart nor hope ; we knew that the country was sound, we saw more and more, year by year, of the incapacity of the Grit Government ; in fact their incapacity was so obvious that we felt that the country would not keep them long in power; we fought them for five years, and, in 1878, we carried the country by an overwhelming majority ; we appealed to the country for a reversal of the verdict which had been pronounced in 1874; we obtained that reversal by the deliberate, sober, second thought of the people, and that verdict has been repeated when we again went to the people. (Loud cheers.) And, gentlemen, who can doubt, looking at the assemblage of yesterday, and looking at the general feeling of enthusiasm in the Conservative ranks ; knowing that in every one of the provinces they are alive to the development of the country, alive to the fact that we have not slumbered during the past, but that we have been active and energetic agents in the development of the country, who can doubt that in 1887 if this Parliament lasts so long, the verdict of 1878 and the confirmation of 1882 will be sanctioned and confirmed by the people of Canada. (Cheers.) I may not be there, gentlemen. It is true that

"The veteran lags superfluous on the stage";

Younger and stronger men must be called upon to carry on the Government, but I am satisfied that whoever may be chosen as my successor, he and those who act with him will move in the same line, will be governed by the same principles, and will be supported by the same party. (Loud cheers.) The Government is resolved to pursue the course that has met with the approbation of the country since 1878. Our Government is resolved not to relax its vigilance. We have carried out our pledges. We have readjusted the tariff ; we have brought into working the National Policy—(cheers)—we have been energetic—our enemies say too energetic—in the construction of the Canadian Pacific railway, and everything that we promised we have carried out. We will pursue the same course in the future. We will make no boasts, but as we have by our acts in the past sought to preserve your confidence so we ask a continuance of that confidence in the future. Gentlemen, the future of this country is safe beyond a doubt. This great Dominion, formed with great care, fashioned with some ability, and conducted with some prudence, has already assumed a proportion which makes us felt in England as adding power to the Empire. I have been attacked, I see, for some remarks I made while recently in England. Gentlemen, whatever I said in England I have already said before in the Parliament of Canada. I have already taken pains to explain my views on this subject at most of the public meetings I have attended, and especially in the year 1875, when I was in Opposition, and when I had the honour of attending the great banquet given in honour of one of our great public men, Mr. White, the member for Cardwell. (Cheers.) I said great is the future of the British Empire, that Empire of which we are a component part and to which we hope to be attached forever and forever.

(Cheers.) It is the fashion in some quarters to sneer at loyalty. I believe that the sentiment of loyalty and the sentiment of patriotism are both requisite in order to make any country a great country. I do not believe in that universal Christian charity which makes every man love foreign nations better than his own. I believe that even under a cloud of misfortune loyalty and allegiance should be the ruling principle in every honest heart. I believe, as was believed in the times of the early Cavaliers, that

> "Loyalty is still the same,
> Whether it win or lose the game,
> True as the dial to the sun,
> Although it be not shined upon."

But when we have loyalty and allegiance of a kind which joins a pure patriotic sentiment to self-interest, then there can be no doubt as to the course we ought to pursue. We are passionately loyal to the sovereignty of Great Britain. We love our Queen and we love British institutions. Our institutions are modelled upon those of England. We draw our inspiration from the great men who have governed England and who are now governing England, and we believe and know that our future prosperity depends greatly upon the continuance of union with the mother country. (Cheers.) It has been represented that I was in favour of federation with the Imperial Parliament. I never have made any such statement, I never had any such opinion. I have stated my personal opinion and belief that Canada must still preserve her Canadian Parliament. Canada is the best judge of the best means of governing herself. I believe that to Canadian statesmen only can be confided the trust of putting burdens upon the shoulders of our people, and that no Parliament sitting in England, however great and able it may be, and although Canada may be represented in it, can faithfully, fully and satisfactorily administer our affairs. The word Confederation means a union by treaty, and I believe that a treaty can be made between England and Canada by which we can have mutual commercial advantages and a common system of offence and defence. The Australian colonies will soon be united in a bond similar to, though perhaps not identical with, the Canadian Confederation. Then what shall we see? We shall see England with her thirty-five millions united to Canada with her five millions, soon to become twice that number, and to Australia with a similar population, and the world will know that if the old Mother Country is attacked, she has two auxiliary nations standing at her back and bound to make common cause with her. (Cheers.) We know that the nations that command the seas command the world. England is now the chief maritime power in the world ; Canada is, already, in her commercial marine, the fourth power in the world, and Australia, that vast continent, surrounded by colonies resting on the sea, must have a navy too. The combined naval forces of those three powers will form the great police of the world. (Cheers.) They will control the seas of the world, and if they control the seas of the world they will keep the peace of the world. It has been said that we are running great risks in venturing to make common cause with England. Gentlemen, if I know the people of Canada aright they are willing to run those risks. But there really is no risk. When any foreign nation knows that the 35 millions of people in England and the 20 millions in the different colonies, forming one great nation, will exert all their military and naval power in one common cause, that fact will prevent possible war with England, and England will be in as complete moral domination of the world as was the Roman Empire in the days of old. (Cheers.) But we are not, as I said before, going to count the cost. Who can look back to the time when the Crimean war broke out and not remember with pride how Canada rose as one man to stand by the Mother Country and by France, when the French Tricolor and the Union Jack were joined together fighting the battles of liberty against absolutism on the shores of the Crimea. There was a rush of Canadians to go to the battle-field, and I had the great pleasure, as a member of the Government of Sir Allan Macnab, to be instrumental in carrying a vote of £20,000, given unanimously out of the public treasury, in order to show that Canada made common cause with England and with

France in the Crimean war. And my friend the Minister of Militia has referred to the fact that at this moment a contingent of voyageurs from Quebec and the Ottawa river and from the North-West have gone to a foreign land to teach the Egyptian people how to navigate their own river. (Cheers.) Gentlemen, I am opposed to independence—(cheers)—not only because it is a treacherous breach of faith with our Sovereign, but because it is a sacrifice as well of the best interests of Canada. In the first place there could be no severance from England ; there never could be a change in our position without a war. In Canada there are men who would fight for the continuation of British connection ; men who would fight as zealously as they fought before in the war of 1812, to which my friend has alluded. There can be no possible change. I for one carried my musket as a boy in '37, and I will shoulder my musket again for the purpose of fighting for British connection. (Loud cheers.) Why, if we are independent we must have an army of our own, we must have a navy, and there will be an enormous expense to support a diplomacy of our own, keeping ambassadors at foreign courts, and besides all that we are lying alongside of a great and powerful people, and I am afraid it would soon be the case of the lion and the lamb. It is said that by-and-bye the lion and the lamb will lie down together, but at the present time, with the United States as the lion and we as the lamb we might lie down together, but the lamb would be inside of the lion. (Loud cheers.) No, no ; let us adhere to the British Crown. (Loud cheers.) We are now the freest people in the world. We do not contribute yet to the army and navy of England. We tax ourselves and we contribute nothing except for our own purposes, for our own Government. With regard to diplomacy, I may say that at this moment Sir Charles Tupper, the able representative of Canada—(cheers)—has been made a joint plenipotentiary with the British ambassador to Madrid in order to attempt to negotiate a treaty of commerce betweeen the Spanish Antilles and British America. We would be unworthy of our record, unworthy of all we have received, of all the kindness which has been vouchsafed to us, were we to withdraw ourselves from our allegiance. And speaking for myself, I have taken the oath of allegiance, and I am not going to break it. (Loud cheers.) No man is justified in withdrawing his allegiance from the Government under which he was born unless that Government fails in its duty to him. As to annexation, I believe there is no large party in favour of it. The United States may be a great and glorious country, but it is not for our or their interests—it is not for their happiness—that we and they should be one country. (Hear, hear, and loud cheers.) It would be a great English-speaking China in North America, instead of there being the good results to both countries which flow from the attrition, the friction, the friendly rivalry which is caused by the contiguity of these two powers. The United States is still a young country, and it may have many phases to go through. A few years ago it was convulsed by internecine strife ; and had we been a portion of the United States before 1860, what would have happened to Canada ? Why our sons would have been cal'ed on to fight their battles against the south ; our progress, our means, our prosperity and our peace and happiness would have been destroyed if we had had to take a part in that great war. I hope and trust that such an event may never occur again in the United States ; but it may occur, and why should we run the risk of annexation and all the possibilities of democratic change and democratic convulsion, when, under the ægis of the British constitution we are certain to enjoy happiness, order, good government and prosperity, governed by ourselves, governed as we wish, *misgoverned*, if we choose, by ourselves, but still perfectly happy and peaceable under the Crown of Great Britain. (Loud cheers.) On this line, on these principles the Ministry of which I am the head are labouring to govern this country ; we will not relax our efforts to promote the happiness of every part of Canada, by pushing forward our great national enterprises, by our railway policy, by the enlargement of the canals, so that a vessel drawing fourteen feet of water may be laden in the upper lakes and sail all the way to England without disturbing her cargo. We will pursue this same course, by every means seeking the development of the Dominion of Canada ; and upon these principles we ask your support, and we know we will get it. (Loud cheers.) I shall now resume my seat, thanking you from the bottom of my heart for your kindness, your self-sacrificing kindness, for your very affectionate regard for myself, for overlooking my many shortcomings, for the kind, generous, loyal support which you have granted to me for the last forty years. (Loud and long continued applause.)

Hon. WILLIAM CAYLEY related some reminiscences of his political career, but his remarks not being audible at the reporters' table the compilers are unable to give a report of his speech.

The CHAIRMAN then called upon Mr. Laidlaw, whose spirited rendering of the following verses to Sir John Macdonald was loudly applauded:—

SIR JOHN MACDONALD, G.C.B.

I.

I sing to-night of one we love, God-gifted with good gifts, and strong
To set our names among the stars and singing, take to grace my song
The name of him the nation hails as one wrought in the heart of fate,
To nurture this fair Canada to grow to proud and great estate,
The mighty lakes and forests wide, blue skies, vast prairies sing one name,
Calling the viewless winds to bear to other lands his deathless fame,
And men that hear the mighty song, sung by the woods and rhythmic waves,
In swift refrain give answer back that only treason's soulless slaves
Would cast one stone to touch the crown of him for whom true men of might
Have buckled on their swords and wrought in many a long and gallant fight!
Ring out your cheers, raise high the bowl, O hearts to-night than winds more free!
A thousand hands stretch out to greet our chieftain, safely o'er the sea.

II.

From east to west we turn glad eyes, and all is vast and grand and fair—
Great cities, where a thousand chimneys pierce the dense, smoke-laden air;
Broad rivers, mighty inland seas, dotted with many a glistening sail,
And smiling farms and happy homes that stretch through many a sunlit vale.
The pine trees towering to the skies, with restless murmur proudly call.
"O loyal hearts, and arms of strength, we've love and welcome for you all.
We ask not what your creed may be; so that your hearts be true and strong.
A new life waits you here, where labour is but freedom, love, and song.

III.

This is the land which our great chief has brought through treason, fight and frown,
And made her brightest of the gems that grace a Queen's imperial crown—
The land whose onward march no foe within her borders or without
Shall stay; whose song of triumph rolls in one prolonged, victorious shout.
This is our chieftain tried and true we greet to-night with loud acclaim,
The victor of a hundred fights, the brightest on the roll of fame.
Full many a loving hand is stretched to join with ours in "Welcome Home,"
To him who comes with honours crowned, and wealth of years across the foam

IV.

Where'er the traitors lurk to-night the sound of ringing songs shall greet
Their tuneless ears, and their false hearts shall own the tribute just and meet
To him who gave with lavish hand his brightest gifts of speech and brain
To make us worthy of the place for which he fought—and not in vain.
Oh shameless souls! Oh coward slaves! who gather gain from others' toil,
Whose watchwords, breathed in whispered haste, were ever "Office" and "The Spoil,"
In many a fight our honoured chief has worsted all your rabble crew.
The people's prayer that he may long be spared for victories anew.
Ring out your cheers, raise high the bowl, O hearts to-night than winds more free!
A thousand hands stretch out to greet our chieftain, safely o'er the sea.

CANADA.

THE MINISTRY.

Dr. FERGUSON, M.P. for Welland, then proposed the toast of "The Ministry of Canada," excusing himself from making any lengthy remarks owing to the already advanced hour. The task which had been assigned to him, of moving the Ministry, had been found to be a rather difficult undertaking when considered in another sense, and in the sense in which their political opponents would like to see the present Ministry moved. They had been found difficult to move out of office, but not difficult to move to speak. He had great pleasure in proposing the toast, coupled with the names of their valiant leader, Sir Hector Langevin, and that of Sir David Macpherson. (Cheers.)

The toast was enthusiastically received, the band rendering an appropriate selection.

Sir HECTOR LANGEVIN, on rising to respond, was warmly received. He said—Mr. Mayor and gentlemen, on behalf of my colleagues, I thank you most heartily for the manner in which you have received the toast of the Ministry. I am glad to hear the mover of this toast say that he did not intend to move us. We intend remaining in our places as long as we have the support that we have now in Parliament and in the country. (Cheers.) We think that what we have done during our long administration of public affairs has been in accordance with the wishes and the interests of the country. Gentlemen, I have to thank you specially on my behalf, and on behalf of my colleagues of the Province of Quebec, for the manner in which you have received us to-day and yesterday, when we were in your convention. We were there as your guests, invited by your committee to be present. We had no right there personally, but your kindness was so great that we felt as if we had been in a convention in our own province. The way you have received us this evening, the way in which we are treated in the distribution of these toasts, shows your kindness to the race which has supported during thirty years our great chieftain, Sir John Macdonald. (Loud cheers.) But there is another fact that I should not forget. Every time the name of our great leader of the Province of Quebec, the late Sir George E. Cartier, has been pronounced in your convention, or here to-night, I may say, every time it has been pronounced in the numerous meetings I have attended throughout Ontario, you have received it with the same veneration and enthusiasm as you accord to the name of our chief, Sir John, the twin brother of Sir George Cartier. It is thus, gentlemen, that you continue to cement that alliance that has been so long existing between you, the Conservatives of Ontario, and we the Conservatives of the Province of Quebec. These things are not forgotten by the people of the Province of Quebec. They know that here, in this great Province of Ontario, we have men who are ready to do justice to them, to stand by them in the same way as they stood by you. (Cheers.) There was a time, as our great chief, Sir John, has just said, when he was not so popular in the Province of Ontario as he is to-day. He had lost a good deal of his popularity because he stood by the rights of Quebec, because he thought justice required it. And, gentlemen, the Province of Quebec never forgot that. (Cheers.) At the time when Sir John had a small band, but a true band, of seventeen supporters from his own province, he had the support of the whole Province of Quebec. And Sir John never forgot that. Until now he has stood by us, and until now we stand by him, and it happens that in both provinces we give him about an equal support, which will keep him in office, I hope, as long as he lives. (Cheers.) When I say as long as he lives you will believe me when I say that I pray God every day that our great chief may be kept at the head of the Government and of the Conservative party of this country for many years to come. At every period of our history Providence has provided a man to guide our affairs, and there is no doubt that Providence has had a special oversight over these provinces and the people of Canada. We are increasing largely. Our country has expanded from a small province to an immense country extending from one ocean to the other, and from the United States to the North Pole. That country will be peopled with a hardy race of men who will make it great and prosperous. Allow me to add just one word more—to repeat to you an expression once used by a man who was a great colleague of my leader, Sir John. I refer to the late Sir Etienne Tache. That distinguished statesman, in speaking of the alliance between this country and England, said he had no doubt that the last shot would be fired in support of the supremacy of England in America by the hand of a French-Canadian. I, too, have no doubt, from the record of the Conservatives of Lower Canada, in the fact that the last vote that will be given in support of Sir John Macdonald will be cast by the ballot of a French-Canadian Conservative. (Loud and prolonged cheers.)

Sir DAVID MACPHERSON—It is a gratification for me to be present to-night to do honour to the leader of the Conservative party. It must be particularly gratifying to our leader, after having shown his ability to carry out the wishes of his supporters in Parliament, to receive as he has been receiving for the last two or three days, the approval of those who undoubtedly represent a large majority in this province and in the Dominion. (Cheers.) His administration of public affairs has been unquestionably able; the policy which he inaugurated has proved a signal success in increasing the prosperity of the country and augmenting the wealth of the people. (Loud cheers.) It is for you to see to it that there shall be no falling away in the support of our leader, and that the policy which has produced such benefits throughout the country, and has been approved by the country, shall be continued. (Loud applause.) What has been done by the Administration is known to you; all they have accomplished is before the country. (Hear, hear.) I need not recount to you any of their acts, but I will tell you what you need not apprehend. You need not fear the disclosure of administrative blunders, like, for instance, the costly steel rail blunder of our predecessors. (Applause.) Nor will you be aked to solve a problem so difficult as the navigation of magnificent water stretches—(laughter)—one end of which is lower by four hundred feet than the other. Ministers will not have to ask your forgiveness for having dug a pit like the Fort Frances lock, and burying hundreds of thousands of dollars therein. Nor have we to hide such a job as the Georgian Bay branch of the Canadian Pacific Railway. Nor will the blush of shame ever be brought to the face of Ministers and their supporters by the discovery of such a corrupt and scandalous job as the printing job of the late Administration, in which even members of the Government were compromised, and which cost two of them and the Speaker of the House of Commons their seats in that House. That printing job was one of the most disgraceful that could be perpetrated by a venal and unclean party. (Loud cheers.)

THE SENATE.

Dr. SULLIVAN, in proposing the Senate, said he rose with great pleasure, although not without some embarrassment, when he beheld the immense assembly before him. He would, before proposing the toast with which he had been entrusted, express on behalf of the city of Kingston his thanks for the honour which had been conferred on that city. After all Kingston had not done so badly. For thirty-four years, from 1844 until the 17th September, 1878, when Sir John, like Nelson, died in the arms of victory, Kingston had been true to the great leader. (Loud cheers.) He was glad, therefore, to accept the honour of proposing the toast. He came here, as they all did to offer the spontaneous expression of his allegiance, and lay on the shrine of Conservatism the offerings of fidelity and loyalty. (Cheers.) Many wondered how Sir John exercised such magnetic influence over his followers. It was in part due to his unvarying kindness and warmth of heart, whether he was victorious or not. The toast which had been entrusted to him was one which called for their respect and reverence. The Senate had been an important part of all constitutional government—the second estate of the realm—one of the pillars of the State. He would simply propose and ask them to honour the toast of the "Senate of Canada."

SIR ALEXANDER CAMPBELL, on rising to respond to the toast, was received with loud cheers. He said—Gentlemen who have preceded me have been telling stories of the past, telling of this and the other achievement, but I stand in the position of having been honoured by the friendship of Sir John Macdonald, and of having known him more closely than anyone present. Our friendship began in 1839, and his friendship has continued for me from that day to this; so that those who have accused Sir John Macdonald of forgetting his friends will find in me a contradiction of that story. (Cheers.) I am glad to have witnessed the honours which have been paid to him to-day and yesterday in that remarkable assembly at the Opera House, and I am sure I have not been present on any occasion when the hearts of the Conservative party were so warmly present with Sir John Macdonald as at these grand gatherings in which I am proud to have participated. With regard to the Senate I may say that I have been a member since its commencement; I have been leader on one side or the other since that time, and if anyone knows anything about the Senate I do. It is a body which has been more or less abused by our opponents, some of whom appear to be in favour of abolishing it altogether; though I do not understand that that is the position taken by leading members of the party like Mr. Blake, Mr. Mowat or Mr. Mackenzie. It is not the opinion of the thoughtful and educated portion of the Grit party, though there are men in that party who entertain what I regard as the dangerous view that the powers now exercised by the Senate and the House of Commons should be exercised by the House of Commons alone. I hope that those views will never prevail, because under such a system there would be no opportunity for that second consideration of public measures which is given by the Senate; for if the Senate has been abused I believe it has been owing to the fact that it has discharged its duties, that it has been useful to the country, though at times it may have been displeasing to a portion of the Grit party. I do not wish to detain you, but as perhaps accounting to some extent for the sentiments of our opponents on this subject I may tell you that when each province came into the Confederation the franchise of that province was adopted as the rule for that province; but when Prince Edward Island came in universal suffrage existed there. On the general rule obtaining as the other provinces it should have come in on that suffrage. But what did the Grit Government do? It carried through the House of Commons a bill insisting on a high franchise, a high property qualification for the voters of that Island, thereby depriving three-fifths of the people of Prince Edward Island of the right to vote. But we rejected it in the Senate, maintaining the old rule, and the people of that Province came into the Confederation on the same principles as the other Provinces. Hence the annoyance which a certain portion of the Grit party feel towards the Senate. I can speak for the Senate as having been in it from its beginning. I have no hesitation in saying that it has discharged its duties fairly and moderately, and with every consideration for the position which it occupies. We know that the Senate does not represent the voice of the people; that the voice of the people is represented in the other House, but care is taken that the expression of the opinion of the people through its House of Commons receives due consideration in the discussion of all questions of importance, or those upon which there seems to be any doubt. I am obliged to you for the toast on behalf of the Senate.

THE HOUSE OF COMMONS.

THE CHAIRMAN then proposed the health of the House of Commons, which was heartily received, the band playing an appropriate air. When the cheering had subsided,

HON. J. A. CHAPLEAU was called upon to respond. He said—Mr. Chairman and gentlemen, I thank you for the applause with which you have greeted the request made by the chairman to me to answer the toast of the House of Commons. I know your applause was not given to the man, to the individual, but it was given to an old soldier of the Conservative party; because for the past twenty years and over I have been a warm personal and political friend of your chieftain and leader, and used to claim the honour of being the youngest member of his "Old Guard." (Cheers.) Yes, Mr. Chairman, I am an old soldier, though my tastes and my connections would make me think that I am still a young man. Let me congratulate you in one word upon the success of your great demonstration to Sir John Macdonald. Your meeting has had the effect of showing Sir John that you appreciate his life work, whilst it holds out a hope to those who have worked, and to those who are working, and to those who are preparing to work in the grand cause of assisting in the development of their country that their labours will be recognized if they have been faithful and true and devoted, as those of your leader have been all his life. This meeting, too, shows that you in the Province of Ontario are, as we are in the Province of Quebec—though perhaps we might be more so than we are—united in your devotion to your party leaders, and that there is not a single note of discord amongst you. I am not going to detain you long at this late hour—(cries of " go on") —but I was asking myself to-night, as perhaps you have been asking yourselves, why all these toasts and all this enthusiasm, when the name, either of the Queen, the Governor-General, the leader of the party, or of the House of Commons was mentioned ? Oh, gentlemen, this is but another form of the old prayer that we are accustomed to make, and this prayer has a greater meaning, perhaps, than most of us realize. What use is there in the whole of humanity saying from day to day " Our Father ; Thy will be done," but to show humanity that there is an authority in the world that has created and sustains all that exists ; an authority that should be recognized by everyone, and whose will must be obeyed if all will prosper. (Cheers.) And when we propose, and when we reply to, and when we cheer the toast given to the leader of our party, and to the grand institutions of our country, we mean to say that the authority in the country, and the men who have worked on behalf of the great sovereign authority, must be listened to, and that the institutions of the country must be heartily supported by every patriotic citizen. (Loud cheers.) You have asked me to respond to the toast of the House of Commons. I cannot say anything for the House of Commons that any one of the constituents of this great Province of Ontario does not know. The Commons is the sovereign power of the peopl·, tempered by the authority of the Sovereign, and wisely controlled by the authority of the Senate. The independence of the Commons is the best security of power for an intelligent Cabinet—nobody has a higher estimation of party discipline than I have, at the same time nobody appreciates more than I do the frank and fearless expression of the opinions of the members of a deliberative body. Servility which despots themselves cannot but despise has no place amongst true commoners. Discipline means duty with devotion, intelligence and loyalty ; servility implies abjection or sordid interest. Party allegiance means a common recognition of the same leader, and a common adhesion to the same political programme. Party discipline requires the faithful execution of the pledge given to the leader and his platform. With party discip'ine individualities disappear, personal preferences sink into the general confidence. Factious coteries, the offspring of favouritism or of jealousy, are the death of party discipline. Their unchecked existence is the premonitory sign of the disruption of a party. A well-disciplined party, intelligent and proud in its allegiance, is the natural ruler and the benefactor of the people. The people are naturally proud, generous and devoted. Carried away by passion or misled by intrigue it may be guilty of ingratitude, but its nature will ultimately bring it back into the right path. It wants superior intelligence, bravery and generosity in its leader; it exacts devotedness, trust and sympathy in a party to remain with it. This is the history of the Conservative party, and of its uninterrupted success during nearly thirty years, and this is the secret of the great power of the right honourable gentleman whom you honour this evening. (Cheers.) Party warfare does not necessarily imply a systematic opposition to every measure proposed by the other party. On the contrary, a party in opposition carries with it the sympathies of the people when it assists the Government in the measures which denote sincere discharge of its duties towards the community. That generous attitude of the Conservative party during the period of 1874 to 1878 aided largely towards the return of the peop'e to its allegiance. That deliberate and dignified struggle for popular favour, that noble rivalry for domination, actuated by a sincere desire of securing the greatest amount of good to the Commonwealth, has won for British parliamentary institutions a stability and a reputation which has survived half a doz·n centuries. A French writer who had followed the debates of the House of Commons in England has said that it was the noblest assemblage of men since the Roman Senate, thus paying a well-deserved homage to that body whose history stands so high in the annals of mankind, whose battles are those of liberty itself. Were it not so young I might say with pride that our House of Commons stands next to its great prototype in England. It wields, in proportion, the same powers, secures the same freedom and rights to all and works with the same smoothness, framing laws suited to the times and to the wants of the country. Powerful as it is, it has, like all human institutions, its faults; it is issued of the people, and to represent it exactly it must have occasional whims and fancies. It changes its affections. It did so in the past, though not often, leaving Sir John aside for a short time, just long enough to regret him, but *Revenant toujours a ses premiers amours.* Sir, it sometimes gets out of temper; it grumbles; it would break the china if there were any about the House; but no one knows as well as its old governor how to bring back sunshine in the household and calm after the storm. Art and nature have combined to make of Sir John the most complete and perfect commoner we ever had. (Cheers.) Strange to say, on that bulwark of the liberties of the people, a leader, when once solidly implanted in the confidence of Parliament, enjoys an authority equal to the power of the greatest potentate. Louis XIV, in his might and in the pride of his absolutism, said:— "*L'etat c'est moi.*" "I am all the powers of the State." Your guest, to-night, gentlemen, our honoured chieftain, might say as truly, though in another sense, were he not so modest, "*La Chambre des Communes c'est moi.*" "The House of Commons of Canada it is I." (Cheers.) He has seen it since its creation; he has worked as an apprentice at the building of it; when he became a master in the art of command, he ruled it in his own way, he has shaped it after his own ideas. No man has exercised so much influence over that body in which are centered all the powers of the State. When he entered the House of Commons, the old assembly under the Union, he saw the battles that were then fought for responsible government. The fight was bitter and protracted. For a moment one could have doubted the ultimate success of responsible government, of free parliamentary institutions. Recriminations were violent, national prejudices ran high, riot invaded the streets, and as if it were an holocaust to liberty, the temple of parliamentary freedom was reduced to ashes. At last calmer counsels prevailed, and the peaceful work of the consolidation of a nation was continued. Sir John came to the front and from that hour to this his influence has been almost supreme, and that great influence he has always exercised on behalf of the material interests of the young colony and of the prestige and authority of old England. (Cheers.) Others may claim a share in the battles of constitutional institutions. Sir John's name is intimately connected with every step in the progress of the country, with every triumph in the direction of self-government, and with every glorious achievement in the different branches of national industries. He can truly say in the words of the poet, speaking of that admirable structure of the State, that he knows:—

> "Who made each mast and sail and rope,
> What anvils rang, what hammers beat,
> In what a forge and what a heat
> Were shaped the anchors of thy hope?"—

(Cheers.) I shall not delay you, gentlemen, drawing a picture contrasting the Canada of young John A. with the Canada of Sir John's latter days—I will not say old days, considering him so young yet. Let me recall you this fact that there are now in Canada people whose income is larger than were the revenues of our country when Sir John first entered public life; let me recall you this other fact that the British colonies were looked upon as wretched colonies, then only a burden to England, and that now we have a standing among the nations of the universe. (Cheers.)

Is it not indeed a singular coincidence; the man who, at the outset of his political career, saw the first battle in favour of responsible government against the arbitrary encroachments of the proconsuls of Downing street has lived to see the representatives of the two great political parties in England assuring him that some form of federation between the Mother Country and the colonies, with a common executive and a common power for the purpose of dealing with matters of common interest, must be devised with the view of advancing the prosperity and happiness and strength of the Empire. How proud the gallant chief must have been of the young country which his labour and his genius have brought to such prominence when he heard a disciple of the Manchester school, converted it is true, making an appeal to that great governing force, the power of public opinion, in favour of that idea of union, that principle of federation "than which," he added, "there is none more fraught with benefit to England, and even to the world." (Cheers.) Who contributed more than Sir John to bring around this change which has enhanced to such a degree the value of this colony even amongst that class of politicians who considered not many years ago, that it would be to England's best interest to let us go adrift ? Mr. Chairman, that which gave us the shape, the form, of a nation was Confederation : that which gave it strength was the building of a railway from ocean to ocean, bringing life from the centre to the extremities, binding together our scattered provinces. What was it that gave it wealth if it were not the development of its resources through the building of our railways and canals ? Every one of these bear the strong imprint of Sir John's genius and foresight. I shall not attempt, gentlemen, to discuss to-night that question of, what shall I say, of that question of Imperial Federation which shall impose itself on the consideration of the statesmen of Canada, as it has already imposed itself on public opinion of England ? The words of annexation are still ringing in the ears of those who have not forgotten the period of 1849. But the sound is one of hollow disappointment bordering on disloyalty. A scheme for the establishment of a commercial zollverein with our neighbours has also passed away. A Pan-Anglo council was dreamt of by one of the Liberal visionaries. But it is evident to any attentive observer that the next generation will solve those problems of the future mode of existence of our country either by the political federation of Great Britain and its colonies or by the peaceful assumption of an independent power by this Dominion. Will it take as much time to be realized as did the idea of Confederation, which dates back to the beginning of this century, when a prominent politician of Nova Scotia submitted a scheme of Colonial Union to the Imperial authorities ? Fifteen years afterwards the movement started from Quebec through Chief Justice Sewell, to be followed in 1822 by the project of Sir John Beverley Robinson, and in 1839 by Lord Durham himself. The period of 1854, following the Democratic wave of 1849, which had crossed the ocean from the European continent, was full of the idea of confederation, as if a feeling of conservation by a closer union of the British possessions had been stimulated against the sudden invasion of Republican ideas amongst the people The unnoticed feeble plant has become a stately and flourishing tree—(cheers)—giving to millions their share of the shelter and the shade, to use the expressions of my poor late friend T. D'Arcy McGee. Has the tree become decayed that we should already think of looking somewhere else for more shelter and shade ? No, far from it. As I said before it is proud England herself who realizes the danger of building up by emigration countries inimical or indifferent to her, "when on both sides the world," to use the expressions of Lord Roseberry, "across the Western ocean and across the Southern ocean, two great countries, empires if you will, are stretching forth their hands in passionate loyalty and devotion to the country from which they sprung." (Cheers.) But we must not be carried away by a sentiment of loyalty, and rush to the conclusion that the disintegration of the Empire is imminent if a new mode of union with the Mother Country is not at once devised. I do fully endorse the noble protest of our High Commissioner, Sir Charles Tupper, when he said, at the conference on Imperial federation, that he had " no hesitation in saying that it would be impossible for any constitutional change to increase that sentiment of loyalty to the Crown, or that love of British institutions which animates Canada from end to end." (Cheers.) That desire to secure for England the immediate co-operation of its great colonies clearly shows the success which those colonies have achieved. And surely one would be very exacting who would not be satisfied with the progress Canada has made during the past seventeen years. Our trade has developed beyond our most sanguine expectations ; our population will soon have doubled ; we have covered the land with our railways ; we have enlarged our canals ; we have opened up all the hidden treasures of mineral wealth ; we have astounded the old continents in laying open to their explorers, their engineers, their tourists, and their savants, the inventory of our riches and our inexhaustible resources; we have united in one common band of fraternal sympathy seven distant provinces covering half a continent; and we have answered the threat of starvation of our neighbours when they stopped commercial reciprocity by a firm policy of protection, which has proved that our Canadian atmosphere was as healthy to manufacturing growth as to commercial and agricultural industries. (Cheers.) To the challenge for the competition of the trade of Asia, we have given the bold answer of a transcontinental railway built in five years, and inferior in construction to no other road on the continent, and far superior to the others with regard to distances between the Asiatic and the European markets. Have we not enough of progress to be proud of, and have we not enough of vast enterprise to consolidate? And, Mr. Chairman, with our rapid growth in national life, our filial affection for the Mother Country has only increased. (Cheers.) Is there not more danger than profit in a new departure. The strongest family ties have often been broken by the indiscreet though well meaning intrusion of pecuniary matters between the members of the family. I fully understand the careful discretion of the right honourable gentleman in dealing with that question, and I would counsel you to trust your destinies to our intelligent and patriotic leader; his past career is glorious enough to be a guarantee that he would direct the nation he has formed into a glorious future. (Cheers.) He has safely passed through enormous difficulties, always saving his good name and the honour of the country. It has been often said that our country was particularly difficult to govern. I would have no objection to admit the proposition. To our statesmen, I would take it as a certificate of ability when I see the wonderful march of Canada in the path of national development. That this diversity of race is a source of difficulties in the political direction of the nation I am not ready to say, but I claim not to be contradicted when I affirm that each of the two great races which compose our Canadian union has, in its past traditions, in its blood, in its genius, all the elements required to make them reach together the highest summits of glory and perfection. (Cheers.) The Norman barons and the Saxon people edicted the Magna Charta, which has remained since the 13th century the political gospel of the world. More glorious laurels were never won than those of Alma and Inkerman; none better deserved and more appropriate was there ever an epitaph than that showing to the traveller the tomb of Wolfe and Montcalm—

> "Mortem virtus communem
> Famam historia
> Monumentum posteritas
> Dedit."

That sublime pledge of peace in glory over the remains of two heroes, standing there as a warning to the thundering cannons of the citadel not to trouble in their sleep the glorious dead of St. Foy and Charlebourg, remains as the inspired motto of the future glory and happiness of the Canadian nation. (Loud and prolonged cheering.)

MR. THOMAS WHITE, M.P., who also responded to the toast, was greeted with loud cheers. He said:—Mr. Mayor and gentlemen, after the magnificent speech to which we have just listened in response to this toast, I am quite sure I will meet your feelings—I am quite certain I shall consult my own—by occupying your attention but for a few moments in further replying to the toast. I feel it a great honour to be permitted to respond to the House of Commons of Canada, to whose confidence, a true reflex of the wider confidence of the great body of the electorate, is due the fact that your honoured guest is at the head of the Government. It has been well said that the difference between a politician and a statesman is, that while the former thinks only of the next election, the latter thinks of the next generation. The tendency to think of the next election is very great, and it is the foundation upon which the demagogue builds his trade and bases his appeals. Arising out of it. I know, as a member of the House of Commons, that in Canada we sometimes are subject to difficulties of apparently a very serious character. We have a magnificent country, but we have varied interests and varied prejudices. In a long line of territory extending from the Atlantic to the Pacific, it is almost impossible but that varied interests should spring up in the different parts of that vast line. Those varied interests give to demagogues, give particularly to those who are in Opposition, the opportunity of creating prejudices against the party which happens for the time being to govern the country. And one gratifying feature of this demonstration—one which I gather from it and carry away from it as a talisman to guide me in public life—is that the people of Ontario, and, I believe, the people of every other Province of the Dominion as well, appreciate the statesman and despise the mere politician. (Hear, hear, and cheers.) The people of Ontario know that Sir John Macdonald has never been a mere provincial politician. (Hear, hear, and cheers.) It is true he has been and is the leader of the party in Ontario, but he has never—in the whole period of his political career, at any time or under any circumstances—attempted to place province against province, creed against creed, nationality against nationality. (Loud cheers.) He has had to oppose throughout his whole career, men who have resorted to these unpatriotic expedients ; and when we find at the end of that career that he is met by a demonstration, the like of which has never taken place in Canada and is never likely to occur again, I say the members of the House of Commons themselves can learn the lesson that the people of Canada honour the men who deal fairly by the whole of Canada, that they are not mere provincials but Canadians, with the aspirations, and hopes and desires of Canadians. (Hear, hear, and cheers.) Another lesson which, as a member of the House of Commons, I gather from this demonstration is that the people of Canada are prepared to stand by the institutions which we possess, guaranteed to us, as they are, by the Constitution under which we live. During recent years the work of Government and Parliament has had special relation to the material development of the country. There are indications that in the future we shall be engaged in discussing questions affecting the Constitution itself. We have already had indications of this in the agitation for what are called Provincial Rights. I think I may say that the House of Commons, composed as it is of representatives of all the provinces, and interested, therefore, in protecting the rights of all the provinces, affords the best guarantee we can have that Provincial Rights run no risk of injury. (Hear, hear, and cheers.) I think there is no motto of the many which surround this room that appeals more to the patriotic instincts of the people of Canada than the one before me :—" The conservation of the rights of the Dominion and the Provinces assured by the Constitution, and subject to it." (Hear, hear, and cheers.) We have in this demonstration which you have given to Sir John Macdonald, in the splendid reception you have given to him, at a time when there is no political excitement in this country, when there is no election, and no immediate prospect of an election coming on—I say we have in it the lesson taught by the yeomanry of Ontario that the young man who devotes himself unselfishly and patriotically to the services of the whole country is certain to meet with the hearty appreciation and the warm greetings of the people whom he serves. (Loud cheers.) As to the Conservative party in the Province of Quebec, I believe that with two such champions as Sir Hector Langevin, the unquestioned leader of the party in that Province, and the gentleman who has just addressed you, that Province, as well as Ontario and the other Provinces, will continue that hearty support to the Conservative cause which it has given in the past. (Loud cheers.) God grant that it may be so ; God grant to the venerable and venerated statesman who dwells in the hearts of the whole Conservative party, and who has the respect, I believe, of three-fourths of the Liberal party as well, that his declining years may be cheered by the thought that the work which he has done has not been void or vain, but that the people, taught by his patriotism, and encouraged by the lessons which he has given them, will go on and complete the great work which he has had in hand in such a way as to make this country all that its most earnest friends desire that it should be. (Loud cheers.)

THE LEGISLATIVE ASSEMBLIES.

Mr. PATTERSON, M.P. for Essex, in proposing the toast of the Legislative Assemblies of the provinces, said—Mr. Mayor and gentlemen, the toast which has been entrusted to me to propose is one which relates to Assemblies which, though not as important possibly as those to which reference has already been made this evening, yet which come more home to the people of the several provinces of this Dominion. Our Provincial Legislatures have control over our educational interests, our civil rights, and our municipal affairs, and the power which they have in promoting the intelligence and prosperity of a country is not to be underrated. There is no doubt that our several provinces are jealous of their provincial autonomy, and while we of the Liberal-Conservative party desire to see a strong Federal Administration, we wish also to see provincial rights fully maintained in all our provinces. (Cheers.) In this respect the Liberal-Conservatives of Ontario are second to none in the sister provinces. (Cheers.) An attempt has been made to cast a slur upon the Conservative party; to mislead the people to believe that we wished to do away with the federative system, and to introduce a legislative system in its stead. I am sure I speak the sentiments of the Liberal-Conservative party in Ontario when I repudiate such a charge. (Cheers.) Any attempt to alter our constitution in that direction would be utterly and absolutely contrary to the wishes of our people. Speaking of our provincial affairs, and referring as I have done to the feelings of the Liberal-Conservative party of this province, I cannot conclude the proposition of this toast without referring to our gallant younger chieftain in Ontario, the leader of Her Majesty's loyal Opposition. (Loud cheers.) While the great chieftain whom you have been honouring to-night is in the full possession of power and prosperity at Ottawa, Mr. Meredith, our Local leader, is still in the cold shades of Opposition. (A voice, "Not for long.") I trust that when the next opportunity comes round we will avail ourselves of the increasing prosperity of our country and our party to place him at the head of Ontario affairs. (Cheers.) Having had the honour of following Mr. Meredith for a time in the Local House, and having watched his subsequent career with pride, I must say that I echo the hope of this audience and of the Liberal-Conservative party in Ontario, when I prophesy for him yet, a long and brilliant career in guiding the affairs of our beloved province. (Loud cheers.) I have pleasure in proposing the health of the Legislative Assemblies of the provinces of the Dominion. (Cheers.)

HON. MR. NORQUAY, Premier of Manitoba, on rising to respond, was warmly received. He said—Mr. Mayor and gentlemen, allow me, on behalf of the Legislature of Manitoba, to return you my sincere thanks for the honour you have conferred on that body by the reception you have given to this toast. I regret very much that my quondam governor and political preceptor, Hon. Alex. Morris, is not here at my side to-night to have preceded me in responding on behalf of our Local Legislatures, and I must take this opportunity here, in his own constituency, of paying that tribute of respect that is due to him for the services he has rendered as a public man, not only to the Dominion of Canada, but to the Province of Manitoba individually. He held the high and responsible position of Lieutenant-Governor of Manitoba for the full term of five years, and having been associated with him during all that time I can speak of the devotion with which he applied himself to the development of our institutions, which were then in their infancy, and the experience that he brought to bear upon that very important subject is duly appreciated by the people of Manitoba to-day. When we look at our constitution and take into consideration its different features, we cannot over-estimate the importance of provincial legislation in its bearing upon the progress of any community. Our institutions, copied as they have been largely from the older provinces, have been sought after eagerly by those who have come to us, and who were desirous of enjoying their benefits in the new land where they have made their homes as they had in the land from whence they came. At the present time we have in Manitoba over sixty municipalities, the whole province being governed by little local governments promoting each its own interests, and contributing by local taxation very materially indeed to the development of the country. I can very well fancy the anxiety and interest that are felt by the people of Ontario in the progress and welfare of Manitoba. Many a loving mother thinks with fond remembrance of the son who, perhaps a little wild and adventurous, but all the dearer to her on that account, has gone to carve out a fortune and establish a home for himself in our Prairie Province and is anxious to preserve that connection which is so dear to all families. Every parent here can realize the anxiety with which the course of that son is watched, and the interest which the fond parents take, not only in his individual success and prosperity, the developing institutions of his new home, but in everything connected with the Province in which he has made his home. At this late hour it is unreasonable to suppose that a lengthened speech must be inflicted upon the audience. I can conceive that the boys are getting restless, and the old men are getting weary. (Cries of "No, no.") We have met on a most interesting occasion, as has been evidenced by the circumstances of yesterday and to-day, and I only regret that the building has not been able to contain all who would have attended to assist in rendering that honour that the Province of Ontario is conferring upon our venerated chieftain—(cheers)—an honour earned by forty years of eminent public service in the interests of Canada—(renewed cheers)—and not in self interest or self aggrandizement. In taking a retrospective glance at the records of the past we find that those who utilize their positions for selfish purposes soon drop out from the ranks of our public men, and lose the esteem of their fellow citizens ; while, on the other hand, those who, like our chieftain, with unselfish devotion and patriotism, devote their energies to their country's best interests, do not fail to receive from an appreciative people the reward that is due for their services. (Cheers.) What prouder or more lasting monument can be built up by any man than to live in the hearts and affections of his people, and to have earned a place in the records of his country as one who enacted or assisted to enact measures for the improvement, the progress and the amelioration of mankind. (Loud cheers.) There have been many milestones in the history of our chieftain, and they are the marks which show what Canada has achieved in the way of progress and development for the last forty years. (Cheers.) I remember two years ago in making a public speech I said that Canada would be blessed by the Almighty in sparing the life of Sir John Macdonald for the term of forty years of public life, like Moses the great leader of old. (Loud cheers.) I am happy to say that wish has been consummated ; a wish which was not mine alone when it was uttered, but a wish of a large majority of the audience I was then addressing. Before sitting down, allow me on behalf of the Conservatives of Manitoba to repeat what was stated in the address presented by me to-day, that we extend an invitation to Sir John Macdonald to visit Manitoba and the North-West, and I will guarantee on the part of his admirers, perhaps not such a large assemblage, but such a greeting as shall not be less warm and enthusiastic than the present. (Loud cheers.)

Hon. Mr. BLANCHET also responded to the toast, and was received with loud cheers. He said :—Allow me to thank you very heartily for the manner in which the toast has been proposed and received. I have had the honour of being selected by my chief, the Premier of the Province of Quebec, to come here and tender to my kind, popular, and patriotic chieftain the respect, the devotion, and the gratitude of the Conservative party of the Province of Quebec, composing two-thirds of the Legislature of Quebec. (Loud cheers.) I am glad and proud to be here to-night to witness this grand demonstration which you of this great Province of Ontario have organized in favour of Sir John Macdonald, who, by his broad, unsectional policy, and wise legislation has made this a prosperous and a happy country. (Loud cheers.) As a Conservative of the Province of Quebec, I am proud of the feelings which you, of Ontario, entertain for your chieftain and mine in Dominion politics, Sir John Macdonald. I am glad that while you are thus honouring him we do not forget the debt we owe to another great statesman—one of the greatest of the Province of Quebec—and that a monument to him to be erected in the capital of this great

Dominion will show to future generations what Canadians think of those who prove themselves to be true patriots and saviours of their country. (Loud cheers.) I hope the people of Quebec will not forget the example which has been set us to-night, and when Sir John comes to us in Montreal next month, the loyal people of that province, attached as they are so closely to British institutions, will give him such a magnificent and hearty reception that he will forget that he is not in his own native province. (Loud cheers.)

THE MANUFACTURING INDUSTRIES.

The CHAIRMAN then proposed "Our Manufacturing Industries," which was received heartily.

Mr. THOS. COWAN, on rising to reply to the toast, was greeted with loud cheers. He said :—I thank you very much for coupling my name with this toast—the most important of all those which have been named to-night. In speaking to it I must, of course, to some extent refer to the question of the National Policy, and I can only repeat what I said to-day at the great convention, that I am glad to know that our exceedingly honoured chieftain has not weakened one iota—(loud cheers)—that he stands as firmly to-day as ever to the Canadian National Policy ; that high above all other planks in his platform, high above all our development, in clear and distinct letters is written, " Here is a Canadian policy for the agriculturists, the manufacturers, the artisans and the workingmen who are making this country"—that is the policy of the Liberal-Conservative party. (Loud cheers.) I can only say that if our esteemed friend whom we are met to honour to-night should live to the age of Methusaleh I hope he will stand by the Canadian National Policy, and he will be Premier of this country. (Cheers.) I belong to the party which is the true Reform party of this country, because it gave us reforms in our fiscal policy which were denied us by the men who called themselves Reformers. We sent deputation after deputation of the best and truest men who live in Canada—we besieged them with deputations, but Mackenzie and Cartwright not only refused to grant our wishes but positively insulted us—(hear, hear,)—and here I am to-day called one of the rankest Tories in all Canada. (Laughter and cheers.) Sir, the question may be asked, why am I a Tory? Simply because I obtained at the hands of the Grand Old Man, who is our honoured guest to-night, substantial reforms that were denied by the men who called themselves Reformers. (Loud cheers.) It is said that we are bloated manufacturers. I cannot see that I am very much bloated yet ; I think I am one of Pharaoh's lean kine. (Laughter.) It has been charged that the N. P. is a grand thing for the manufacturers, while it is a hardship for the artizan—th se who say so all the time forgetting that the beauty of the N. P. is that the man who comes into the country with his own skill and labour stands in exactly the same position as the man who comes with his millions of capital. (Cheers.) We say to manufacturers, come with your money; Canadian towns are willing to encourage you with bonuses to start industries in their midst; and we proclaim to the hornyhanded son of toil who handles the lathe or the plane that there is no let, no hindrance, but that here all stand upon the same basis. (Cheers.) It is said that we manufacturers are making money. I hope we are. At the same time we have overproduced to some extent, and the consumer is able to-day to buy his cottons and his woollens, his coffee and his sugar, and all the necessaries of life cheaper than ever before in the history of Canada. (Cheers.) I belong to the party that joined the Conservatives with the N. P. when things looked blue. In the old election of 1874 I fought against our esteemed and worthy chieftain, and we thought the millenium had dawned when we defeated him. But the great mistake was that we did defeat him. Why? Simply because we rejected the man who was willing to advance the interests of the country. Those of us who left our party and fought for the N. P. made great personal sacrifices. We were in power, and had the dispensation of patronage, and in espousing the cause of the N. P. we deserted the party in power and joined the ranks of the party then in the cold shades of Opposition.

I am glad to be here to join in this honour to our chieftain. Why is it that he holds his proud position so long in defiance of all opposition ? I will tell you why ! It is because he is the youngest man in the Dominion. (Cheers.) I say he is the youngest because he is the most progressive man, modern in his ideas and always to the fore with such a policy of true reform as is best suited to the progress of the present times. We know very well that in the old time when we went to the office of Mr. Mackenzie and asked for a change in the tariff, when we sent the best men that could be found in Canada, they were not only repulsed and refused, but they were actually insulted. But I know that to-day the son of the humblest citizen in Canada can go to Sir John Macdonald or to Sir Leonard Tilley with his cause and he will have a fair hearing. (Cheers.) Another reason of Sir John's success is that not only is he the most progressive man in Canada, but he knows how to gather men around him in whom he can trust, and in whom the people can trust. Alexander Mackenzie, whose name I always mention with a feeling of reverence and honour, managed the whole Government himself; Messrs. Blake and Cartwright did not stand by him as they should. But Sir John knows that when a question of public works comes up he can trust Sir Hector Langevin ; when other questions come up they can be dea t with by his respective colleagues ; Sir John knows his men, and that is one great reason for his success. Sir Richard Cartwright said that the Saskatchewan valley was only a huge projection of the great American desert ; and it cost us hundreds of thousands of dollars to contradict that lie about our country ; and we proved by experimental farms along the whole line of the Canadian Pacific railroad that the country is capable of producing the best wheat, and the largest quantity per acre of any part of Canada (cheers) ; and in the presence of my esteemed friend, Mr. Norquay, I will say that it is capable of producing the best men in the world. (Hear, hear, and loud cheers.) I am glad to be on this platform with the Premier of Manitoba. Last year the editors of some small country newspapers, the secretaries of small Grit organizations, the secretaries of so-called agricultural clubs, who would not know which end of a plough to hitch a horse to—(laughter)—called themselves the representatives of the farmers of Manitoba. But our good friend Norquay calmly, coolly and deliberately looked over the whole scene, and having looked it over he said, "Never mind the racket the thing will come all right." (Hear, hear.) And to-day in Toronto he received a welcome of which any man might feel proud. I well remember the occasion on which I first met my honourable friend. It was at the opening of a branch railroad in the Prairie Province, and he was to drive the last spike, and, sir, when he took off his coat and went at the business in a true workmanlike manner I should have said that he had done nothing but drive "last spikes" all his life. (Cheers.) But later on in the day, when he stood on a flat car and delivered the opening oration I fully made up my mind that he had devoted his life to making speeches from a flat car. (Cheers and laughter.) As between the two parties you have the Conservative party wafting the olive branch of peace between the different provinces and saying we are all Canadians and citizens of a common country. (Loud cheers.) The policy of the Opposition has been exactly opposite, they have sought to array the provinces against one another, to arouse local enmities and dissentions. As between the two parties no patriotic Canadian can be long in choosing the one which is led by the man in whose honour we have assembled to-night. After again thanking the meeting for the honour they had done him, the speaker resumed his seat amid loud applause.

TRADE AND COMMERCE.

The CHAIRMAN then proposed "Trade and Commerce," which was duly honoured.

MR. ROBERT HENRY, Brantford, was called upon to respond to this toast. He said it afforded him great pleasure as an humble member of the great Conservative party to be present with those assembled from all parts of the Dominion to do honour to our great leader, the Right Hon. Sir John Macdonald, at this magnificent demonstration. It was no more than an expression of the opinion of a vast majority of the people of Canada to say that he congratulated their great leader upon the honours conferred by her Majesty, honours worthily bestowed and honourably won. (Cheers.) He hoped that he might be long spared to rule over the destinies of Canada. He (Mr. Henry) thanked the committee for associating his name with the toast of the trade and commerce of this country. No one can deny but that depression exists throughout the country at the present time. But on the other hand he was bold to say that never had the commercial and manufacturing interests of the country been in a more prosperous condition than during the years between 1878 and 1884. (Hear, hear.) Allusion had been made to the great benefit derived from the National Policy, and he believed that the adoption of that policy was in the true interest of the people of Canada. He concluded a short and forcible speech by saying that in so far as Governments could legislate in the interests of trade and commerce, those great interests were safe in the hands of Sir John Macdonald and the able and painstaking Ministers with whom he had surrounded himself. (Cheers.)

THE LADIES.

SENATOR TURNER, of Hamilton, in proposing the toast of the ladies, said:— Before proposing the toast placed in my hands, allow me to congratulate our right honorable guest on his improved health, his splendid forty years record as a politician and his brilliant accumulation of Imperial honours—honours justly earned from an Imperial as well as a Dominion point of view. John A. (I like the good old name) has been mainly instrumental in laying the foundation of our Dominion—the Great Britain of the west, whose advancement in national importance will ere long astonish Europe. (Hear, hear.) Compare the United States before immigration struck their prairies with what they are to-day, and judge for yourselves what the Dominion will be in a few decades hence, now that we have not only gained entrance to, but have a railway through, prairies second to none in the world as to extent and fertility, and a homestead and land policy unequalled in liberality. The toast I have the honour to propose is The Ladies, only second in importance politically, as well as socially, to the toast of the evening. The question of woman suffrage has been mooted here as elsewhere, I presume, so far as the Dominion is concerned, without their consent. They always have been, are now, and will continue to be, a power in legislation, and I trust will not willingly give up their quiet, persuasive powers or the pleasures of the curtain lecture in exchange for the doubtful honours pertaining to an election campaign. Any Dominion government having the confidence of the ladies may control Parliament, but the tenure in office of any administration without their confidence is not worth a week's purchase. The ladies are now, and may they long continue to be so, the power behind the throne of our Dominion.

W. R. MEREDITH, Q C., M.P.P., on coming forward to respond to this toast said:—Mr. Mayor and gentlemen, I do not know why having the misfortune, if I may use that expression, to be a married man, I should be called upon to respond to this toast, for I am sure that in such a gathering as this there are many young Conservatives who would gladly come forward to take my place. But when I am called upon, I respond most heartily, and I do it perhaps not exactly upon the ground that Mr. Turner has taken in moving the toast, in regard to the proposition that has been made to the Dominion Parliament for the admission of women to the franchise. I do not know whether this measure will become law or not, but this I do know, that the women of this country exercise a most important part in controlling the destinies of this country, through the influence they have over their husbands. And, as has already been said most eloquently to-night, if we are entitled to appeal to the old men of the country, and to the young men, too, we are entitled to appeal to the mothers and to the wives and daughters of this land in the interests of the country. I shall not at this hour detain you at any length, but I cannot take my seat without expressing the great gratification which it afforded me of seeing such a gathering upon this platform of prominent men from all the different provinces of the Dominion. We know what attempts have been made in the past to spread discord in the ranks of the Conservative party. We know that, in 1881, when the Reform party went to the country, without a policy, and without a platform, they returned to that old cry which has been their battle cry of old, the cry of French domination. And although they appealed strongly to sectional feeling, they were unable to stir up the hostility of our people to their fellow citizens of Quebec. I was glad to hear the words that fell from the lips of a former Premier of Quebec, Hon. J. A. Chapleau. I reciprocate the patriotic sentiments which he has uttered in your hearing to-night, and I believe a vast majority of the people of Ontario reciprocate likewise. Parties are but a means to an end, and I believe that it is the Conservative party by whose policy and principles the interests of this country can be best advanced, and by which we can be consolidated and bound together as one people. I am willing for that to stay in the cold shades of Opposition, and even to submit to be driven from public life altogether, so long as I can resist anything tending to introduce discord into the ranks of this great Confederation. (Cheers.) The great North-West has to be peopled; and unless we can fill it with population I do not know what the future of that country will be; and the man who would do anything to check its progress does a deed which will militate greatly against the people of this country. Largely by the policy of the present Government we have bound the interests of the people by the Canadian Pacific railway. In the providence of God we have a great duty to perform in that country. There are millions of acres there to occupy and till. The destiny of this country is a great one; the Liberal-Conservative party understands what that destiny is, what the giant energies of our people are, and they are willing to assist them in this great work. (Cheers.) I say to the men and women of this country, put your shoulders to the wheel and heartily assist the party, whose policy is to develop this country in the present as well as the future. I believe that by adopting the false and foolish cries of other men the result would be to put back this country at least fifty years in the race of progress. (Hear, hear and cheers.) To-night we have been demonstrating that confidence in our party and honouring our chieftain; the great thing to be done is to accomplish the ends for which these parties are created. I say to you that when you go to your homes, warm with the enthusiasm which has been created here, when the hour of battle comes you should be ready to go forth in battalions like a well-trained army, and if you do so you will sweep the enemy from before you like a whirlwind. (Loud and repeated cheers.)

The toast of "The Caterers," Messrs. McGaw & Winnett, was then proposed and heartily honoured.

THE PRESS.

"The Press" was proposed by the chairman, and having been duly honoured was responded to by

Mr. CREIGHTON, M.P.P., who claimed that the proud position now occupied by the Conservative party of Canada was largely due to the efforts of the Conservative press. (Hear, hear, and cheers.) A portion of the Canadian press had pursued a course inimical to the true interests of Canada; but, on the other hand, there was a large and respectable portion of the Canadian press, viz., that supporting the Conservative party, which had at heart the best interests of the country. (Cheers.) Of the latter *The Toronto Mail* by right occupied the foremost position as the most progressive, enterprising, and enlightened newspaper in the Dominion. (Hear, hear, and loud cheers.) Next to *The Mail* came the Conservative county papers which had done much to accomplish the ends and objects of their party, and which deserved to receive their hearty support. (Loud cheers.)

The toast of "The Chairman" having been proposed by Sir John Macdonald and very cordially honoured by the audience, the meeting then broke up with cheers for the Queen, Sir John Macdonald and Mr. Meredith.

THE MONTREAL BANQUET.

The Junior Conservative Club of Montreal having resolved to entertain the Conservative leader at a banquet, Sir John was invited to attend a reception in the commercial metropolis on Monday, January 12th, and a banquet at the Windsor House on the following evening. The reception accorded the distinguished statesman by the people was without parallel in the history of Canada. On the arrival of the train carrying Sir John at the Bonaventure station on the evening of the 12th, the city was in a blaze of illumination and the enthusiasm never for a moment flagged. Sir John, Lady Macdonald and party were escorted through the streets by a torchlight procession. The banquet was the largest and most brilliant assemblage of the kind ever held in Montreal. The splendid dining-hall of the Windsor was crowded to its utmost capacity; all the leading men of the Conservative party of Quebec were present, and many from the other provinces. Brilliant speeches in both French and English were made, in response to the various toasts, but in order to confine this book within reasonable dimensions, only those of Sir John and the Minister of Finance are given.

The toast of the evening was received with unbounded enthusiasm, the vast audience rising to their feet and cheering loud and long. Again and again was the cheering repeated, and Sir John could not get an opportunity to reply until the audience had fairly exhausted itself. When quiet was restored, Sir John, who was visibly affected by the warmth of his reception, said:—

Mr. Chairman and gentlemen,—I cannot hope to convey to this magnificent assembly my deep sense of the honour that has been conferred upon me. I wish I could convey to you my feelings of exquisite pleasure, of complete happiness at the demonstrations of yesterday and to-day. But as my words are all too feeble for that purpose I shall not make the attempt. I shall only ask you, and I know that you will believe me, to accept my assurance that *ab imo pectore*—from the bottom of my heart, I feel the utmost gratification at your kindness, at the honour you have conferred upon me, at the distinctions you have paid me to-day and yesterday. (Cheers.) To see as it were the population without distinction of race, or I might say of politics, surging along the streets of this magnificent city to show that, even if they could not give him their political confidence, they appreciated the honest and earnest exertions of a public man, was not only gratifying to myself but must be gratifying to all the lovers of their country when they see that public service, well-meant service, was greeted as mine was greeted yesterday and is greeted at this moment. (Loud cheering.) As I said or attempted to say yesterday, because the dimension of the meeting was too enormous for me to reach all who were present, and therefore I may now repeat my remarks, the reception of this great demonstration on the anniversary of my birthday sinks deeply into my heart, and, as I also stated, no place could be more appropriate, if my friends wished to celebrate such an anniversary than the great city of Montreal. (Loud applause.) On the 11th of January I was three score years and ten. Forty years ago last November I commenced my political life as seventy years ago I commenced my natural life, (Cheers.) My political life began in Montreal. (Renewed cheers.) Here I first entered parliament; here I made my first attempt at a speech; here I first took office under the Crown, and forty years afterwards I have the immense gratification of finding in the city where I commenced my political career such a magnificent, such a overwhelming demonstration as I am honoured with to-day. (Loud cheers.) To few men has been vouchsafed such a concurrence of gratification, such an overwhelming amount of honour, as has been conferred upon me by the Crown and by the people during the last few months. You, sir, have kindly alluded to the fact that I was honoured by Her Majesty, the gracious sovereign of us all—the beloved sovereign of us all—(loud cheers)—that I was honoured with this star and with this ribbon ; and great as the honour was in itself, I felt that it was increased when Her Most Gracious Majesty, with gracious words, invested me personally, with her own hands threw the ribbon over my shoulder, with her own hands adorned me with the star. (Loud and enthusiastic cheering.) And, sir, I believe, I am proud and happy to believe that great as the gratification was to myself personally, that gratification was shared by the majority of the people of Canada. (Cheers.) They felt that this distinguishing mark of Her Majesty's approbation was conferred not upon John A. Macdonald, not upon the Premier of Canada, but upon the man who for years had represented the majority of the people of Canada. (Cheers.) Her Majesty was conferring a distinction upon Canada by conferring an honour upon me, however I as an individual might be unworthy of that great distinction (no! no!) Oh! Mr. Chairman, I am not going to affect the modest, I am not going to say I am altogether unworthy of it. (Loud cheers.) If I said so it would be a mere affectation of modesty, and, moreover, it would be impugning your judgment, gentlemen. (Cheers.) Whatever may have been my original humility and shyness, I had to yield my own opinion as to my insufficiency to the consensus, to the action, to the opinion of the majority of the people of Canada that I was worthy to hold the proud position that I have held so long, of being the First Minister of Canada. I yielded to your opinion, gentlemen. I gave up my own modest estimate of my own worth. (Cheers and laughter.) I accepted your judgment, the judgment of the people of Canada, as far superior to my own. (Renewed cheers.) I had intended, Mr. Chairman—of course there is a certain place paved with good intentions—to have gone on to show to you, to make it plain to every capacity, that the honour was not undeserved. (Hear, hear.) But you, sir, have relieved me of that painful necessity. In your eloquent and too flattering remarks you have gone over many of the events connected with the progress and development of Canada in which, more or less, I had some share. (Hear, hear.) I had, from a necessity or supposed necessity, felt that I must show myself on an occasion of this kind like an Indian warrior chief, who feels that he must come in and display his wounds and count the scalps he has won in the combat, but I am saved the necessity. I need not glorify myself—you have glorified me, and I am proud and happy to say that this grand meeting has not disapproved of what you have stated. (Loud cheers.) Mr. Chairman and gentlemen, I am three score years and ten ; I have nearly run my course. (No, no.) I hope that you are all true prophets (laughter and cheers), but when a man is three score years and ten he has about to begin to remember that perhaps it may be as well that he should make way for younger and stronger men. (No, no.) Well, gentlemen, I intend to stay for a while. (Loud cheers.) However desirous of rest, I must yield, faithful to my party, to the unanimous voice of my party. But, gentlemen, if you are good Christians, if you desire to treat your enemies well, how can you be so cruel as to desire that I should remain in public life. (Cheers and laughter.) Those who are in opposition to us have declared, rightly or wrongly, that as long as John A. is in office, they must stay out. (Cheers.) How can you be so cruel, how can you treat your fellow-citizens, the Grits or Rouges, or Opposition of Canada, so cruelly as to desire that I should remain longer in public life ? (Cheers and laughter.) However, here I am, strong for my years, strong in health for my three score years and ten, and, thanks to a kind Providence, and thanks to the great care of a good wife—(loud and enthusiastic cheering, the whole audience rising) -I feel as old Adam said, like a lusty winter, frosty but kindly. At any meeting of this kind it would be out of place for me to go over the events of my political career, and, as I have already said, you have relieved me of the necessity.

At a political convention at Toronto the other day—one of unexampled power and magnitude in its political significance, where four thousand gentlemen, every one a representative man, coming from every one of the constituencies and counties of Ontario, met me—I felt it my duty to enter at some length into the whole of my political life, the development and progress of old Canada during that life, the formation of the present Dominion in 1867, and its progress ever since. You are a reading public, and I have no doubt that some of you even take the trouble to read the *Globe*, and while I do not ask you to take the portrait of me in that paper as exactly correct—(laughter)—while perhaps you may think the shadows are put in too strongly for correct portraiture, still there you will find an unwilling witness to the important share I have had in the political events of Canada for the last forty years, whether it has been for good or evil, whether it were right or wrong. One thing is clear, that this country has grown. It has developed. It has grown from four small isolated provinces without credit, with a small population, without much hope, without cohesion, and without ambition, to one Dominion. (Loud cheers.) During my time, during the time that I have been in the Government, we have seen the two races, the French and the English races, who were formerly drawn up in hostile array against each other, ready to fly at each other's throats, we have seen them here to-night as we have seen them before during the time that I was a public man, going side by side as fellow-subjects and as friends, as constitutional supporters of the British system introduced into Canada. I, sir, have seen all this, and I have had something to do with it. (Loud cheers.) Sir, when I first went into Parliament, when I first came to Montreal, what did I see? I saw slaughtering in the streets. I saw people killing each other, or trying to kill each other. I saw the troops called out to keep the peace, because there were two peoples opposed to each other, civil war in fact, and now what do we see? And, sir, I am proud to say, that if there has been a union between these two races, if all the old enmities are vanished, if we feel that we are common subjects of our common sovereign, it is because by the joint action of men like Sir George Cartier representing the French-Canadians—(loud and enthusiastic cheering)—and by the co-operative action of men of the British race like myself, that we find ourselves one happy, contented, united people, united on political questions without reference to religion, using our own independent opinions. We find men of both races in both the great parties without dividing the country. And, sir, that is what we fought for, what Sir George Cartier and myself after many impediments, after much obstruction, succeeded in carrying out. (Loud cheers.) Why, there are men in this room who remember the politics of not thirty years ago; how I was hounded down in Upper Canada, how I was called a traitor to my race, a traitor to my religion, a traitor to the best interests of my country; how it was said that I was subservient to the Pope and Popery, that I was under French domination, that I basely sold the interests of my race, and the interests of my people for the sake of office, and for the sake of position. That attack, gentlemen, I had to bear, and Sir George Cartier had to receive the same treatment from his own province. It was said to him that he wore the gown and was sold to the Orangemen of Upper Canada. But both of us rose superior to these attacks. We joined hand in hand We were, in fact, called the "Siamese Twins"—(laughter)—and we never, during our long life of political co-operation, for one moment had a single difference of opinion, a single quarrel or conflict as to our mode of action. (Loud and enthusiastic cheers.) We were satisfied to be unpopular for the time in our several provinces. We rose superior to the dread of losing the mushroom popularity which can easily be gained by pandering to the popular feeling of the day. We knew that we were right, gentlemen, and what do we see now? You see me here, the First Minister of Canada, come from Upper Canada, an Englishman, or a Scotchman rather, and a Protestant, and you see me here greeted as a man almost never has been before, and greeted in the Catholic province of Quebec. (Loud and long continued cheers.) And in a few days, Mr. Chairman and gentlemen, I shall have the pleasure, the melancholy pleasure, of unveiling in Ontario by the unanimous voice, I think, of the Parliament and the people of Canada, and with the unanimous assent of the people of Ontario, of unveiling the statue raised to the memory of Sir George Cartier. (Loud cheers.) Let it then be an encouragement to all public men, let it be an encouragement to all who think they would like to become public men, and who desire to serve their country in a public position, to look back on the career of Sir George Cartier and myself. (Cheers.)

Mr. CHAIRMAN and gentlemen, I have already stated that I would not over again make an historical account of what has happened during my long and diversified career. (Loud cheers.) You, sir, as I have already stated, have relieved me, and in a few days you will have an opportunity of procuring in a convenient form the speech that I made at Toronto. (Cheers.) Mr. Chairman, when I spoke of the honour that was conferred upon me by her Majesty, I intended at the time to have alluded to the sneers of some of the Opposition press at the honour so conferred. They were good enough to say that I was only running after such honours, that I was kneeling and bowing to Imperial statesmen for the purpose of getting these honours. I can state here, and I can prove it, that of every honour I have received, of every mark of distinction that has been conferred upon me, not one has been granted in response to a request on my part. (Cheers.) The honour of K.C.B. was conferred upon me before I knew it. I was a knight and did not know it. (Laughter and applause.) A fortnight before I was aware of the gratifying fact it had appeared in the London *Gazette*. Afterwards, when I was made privy councillor, one of Her Majesty's sworn advisers according to the constitution of England, I received that honour as all the others did who were connected with the Washington treaty. Sir Edward Thornton, Mr. Mountague Bernard, and myself, received the honour at the same time, without any signification, without any previous notice that such an honour was to be conferred. And in the crowning honour of G. C. B. the first intimation I received of it was a note from Mr. Gladstone, the Liberal Premier of England. (Cheers.) He knew that I was a Conservative and he was a Liberal. He, knowing that I was a supporter of the National Policy and he a free trader, knowing all the charges that had been brought against me of corruption and scandals and all the rest of it—(cheers)—addressed me a letter which was placed in my hand, and which stated that "in acknowledgment of long and distinguished services her Majesty has graciously authorized me to offer you the honour and rank of G. C. B." (Loud cheers.) I know there are gentlemen who sneer at such honours, sneer at honours conferred by their sovereign upon one of themselves. But when they were in power they did not hesitate to ask for honours for Sir William Howland, one of my former colleagues, but who returned to the Grit ranks; for Sir Albert Smith, for carrying into effect, as Minister of Marine and Fisheries, the fishery clauses of the Washington Treaty, which every one of my opponents, including Mr. Mackenzie and Mr. Blake, described as being a crime on my part. They called me a Judas Iscariot and a Benedict Arnold. Yet, gentlemen, when the award was made they did not refuse the money. They took the money, the thirty pieces of silver. (Laughter.) They took the money and they asked that Hon. Albert Smith should be knighted for what Peter did. (Cheers and laughter.) But then, gentlemen, the crowning honour of all that was conferred at their special request was the honour conferred on Sir Richard Cartwright. He was an old Tory, the son and grandson of old Tories, and if it be true, as we believe, that grandfathers and fathers can look down upon what is going on among their descendants, how they would shudder, those old U. E. loyalists, who had sacrificed everything for their country and their Conservative principles, when they would see the honour conferred upon him because he had sold his party. (Loud cheers.) Ah, yes, gentlemen, he was a knightly man was Sir Richard Cartwright. We know that knighthood is an order of chivalry, and that a knight should be a chivalrous man, and the first duty of every man is to be true to his allegiance, to be loyal to his party. (Cheers.) The duty of all true knights when occasion calls for it is to surround the sovereign and the Crown, and if necessary to fight in defence of that Crown. But Sir Richard Cartwright has set himself up as the champion of independence. He has been set on to try how such a thing would be received by the people of this country. Mr. Blake will not commit himself to the policy yet. He waits to see how the cat will jump. (Laughter and cheers.) And so they tried it the other day. And, gentlemen, only think of it, the man who is a Privy Councillor of Canada, who has sworn allegiance to her Majesty, *her heirs and successors*, he man who has accepted the order of knighthood at her hand, who is supposed to have knelt at her feet, kissed her hand, and received the acolade on both shoulders, saying, " Rise Sir Richard Cartwright, true, faithful and loyal." Fancy him preaching independence. Fancy him casting aside the loyalty he has sworn to maintain and still flaunting the title of K. C. M. G. (Laughter and cheers.) And, Mr. Chairman and gentlemen, when reading of this I think of the language put into the mouth of the Lady Constance by Shakespeare when she addressed the Duke of Austria after he had deserted the cause of Prince Arthur.

> "Thou cold-blooded slave,
> Hast thou not spoke like thunder on my side?
> Been sworn my soldier ? bidding me depend
> Upon thy stars, thy fortune and thy strength ?
> And dost thou now fall over to my foes?
> Thou wear a lion's hide ! Doff it for shame,
> Aud hang a calfskin on those recreant limbs."

(Laughter.) Aye, sir, when I am speaking on that subject I may as well discuss the question of independence. Sir Richard Cartwright will have to drop the title if we become a republic I suppose. (Laughter.) I wonder if he ever thought of that? (Renewed laughter.) I wonder if it ever crossed his mind that he would cease to be a gentleman with a star on his breast and with a mark on his brow ? (Laughter.) Gentlemen, we want no independence in this country except the independence that we have at this moment. (Cheers.) What country in the world is more independent than we are ? (Cheers.) We have perfect independence. We have a sovereign that allows us to do as we please. We have an Imperial Government that casts on ourselves the responsibilities as well as the privileges of self-government. (Cheers.) We may govern ourselves as we please, we may misgovern ourselves as we please. We put a tax on the products of the industries of our fellow-subjects in England, Ireland and Scotland. If we are attacked, if our shores are assailed, the mighty power of England on land and sea is used in our defence, (Applause.) What thing more can we have ? Aye, we can have one thing more. We can upset the Conservative party. We can have an army and navy of our own, commanded by a series of Sir Richard Cartwrights. (Laughter.) But I don't think, Mr. Chairman and gentlemen, from the just plaudits that you gave to my Minister of Militia, that you will be very willing to make the swap. (Laughter and cheers.) Aye, but they may say, "We shall want no armies and no navies." Look around the world, gentlemen, and what do we see to-day ? We see the nations of the world drawn up in hostile camps, and one is almost inclined to believe with Hobbes the philosopher of Malmesbury, that war is the natural state of man, and that peace is but the sickly exhibit of an exhausted civilization. (Hear, hear.) Look at Europe at this moment. Look at the smaller countries with a diminutive population. Look at Belgium with her army, although her neutrality is guaranteed by the other powers. Look at Holland with hers. Look at little Switzerland with her army, although her neutrality is guaranteed. And, gentlemen, in our own case we should be compelled to have an army, a navy, a diplomacy ; we should have to pay the enormous cost of walking alone. Independent, and yet we never could be certain but that at any moment a convulsion or fit of emotion in the neighbouring Republic might absorb us into the great republican net. (Hear, hear.) Where would then be our country, our independence, the glorious state of order and prosperity we have now ? Here we are, free from all the complications of Europe. England will never go to war unless she is obliged to in defence of her own honour, and if England goes to war we can defend our own shores, and as experience has proved, the young men of this country, and the Parliament of this country, the representatives of the people, will vie with the whole of our people in coming to the support of the Mother Land. (Loud cheers.) The history of Europe has shown that by slow degrees the nations are growing larger, and that England is circumscribed, notwithstanding her great power and wealth, by the territorial limits of the British Isles. (Hear, hear.) With her enormous energy, with her healthful climate and healthful people, that population, if there was only standing room enough, would keep its pace with any nation in the world. (Loud cheers.) But Great Britain cannot hold the people she has now, and she must send her surplus population to other lands. (Hear, hear.) She has found out at last that colonies are not mere sources of worry, vexation and danger. (Cheers.) At this moment the different parties in England are contending with each other as to who shall have the greater merit of encouraging emigration to the colonies, and we may look forward, notwithstanding the opposition of our own friends at home, to the people of England still sending their surplus population to Australia and Canada. And if England, by her territorial limits, is bounded and confined, she will receive expansion and strength enough from her colonies, to equal, to match and to over-match any nation in the world. (Cheers.) We have enemies in our camp. It is not an enemy that has done Canada such dishonour, but it is her own familiar friends, those with whom we have taken counsel, those of her own lineage, those living in this country. These are the foes of Canada who have insulted her and maligned her climate, the friends of every country but their own. The present Opposition by every falsehood, every insinuation, have attempted to divert immigration to other countries than Canada. (Cheers.) I have been, and those connected with me have been objects of obloquy for years. Our characters have been attacked, our private conduct maligned and misrepresented, our families, our domestic relations have been insulted. But we have borne it all, and we are quite willing to bear it all, because I know well that the people do not believe them, and we can outlive their calumnies. (Cheers.) But when I find that the Opposition, not satisfied with the loss of office, not satisfied with abusing us, going so far as to abuse our country, I feel inclined to use the language put into the mouth of that grand old American lady who, when the Union flag was pulled down, raised it up in presence of the Southern army, and as the Southern soldiery poured in their shot on the flag, she cried in language which I envy,

"'Shoot, if you must, this old gray head,
But spare our country's flag!' she said."

(Loud and long-continued applause.) Mr. Chairman and gentlemen, since 1867 we have conducted the Government, the party to which I belong, with the exception of five years. During those five years, as I think you will admit, the Government underwent five years of continual degradation, continual loss of credit, loss of population, loss of industry; without development, without hope. But when, following up the policy of the party to which I was an exponent, following up the National Policy which you have cheered so loudly to-night, we declared that we should have Canada for the Canadians, and that such a policy would open up new avenues of trade; when we declared that we were going to make British North America one vast Dominion, not a mere geographical expression, gentlemen, but a living body of British subjects under one crown and having one interest—I ask you, gentlemen, if the promise thus made to the country has not been fully carried out? (Cheers.) Aye, sir, when we did announce our National Policy, not a policy taken up merely in opposition to the existing Government, but one which Sir Alexander Galt years and years ago, as Finance Minister, announced was the policy of the Conservative Government, to introduce a measure for the interest of Canada, a policy that would make us independent of foreign nations by giving us manufactures here—that was a policy we always declared and steadily insisted upon. (Cheers.) "Ah, but," they said, "why did you not introduce it from 1860 to 1865?" The answer is obvious. We were in no danger during those years. The United States was convulsed with civil war. They sent nothing to us, but we sent everything to them. (Hear, hear.) The moment that great nation had shaken itself free from its temporary dissension, and started anew in that career of wondrous prosperity under the protective system which still exists, then we had to face the altered state of affairs. Our infant manufactures were being crushed, our best class of population going to the United States, our farmers shut out from the American market, and we were liable to be swamped and ruined at any moment if our people had a bad crop. Under these circumstances we introduced the National Policy, announced years ago, with the result which you know. And, gentlemen, it is shocking to observe the fiendish glee with which the Opposition papers chronicle every failure that now takes place. If a tradesman's wife mismanages things, if a shop is shut down for a week in order to clean the machinery, it is published in all the papers as another stoppage under the National Policy. (Laughter and cheers.) We are suffering now, it is said, from a time of depression, but if you look to the protectionist United States you see them suffering still more, and the number of insolvencies greater than amongst ourselves. (Hear.) If you look to free trade England you will see a degree of misery among the working and industrious classes to-day, a severe depression with which there is nothing in the United States to compare. But if you look to Canada, we are suffering from depression it is said. What is actually the case with Canada to-day ? why, we are suffering actually from too much plenty. (Cheers.) Too much plenty I say, gentlemen. We have got more wheat and flour than we want, and therefore the price is low. (Cheers.) We have got more cotton goods than we want—(cheers)—more cotton goods than there are backs to make shirts for—(laughter)—and, therefore, the price of cotton is low. We have got more woollen goods for the time than the people can consume. But, Mr. Chairman, that is a happy kind of misery. (Cheers and laughter.) We won't suffer from starvation as long as we have too cheap wheat and flour. We will not want for clothes as long as we can buy our shirts and greatcoats at too low a rate. (Cheers.) Mr. Chairman and gentlemen,—I feel that I am occupying your time too long—(cries of "No")—but there is one other thing, one other item in our policy to which I have not yet alluded,—that is the carrying out of the Canadian Pacific Railway. (Loud cheers.) I fell in 1873 an advocate to the advancement of that great railway for uniting all the provinces of the Dominion, I rose in 1878, without a change of mind—(cheers)—and without a change of principle. (Cheers.) Like the Bourbons, I had forgotten nothing, and I had learned nothing (Laughter.) I had not forgotten that in 1873 we had promised a National Policy. I had not forgotten that in 1878 we had promised to complete a railway across this continent. In 1878 we came back, not having fallen at the feet of Gamaliel Cartwright or Gamaliel Mackenzie. (Cheers and laughter.) In the depths of our ignorance we carried our policy, but ah ! how ignorant you must all be to get the approbation of the country in so doing. (Cheers.) And to-day, gentlemen, look at the Canadian Pacific railway. In the whole annals of railway construction there has been nothing to equal it. (Cheers.) In the original contract of 1873 we gave ten years to build the road, and now the ten years have hardly expired, and the road is to be finished in 1886. (Cheers.) The contractors are Canadians, gentlemen,—(cheers)—men who had made their money in Canada, and men who are principally Montrealers. (Loud cheers.) They are men who had made more money than they knew what to do with—(laughter)—men who might have pleased themselves in going to Europe as some Americans go, for they say that Paris is the heaven to which all good Americans go. (Laughter.) Men who might have gone to spend their lives in domestic or foreign felicity as others have done. (Laughter.) They ventured their all, they ventured their fortunes, their ability, their credit and all they had for this grand line of railway. (Cheers.) They have been successful, gentlemen. But why were they successful ? I will tell you. Because they were Canadians to the core. (Loud cheers.) They were resolved not to rest or to let their minds rest until they took hold of this great enterprise. And among the many things that I perhaps in my idle vanity may pride myself on, I pride myself on none more than on this—that I was able to exhibit some degree of thought-reading—and there are some thought-readers here, for I am looking at one this moment—(laughter.)—when I put my eye upon the men in Montreal that would be most likely to complete this grand railway—(cheers)—and long after we are gone to our graves, in the history of the development of Canada, in the history of the progress of Canada, in the history of this mighty empire, the mighty empire it is going to grow to in our day or in the day of our immediate descendants, the names of these men will be regarded as men and as patriots deserving of all the credit and of all the honour that their earnestness, their devotion, and ability and perseverance entitles them to. [A large diagram was here exhibited behind Sir John of the Canadian Pacific railway. Sir John, pointing to the map continued.] Here, gentlemen, is a small town called Montreal —(laughter,)—and running your eye along the diagram you will see how far the road is finished. At one point there are six miles to be graded, the rails have to be laid on another part, and there you have, gentlemen, an idea of the Canadian Pacific railway. Look, gentlemen, and you will see the very few spots that remain to be finished, and if you take good care of your health, if you don't go to too many banquets in honour of Sir John Macdonald—(loud laughter)—if you go to bed early, and rise early, and obey your wives' injunctions, every one of you, old and young, may hope to travel over, personally to travel over, that great road. (Cheers.) Gentlemen, it is not a vision ; you have almost a physical view of its completion now. Now every one of you next year can travel over that road, and you will bless your stars that you belong to a country where we have men so strong and so able, and so energetic as to be able to build thousands of miles of railway in six short years. (Loud cheers.) In my Highland country, in days before the rebellion of 1745, there were very few roads. My countrymen then did not want many roads there because they used to go down to the lowlands and—not steal, gentlemen—but walk away with their neighbours' cattle. (Laughter.) They did not want to leave any tracks behind them to the highlands. Marshal Wade went up there and made a military road, and somebody said

"If you had seen those roads before they were made,
You would lift up your hands and bless Marshal Wade."

(Laughter.) Now, gentlemen, you can all, I know, lift up your hands and bless the syndicate—I suppose you have heard that word before—(laughter)—you will bless the syndicate who have built that railroad, which is a credit to Canada. (Cheers.)

Gentlemen, I have to return you again my sincere, my ardent, my respectful, and my heartfelt thanks for this crowning honour. I shall remember it as long as I live, as long as my memory holds its seat, and I hope, and believe, that in future years you will look back with some degree of pleasure on this assemblage as one in which you have taken a part, in which you, gentlemen, have met to do honour to a man who with all his faults and sins of omission and commission loved his country with a passionate love—(loud cheers)- who to his short-comings can, at all events, plead that which was all powerful with the Divine Master, and who can therefore hope that much will be forgiven him because he loved much.

SIR LEONARD TILLEY'S SPEECH.

The toast of the health of the Minister of Finance was enthusiastically received, and in reply Sir Leonard Tilley said that their devotion and attachment to their leader was too well known to need any remarks to prove them, and he would have been willing to have taken and accepted this magnificent reception given to Sir John, as the leader of the Government, as sufficient proof of their approbation of the conduct of all his colleagues. They were devoted to Sir John because of his devotion to his country and his affection for his people, a devotion that had been manifested for over forty years without respect to creed or nationality. Their attachment to him was strong on account of the consideration he had always shown to his colleagues. As members of the Government, they were extremely gratified at the magnificent reception which had been given to their chieftain by this representative assembly in the chief city of Canada and the banner province of the Dominion) (Cheers.) He desired to be brief, but in the interests of his country he asked for ten minutes to answer some statements which had been made by an ex-minister less than six weeks ago in the city of Montreal—statements that had been published broadcast in the United States, that had been commented upon in England, Ireland and Scotland, that had been made, as stated by the newspapers of those countries, on the responsibility of a man who had held the position of Finance Minister of the Dominion of Canada—statements damaging to the position and credit of this country—(cheers)—statements which were without foundation and were not warranted by the truth, although the gentleman to whom he referred had prefaced his remarks by the assertion that as an honest man he must give his audience the information. He would take only two of the statements made by that gentleman and would give evidence to show how baseless they were. He had alleged that the taxation of Canada had nearly doubled within late years, and that the taxation of the people of Canada per head is nearly double that of the United States, and that Canada is fast becoming one of the most heavily-taxed countries in the world. He desired to give them facts which would go to the country, and would show how fallacious were the statements to which he had referred. (Hear, hear.) The taxation per head necessary for the payment of the expenses of the country, collected from customs and excise, which covered nearly the whole of that taxation, was less per head now than during the five years when Sir Richard Cartwright was in power. The net interest paid by the people of Canada in proportion to the population, notwithstanding that since 1879 $55,000,000 had been spent on the Pacific railway, on canals and other public works, was less the last fiscal year than when Sir Richard Cartwright surrendered the seals of office. (Cheers.) He had stated that the taxation of Canada nearly doubled that of the United States. How false was the statement. It must be remembered that we occupied a very different position from that of the United States in this respect, that the Dominion had undertaken to pay the interest on the debt of the provinces, and further to pay a sum sufficient to meet the expenses of the different provinces, leaving scarcely any local taxation necessary for the provincial requirements, while in the United States the taxation for the expenses of the different states amounted to 40 cents on an average on every $100 of real and personal property in the Union. (Applause.) This was not mere guesswork. It was shown by returns laid before Congress which had been printed and published. In the first place we in Canada had collected less per head than the United States had in the last year, and the necessary taxation from 1876 to 1884 had been just about the same as it was last year in the United States, while we had taken out of a taxation equal to that of the United States enough to pay nearly the whole of the expenses of all the provinces in the Union, and one-third of the taxes collected from the people of this country last year, and which had been paid into the Dominion treasury went to pay the interest on the debts of the provinces and subsidies for their maintenance. (Cheers.) Instead of our taxation being nearly double that of the United States, we had within the last few years collected on an average within a cent or two of the amount per head collected in the United States, and out of that had taken sufficient money, nearly a third of the total amount collected, to pay the expenses of the local legislatures, while in the United States they had an additional taxation for the maintenance of the different States, amounting to 40 cents per hundred dollars of all the real and personal property in the country. Further than that, in 121 of the cities of the Union, the average taxation was $1.90 for every $100. He did not know what the taxation was in Montreal, but in Ottawa, which was considered the most heavily taxed city in the Dominion, it was but $1.90 per $100. Notwithstanding these facts, Sir Richard Cartwright had not hesitated to assert before what he presumed to have been an intelligent audience in the City of Montreal, that we had collected double the amount of taxes collected in the United States. He (Sir Leonard Tilley) was prepared to meet those statements with figures and proof in Parliament, but he would not detain them by doing so to-night. (Cheers.) Sir Richard Cartwright had also declared that the taxation of Canada approached that of the most heavily taxed country in the world. The statement was not true. Compared with the different countries in Europe, we occupied a proud position, our taxation being far below that of Great Britain, France, Russia, and, considering her military laws, I might add Germany, while the very lowest taxation of our sister colonies in Australia was 75 per cent. more than ours, some of them reached three and four times the amount per head, and the average taxation in the Australian Colonies was £2 10s per head, while ours was about £1. In comparison with our fellow colonists in Australia we occupied a proud position, our debt being only about a third of theirs, notwithstanding the vast liabilities we had incurred for the deepening and enlargement of our canals, and the construction of our magnificent railway system from ocean to ocean. There was scarcely a country to-day in which the taxation was lighter than it was in Canada. (Cheers.) In China, Japan, British India and other such countries, the taxation was dollar for dollar lighter, but the important point was how many days work of the people did it require to pay the taxes. Allowing for that, we in Canada were to-day, with but few exceptions, the lowest taxed people in the world, considering that we are giving one-third of the money we collect to the provinces. (Cheers.) These facts were susceptible of proof. He had the proof in his possession, and he had reason to know that Sir Richard Cartwright had it in his possession, notwithstanding which he as a man holding a responsible position, an ex-Minister of the Crown, which gave more importance to his utterances than would be given to those of a less important person, had not hesitated to make the statement to which he referred. It was a crying shame that any public man should make such assertions without foundation in order to damage our credit, prevent emigration from coming to our shores, and injure the country of which he was a citizen. (Cheers.) These men might slander them as members of the government, and he did not believe they could establish an action for damages because they could not prove damages. (Cheers.) But what penalty should be meted to the man who slandered his country and damaged its credit? Let the intelligent men of Montreal and of the province of Quebec, let the electors of Ontario and the outlying provinces tell those men that the penalty was that they should not come into power on a platform such as that, that though they might have ability for certain positions in life, the people could not accept as rulers men who would defame Canada, misrepresent her, and damage her credit and reputation. (Loud cheers.) They should say as the electors of Lennox had recently said—(cheers)—that if these men expected to get into power they must abandon the policy of defaming the character of Canada and the Canadians, and must stand upon higher and broader ground. (Cheers.) He thanked them as a member of the executive of Canada for this renewed expression of their confidence. Nothing could be more gratifying to a public man after a career of forty years, amidst abuse and misrepresentation, than such a demonstration as this, even if he had never received any other expression of approval of his conduct, any other reward for his toil and labor and anxiety, and none could appreciate the extent of that labor better than those who had been acting in concert with their chief in the administration of the country, and knew his trials and difficulties. (Cheers.) The demonstration at Toronto the other day, and the expressions of good-will last night and to-night were felt, he was sure, by their chieftain to be ample compensation for all he had done and suffered for his country. (Cheers.) These demonstrations strengthened the hands of the government. Their chieftain had had no reason to change the policy adopted in 1879. He had, as stated at Toronto, nailed his colors to the mast, and if the ship went down he and they, the officers and crew, would go down with it. (Cheers.) He had no doubt as to the future of this country, with its great natural resources, with a hardy population and a well educated people. He concluded amidst loud applause by again expressing his appreciation of the magnificent demonstration tendered the premier and the government, and was enthusiastically cheered upon resuming his seat.

EXTRACTS FROM A SPEECH OF

THE HON. JOHN CARLING.

The Honourable John Carling, Postmaster-General, addressed a mass meeting of his constituents at London on the occasion of their meeting to select delegates to attend the Toronto Convention. As he dealt largely with figures going to show the steady advancement of Canada, some of the tables given by him are appended :

	1871.	1881.
Shipping	$ 25,047,190	$ 39,442,450
Animals and animal products	179,861,227	220,062,480
Field products	100,627,319	151,826,612
Various products and furs	26,837,313	45,956,193
Products of the forest	45,919,088	79,345,017
Raw mineral products	4,777,580	8,705,075
Industries	221,617,773	309,676,068
Fisheries	10,754,997	16,958.189
Total	$619,437,487	$872,011,087

As to the industries of the country and their growth, the following figures were given from the census returns, Mr. Carling stating that he had information which justified him in saying that there had been an increase since of upwards of 30 per cent.

	1871.	1881.
Capital Invested	$ 77,324,020	$165,302,623
Hands employed	187,942	254,935
Amount of yearly wages	40,831,009	59,429,002
Value of raw material	124,901,846	179,918,591
Total value of articles produced	221,617,773	309,676,068

The progress of railways since Confederation was given as follows :—

	1868.	1883.
Miles	2,586	9,650
Money invested	$158,400,000	$494,300,000
Locomotives in use	485	1,380
Tons of freight carried	2,260,000	13,270,000
Number of persons carried	2,920,000	9,579,948
First-class cars	310	676
All other cars	4,588	21,800

TELEGRAPHS.

Miles of wire	8,507	39,350
Miles of poles	7,000	24,000
Messages sent	690,000	4,100,000

Mr. Carling dealt with some figures connected with his own department, as follows :—

"I will take the Post Office Savings Bank, which, I suppose you know is used, by the working people, mechanics and servant girls, in which they can deposit $1 and draw at the rate of four per cent. In 1874, when our opponents came into power, there were in the Savings Bank $3,204,965, and I wish you to notice the decrease of the next year, when it sank down to $2,926,090. In 1876 it continued to dwindle and stood at $2,740,952. In 1877 it was but $2,639,937, and in 1878 $2.754,484. Now notice the result in the next year, when the Conservative party had been restored to power. In 1879, the figures rose to $3,105,190, and continued to go up, as follows :—

1880	$3,945,669
1881	6,208,226
1882	9,473,961
1883	11,976,237
1884	13,245,552

"In December, 1884, the figures may be said to have reached in round numbers $14,000,000. Does this not show how the country went down and then came up again as soon as the Conservative party was restored ? (Cheers.) These figures do not include the deposits in the Government savings banks, which are established at Toronto, Halifax, and in the lower provinces, and which amount to $16,000,000. It will be seen, gentlemen, that the Government have in their keeping thirty million dollars of the savings of the people, (cheers) and in these Government savings banks there have been increases of $10,000,000 since 1878. You may also add to these figures the large amount of $16,000,000, in deposit in loan societies, representing an increase of $15,000,000 since Confederation, and $8,000,000 since 1878. Besides, there is the immense amount in chartered banks, the figures of which I have not at present got. I may also say that the number of post-offices has increased from 2,586 in 1868, to 6,856 in 1884 ; the number of miles travelled in 1868 was 8.447,000, while in 1884 the number had increased to 19,465,121. In the year 1868 the number of letters and postal cards carried was 15,430,000 ; in 1884 they had increased to 78,340,000."

Referring to the credit of the country, the following comparisons were given:—

Stock.	Rate of Interest.	Selling Price.
Canada	4	107
Austria	4	88
Hungary	4	76¾
France	4½	107¼
Norway	4	101½
Sweden	4	101¼
Portugal	5	89
Spain	4	60⅝
Greece	5	89
Italy	5	95
Russia	4	83
Prussia	4	102¼

This table shows Canada's credit as compared with the other colonies :—

Stock.	Rate of Interest.	Selling Price.
Canada	4	107
Cape Colony	4	93½
Ceylon	4	104
Jamaica	4	101
Mauritius	4	104
Natal	4	90

New South Wales	4	105½
New Zealand	4	105
South Australia	4	104½
Tasmania	4	101
Trinidad	4	101
Victoria	4	104
West Australia	4	101

Coming to the charge so often made against the Government's fixed policy that it has increased the price of goods to the consumer, and thus enhanced the cost of living, Mr. Carling gave the following particulars:—

	1878.	1884.
Sugar retailed at per pound	$ 09	$ 05
" "	10	06
" white "	11	07
Syrup for table use per gal	1 00	60
" ordinary, "	80	50
Tea, per lb	1 00	60
" "	75	50
" "	50	30
Coffee, per lb	30	20
Rice, "	06	05
Flour, per 100 lbs	3 00	2 00
Starch, per lb	13	10
Soap, 2½ lb. bar, each	20	13
Canned salmon "	25	15
" lobsters "	20	12½
" apples "	25	12½
" corn and peas, each	25	12½
" tomatoes, each	25	12½

Suits of Canadian tweeds, strong and well made:—

1880	$10 00	$12 50	$17 00
1884	8 00	10 00	12 50
Reduction	2 00	2 50	4 50

MEN'S OVERCOATS.

1880	$10 50	$15 00
1884	7 00	9 00
Reduction	3 50	6 00

MEN'S UNDERWEAR.

Pure wool undershirts and drawers.

1880	$1 00 to $1 12½
1884	75

Union undershirts and drawers.

1880	50c. to 75c.
1884	30c. to 50c.
Reduction	20c. to 25c.

Canadian tweeds for men's and boys' suits.

1880		75c. to $1 00
1884		50c. to 75
Reduction	25c.	25

CANADIAN BLANKETS.
(Weight from 4 to 10 lbs. each.)

1880	65c. to 75c. per pound
1884	45c. per pound
Reduction	30c. per pound

GREY FLANNEL.

1880	35c., 37½c., 45c. per yard
1884	25c., 30c., 35c. per yard
Reduction	10c., 7½c., 10c. per yard

CHECK FLANNEL.

1880	37½c. to 40c. per yard
1884	25c. per yard
Reduction	12½c. per yard

FACTORY COTTON.

1880	5c. to 6c.—30 inches
1884	3¼c. to 4c.—30 inches
1880	7c., 8c., 9c., 10c., 12½c.—36 inches
1884	5c., 6½c., 7c., 8c., 9c. —36 inches

WHITE COTTONS.

1880	8c., 9c., 11c., 12½c., 16c.
1884	6c., 7c., 9c., 10c., 12½c.
Reduction	2c., 2c., 2c., 2½c., 3½c.

COTTON SHIRTING.

1880	12½c., 15c., 25c.
1884	7c., 9c., 10c., 12½c., 15c.

DUCKS AND DENIMS.

1880 (imported)	25c. to 40c.
1884	12½c., to 20c.
Reduction	12½c., to 20c.

I.

List of Delegates from the various Constituencies appointed to attend the Convention.

ADDINGTON.—John M. Bell, M.P., George Dennison, M.P.P., Dr Beamish, John Clark, John S. Miller.

ALGOMA.—Thomas Marks, George Marks, W. H. Langworthy, Napier Robinson, S. J Dawson, M.P., William Vigars, R. Vigars.

BRANT (North Riding).—William Shaver, G. D. Farmer, N. O. Gurnett, G. J. Williamson, J. R. Currie, A. Tew, Richard Bass, L. B. Lapierre, A. Muma, Wm. Sewell, Thos. Scott, H. R. Nixon, J. Shuert, Benjamin Bell, W. H. Howell, R. Lawrason, J. P. Lawrason, George Howell, William Ellis, S. B. Lawrason, William Robb, William Mullen, Henry Howell, S. Atmore, Edward Kenwick, Frederick Snider, R. S. Stevenson, Richard Green.

BRANT (South Riding).—Edward Brophy, James Pollock, Dr. W. T. Harris, H. Lemmon, H. McK. Wilson, D. Curtis, J. Elliott, A. Watts, J. J. Hawkins, R. Henry, G. Watt, Thomas Watt, John Strickland, H. H. Rothwell, Hugh J. Jones, W. G. Elliott, Alexander Fair, Thomas Palmer, W. Hunt, G. A. Pearson, Herbert Johnston, Robert Wilson, Thomas Elliott, C. Thomas, W. G. Culbard, H. J. Matthews, C. Jarvis, D. Hawkins, M. S. Smith, William Slingsby, A, H. Baird, T. W. Munn, Joseph Bullock, Oct. Egelow, D. A. Adams, R. Thompson, James McDonald, J. H. Fisher, J. Baker, T. H. Jones, Joseph Robinson, D. Patton, R. McDonald, Paul Moore, P. Hill, J. D. Eddy, W. F. Miles, William Bonny, T. Lloyd Jones, B. F. Haun, Reginald Walcot, P. Huffman, W. Duncan, F. A. Smith, J. E. Brethour, Abraham Muma, James Ferris, W. Ferris, H. Tutt, R. Walker, John R. Ellis, John Phipps, W. M. Scott, J. Forde, A. McMenns, J. W. Gable, V. McKenzie, Q C., M. W. Hoyt, Jno. Montgomery, James Weyms, William Smith, J. S. Hamilton, R. S. Dunlop, H. Griffiths, Samuel Clever, G. Runner.

BRUCE (North Riding).—W. A. Hargreaves, Samuel T. Rowe, A Colborne, John Crowe, A. Taylor, A. McCulloch, Dr. Thomas, C. A. Richards, John Beeton, Dr. McNamara, W. H. Ruby, John George, J. C. Miller, H. Hilker, J. Howe, O. Megraw, M McBride, Rev. Dean Cooper, A. Freeborn, William Marnion, James Allen, William Beatty, J. Johnson, A. Johnson, J. E. Murphy, George E. Smith, Dr. Scott, M. McKenzie, A. Lindsay, J. T. Conaway, D Robertson, A. McNeill, M.P., D. G. Miller, Allan Thompson, Joseph Adams, W. J. Conron, John Follis, John Bearman, John Fortune, W. C. Valentine, George W. Mallock, Dr. S. McAiton, John F. Dinsmore, A. M. Tyson, Dr. Wigle, F. W. Patteson, —— McCaul, H. T. Potts.

BRUCE (West Riding).—Robert Wilson, Donald Reid, L. Rightmeyer, A. Denholm, Robert Baird, J. H. Scott, A. J. Evans, S. H. Marshall, Henry Collins, C. R. Barker, George M. McKendries, Dr. Martyn, D. Buchannan, L. O'Hagan, Dr. Bradley, John Hewitt, John Shier, L. T. Bland, William Sturgeon, Thomas Blair, John Nesbitt, George Shane, Robert Ballantyne, John Hunter, William Collins, Thomas Wilson, William Wilson, Angus Munn, Robert Thompson, Dr. Smith, George Daniels, William Blair, Amos Hilker, F. Hood, Robert Co oper, R. McLennan, John Biggar, John Darling, S. Mason, T. J. Stewart, John Rouson, S. Corrigan, William Taylor, Edward Neil, Dr. Tennant, Thomas Wallace, Dr. Garnier, Robert Ellis, William Ellis, H. Chambers, R. Hanneton, John Grundy, F. Grundy, R. Webster, Thomas Webster, W. Johnston, R. Graham.

BRUCE (East Riding).—Charles Schurter, Richard Rivers, H. Hinsperger, William Dickinson, D. Schwan, Frederick Weigle, A. Seegmiller, P. A. Jiemert, S. Murray, James Schmitt, J. H. Buck, George Herniger, Joseph Guittard, G. Taylor, J Flemming, J. Hundt, W. Coluir, R. Coluir, G. McDaniel, H. Ballagh, J. Goodfellow, W. Ballagh, F. X. Keefer, A. Slivemaker, William Scott, William Cross, T. Stephens, G. H. Coo, R. Douglas, J. Donohoe, J. Nixon, W. R. Thompson, H. Wilson, J. McCallum, J. Ferguson, George Sirss, George Hollinger, A. Todd, J. Hampton, J. Gateman, J. C. Eelsford, A. Johnston, T. Toner, John Lambatus, James Ward, R. Long, J. Cook, N. B. Clement, James A. Lamb, B. Cannon, J. Hanmore, J. Telford, H. H. Perdue, B. McCartney, J. Messinger, H. Goodeve, S. McNally, A. Shaw, J. G. Cooper, G. Bradley, W. A. Green, E. H. Sheffield, C. W. Stovell, C. S. Harris, A. McLean, J. Fulton, J. A. Rittinger, C. F. Huycke, H. Beattie, F. Gugisberg, J. Wanless, W. Richardson, J. Vaner, A. B. Klein, W. Nelles, A. Symons, Thomas Cunningham, John Cunningham, W. Trotter, R. Chambers, J. Weighter, Jacob Weighter, H. Cargill, James McKee, W. Bradley, J. Brockie, Edward Wynn, James Stark, W, Clark, R. Glancy, H, Spitzig, E. Wellyson, J. Doyle, R. Garland, W. A. Reed, J. Gamice, D. Pinkerton, George Lisksem, R. Russell, T. Splan, G. Collins.

BROCKVILLE.—John F. Wood, M,P., W. H. Jones, James Reynolds, Dr. O. H. Moore, Samuel Keefer, J. C. T. Cochrane, Hon. W. J. Christie, Robert Fitzsimmons, H. F. J. Jackson, Robert Lipsett, John Stagg, Herman Shepherd, David Mansell, H. T. Fitzsimmons, F, L. Kincaid, Thomas Price, George Hutcheson, John Culburt, Dr. Le Fevre, R. P. Cooke, Isaac Ritchey, Edward Jobling, Henry Burniston, George Baker, J. W. McIntosh, W. H. Harrison, Alexander Crenning, John Ringland, M. J. McNamara, R. C. Jamieson, Thomas Ayres, Wesley Dickinson, Thomas Bennett, George R. Webster, James A. Hutcheson, Dr. Pickup, William Montgomery, John Stracey, George Stracey, George Barr, B. W. Richards, A. R. Allan, R. M. Fitzsimmons, N. B. Colcock, John Kyle, W. R. Bain, D. V. Beacock, Ralph Davis, Dr. Allen, George H. Weatherhead, Alfred Stagg, Walter Bell, Terence Sparham, Robert Wright, George Wesley Baker, Capt. W. Cook, C. J. Sheriff, Ellswood Smart, James Williams, Lawrence Black, Robert Graham, Charles Stevenson, H. Hillis, Hugh Wilkinson, William Stafford, Robert Jelly, Robert Barlow, Hugh Morrison, Edward Davis, John Forth, N. E. Brown, John Kendrick, Samuel Simpson, Daniel Ross, Joseph Stacey, Stafford McBratney, John Barry, Thomas Smith, Dr. Horton, John Checkley, Fred. L. Moore, W. J. McLean, John Moles, Chilion Jones, C. E. Jones, William Wilson, Erastus Rowson, Alexander Miller, Robert Boyd, James Perry, H. A. Bradfield, Cephas Godkin, Adam Cunningham, James Henderson, J. S. Sherwood, William Burrows, Charles Pritchard, Samuel Connor, Richard Johnston, John Paul, Daniel Scott, Samuel Cooper, Charles Goff, John Burns, Joseph Miller, Isaac Paul, William E. Davis, L. de Carle, William Davis, R. R. Heather, W. J. Connor, Thomas Petham, Joseph Robinson, Henry Robinson, Joseph Paul, Robert Sturge, Henry F. Bolton.

CARDWELL.—R. Evans, T. Fisher, J. Switzer, Joseph Durragh, John Hewvey, John Kelly, John Kidd, Joseph Leggatte, John Mason, Joseph Morrow, Dr. Allison, Jas. Alexander, S. Barber, Thomas Babe, R. Davis, William Elgie, J. Hassard, T. McCourt, William Stubbs, T. White, W. Willoughby, Thomas Vanwyck, — Atcheson, — Brown, — Hilliard, R. Allen, H. Carson, G. Harshaw, R. Jackson, H. Lafferty,

II.

J. McGuire, James Mills, W. S. Pigott, James Snell, Joshua Tate, Robert Wilson, E. W. Hammill, J. Allen, R. Duggan, P. C. Campbell, — McCourt, — Stewart, G. Verner, John Vance, James Brown, J. Wallace, — McCabe.

CARLETON,—William Kidd, Dr. R. C. Church, G. W. Monk, H. Brownlee, William Mosgrove, John Thompson, A. Stewart, James Hickey, A. J. McNab, McL. Stewart, John Nelson, H. C. Monk, Thomas Graham, G. M. Patrick, H. Sykes, A. Abbott, William Graham, C. W. Monk, William Watts, Robert Beckett, John Pratt, W. H. Berry, George Acres, George H. Morgan, William Boucher, William Richardson, R. Richardson, John Craig, George Dickinson, Capt. P. Davidson, Dr. Spotter, Dr. Groves, Ira Byce, Thos. Tubman, A. Bradley, J. Kempt, J. Shore, R. Fuselle, Robert Cherry, J. R. Simpson, J. Simpson, R. H. Grant, James Hodgins, George Burrows, James Cathcart, Dr. Scott, Dr. Beattie, H. Rielly, H. Bene t, W. Butler, H. McElroy, James Mills, J. Headley, J. Grierson, S. Sullivan, James Clarke, Thomas Clarke, James Beaman, John Boyce, E. Skead, John Rochester, ex-M. P. J. A. Cowley, W. F. Powell, William Scott, jr., G. B. Hopper, J. Heney, William McKay, H. Church, Dr. Hill, J. Dawson, J. R. Booth, W. H. Perley, William Roland, J. Foster, Thomas Sheldon, Dr. Potter, James Rochester.

DUNDAS.—James Collison, William Lock, A. Broder, M.P.P., Alexander McKay, Dr. Steacy, Charles Durant, J. S. Marcelis, William Whittaker, Dr. Hickey, M.P., A. Farlinger, H. C. Kennedy, C. A. Myers, A. H. Merkley, J. P. Whitney, G. S. Hickey, Adam Harkness, Allan J. Ross, Hugo P. Ross, Arthur Patton, George W. Brouse, Daniel Abbott, W. Henry Patton, James Powell, Hiram Wallace, P. Everette, W. B Abbott, Samuel Lasue, W. Fisher.

DURHAM (East Riding).—Col. Williams, M.P., D. Chisholm, James Evans, W. G. Stephenson, J. P. Cherney, H. A. Ward, William Gracey, Henry White, Henry Shepherd, Thomas Leonard, Robert Elliott, Charles Smith, Thomas Walker, A. F. Winslow, Thomas Chalk, Robert Chalk, Joseph Eakins, John Lydon, A. F. Ogilvy, R. A. Mulholland, Major McLean, Joseph Gallagher, Dr. Wright, Captain Jones, James O'Neill, J. W. Stepheason, J. B. Trayes, T. T. Baines, John Holmes, W. Craig, sr., T. H. Ambrose, William Gamble, L. Misson, J. P. McKenny, John A. Brown, Capt. Lowry, J. H. Clarke, William Allen, James Addy, Charles Masher, J. G. King, James Christopher. J. M. Hunter, Mark Boyd, Allan Adams, Colonel Adams, William Gibson, H. H. Meredith, F. M. Beamish, J. N. G. Lodge, John McCormack, W. Killaway, John Mulligan, William Craig, jr., R. G. Mulligan, A. Ogilvy, F. M. Benson, Johnston Beatty, George Beatty, Marshall Thompson, William N. Wilson, Robert Maize, Paul Oke, M. Rosercan, R. Carscadden, Alexander Beatty, James Woods, Henry Bryce, Alexander Walker, S. O. Taylor, William Thompson, Herbert Beatty, Robert Woods, William Woods, William Salisbnry, D. G. Trew, Robert Leith, Alexander Noble, Alexander Waleh, J. H. Gardiner, John Martin, Major Howden, J. B. Collins, H. B. Weller, A. Ferguson, James Kerr, William Vance, S. V. Hutchins, George F. Elliott, James Fitzgerald, F. W. Wallace, H. Allen, J. B. Smith, Dr. Turner, Robert Vance, George Campbell, C. H. Winslow, W. H. Lough Thomas McCamus. Charles McNeill, S. E. Ferguson, R. Sanderson, James Williamson, Joseph Thorndyke, Samuel Graham, Samuel Staples, Robert Touchburu, John Cairns, Thomas O'Brien, J. C. Williamson, Joseph Armstrong, Major Hughes, J. J. Preston, John Vance, W. J. White, Charles Reynolds, Johnston Morton, George McCartney, William Shaw C. H. Brereton, M.P.P., Robert Grandy, Capt. Preston.

DURHAM (West Riding).—S. Washington, H. T. Philips, L. Rodgers, J. Virtue, J. Stainton, Thomas Stainton, W. A. Thorn, J. Pye, W. Clemence, J. Bingham, J. Byers, J. Hooper, William Jacks, E. W. Lee, J. Garhatt, J. Maroney.

ELGIN (East Riding).—Dr. W. Marlatt, T. W. Dobbie, ex M.P.; Thos. Arkell, ex M.P.: T. W. Crothers, J. H. Martyn, Leonard Jones, J. G. Munn, John Coyne, R. McCully, C, O. Ermatinger, M.P.P. J. Crocker, G. T. Clavis, Nelson McCall, Mayor Horton, John Doyle, Hugh Daley, J. M. Kirby, H. N. Reddings, F. Ellison, S. H. Shaw, Dr. McLean, J. McConnell, James Martin, J. Sissler, J. Andrews, J. Squance, — Shepherd, Angus McLarty, J. J. Blackmore, Albert Miller, E. A. Miller, F. Nichol, — Youell, Major Ellison, R. C. Wade, James Mitchell.

ELGIN (West Riding).—E. R. Hogg, D. B. McColl, C. Baker, A. Wismer, J. Kelley, G. Zoller, G. Munroe, P. Schleihouf, D. McKillop, D. McCallum, M. Baker, J. Smails, George A. Schnely, D. McIutyre, J. Mc-Millan, R. Jameson, J. McGregor, J. McLarty, J. McDonald, J. Bishop, J. Henry, W. Bachus, John Beatty, John L. Gosnell, John Heywood, W. Curtis, George Scott, J. A. McArthur, J. Lather, A. Marcus, R. L. Pomeroy, S. E. Walker, F. Johnston, D. Gesner, George White, E. McCollum, William Fentou, N. Rose Fred. Atkinson, John Irwin, S. Burns, William Attridge, T. Newcomb, M. Hall, A. B. Barr. John McKim, F. Poulin, L. Johnston, Alexander Clark, H. Buller, D. Desmond, J. Harkney, James White, D. G. Willson, J. C. Nation, E. Brien, Alexander Goff, William Walters, Thomas Sinnett, Israel Smith, jr., F. Guyett, C. Stammers, M. Arnold, D. P. Holmes, John Winter, J. Everett, J. N. Willson, Jacob Maw, E. Barton, J. Shaw, J. Green, jr., Thomas Buller, George Pearce, J. Everett, T. Armstrong, A. M. Waltou, S. H. Spencer, W. Desmond, M. Wilson, D. Lattimore, Thomas Sheppey, J. Crowder, L. Spencer, E. Brown, J. Sinnett, J. Cain, J. Smith, R. Alexander, D. S. Williams, II. Leirely, James Winter, R. Watt, James Leatherdale, T. McCollum, Fred. Arnold, W. Simpson, J. Boothroyd, R. F. Green, Alexander Whitsill, J. Lampman, Yeates White, B. W. Wilson, A. Dean, T. Brown, P. H. Bowyer, J. Taff, George Rockey, T. B. Shoebottom, C. E. Scane, George Murray, T. F. Kyle, Lewis Rowe, J. Cooper, W. H. B. Morgan, Dr. Marr, Isaac Bunker, J. E. Beddard, D. Patterson, C. W. Fox, J. R. Craig, J. McPherson, William Grant, L. W. Fish, N. B. Huffman, J. Grant McKay, William Summerville, J. E. McKinley, Thomas P. Watson, R. Porter, R. A. Clarke, O. A. Brennan, T. G. Guest, H. Lumley, D. Cochrane, George A. Barnard, W. Baird, Jas. Vair, S. R. Stewart, A. D. Hurdon, J. S. Gadd, F. X. Schindler, Robert Bowyer, W. R. Laudon, W B. Rowe, James Drake, J. C. Moore, George Addiman, J. C. Wallace, L. W. McIntyre, A. D. Urlin, A. McKillop, W. Backwill, P. J. Henry, Thomas Linton, A. W. Bowlby, D. Curtis, J. L. Pearce, A. McIntyre, F. A. Hunpage, H. Lane, D. J. Thompson, D. C. Clay, A. Patterson, D. McLean, D. Patterson, A. McGeachy, James Welch, D. McPherson, James Hood, John Kerr. J. C. McRae, D. McPherson, James McWilliams, E. Roach, R. Bobier, D. Bobier, A. Bobier, W. Moore, Benjamin Crane, G. Trotham, S. Bachus, Steven Bachus, M. Conn, A. Lum, James Buchanan, E. Sifton, J. Pearce, D. McColl, S. E. Burwell, A. P. Campbell, J. Andrews, C. Munroe, J. Fowler, Thomas Warran, J. Mills, A. Kerr, T. Burch, D. Campbell, J. Williams, W. Wallace, H. McAlpin, T. Nichol, H. Brooks, T. Travers, R. Miller, W. Morris, T. W. Kirkpatrick, W. McCallum, J. Streib, J. Jameson, D. Somerville, M. Mills, J. Livingston, J. Mahau, Dr. W. B. Brock, J. H. Greer, William Paris, J. C. Schleihouf, A. McKillop, A. Patterson.

ESSEX (North Riding).—A. B. Marcutette, H. F. Allmet, Col. A. Rankin, John McEwan, Denis Rochelow, Noe Jely, Loon Boudy, Thomas H. Wright, Thomas McWhiuney, Edward Boismier. Jos. St. Louis,

III.

Henry Morand, H. Mailloux, C. Janisse, P. Leduc, J. Janisse, A. St. Louis, M. McCarthy, Thomas Halford, A. Halford, Samuel Goyeau, John Cada, John McHugh, C. Lappan, J. E. Doyle, D. Gauthier, P. Strong, J. A. Hogan, T. Sylvester, P. Trembly, J. Desjardines, B. Dupuis, Dr. C. E. Casgrain, J. C. Patterson, M.P., Sol. White, M.P.P., Dr. Carney, Dr. Aikman, Dr. Slater, Dr. Coventry, T. A. Bourke, D. B. Odette, M. A. McHugh, J. H. Wilkinson, George Campbell, J. W. Drake, James Nelson, Joseph White, jr., J. W. Tringham. William Stokes, Dan McLean, Charles Fox.

ESSEX (South Riding).—S. E. Martin, J. H. Morgan, Thomas Ouilette, T. B. White, William Pattipace' P. McQuade, Joseph Beniteau, L. Odette, John Thrasher, J. Hunstead, Samuel Jones, Henry Banks, P. Nevin, John Lovegrove, George Taylor, J. Wright, L. Cuddy, A. Rondeau, John Lincau, P. Ouilette, John Kolfage, John Heard, H. Anderson, C. S. Wigle, M. Twomey, P. Leighton, George Bailey, C. H. Fuller, D. Brown, Joseph Reneave, G. Pulford, J. Campeau, G. Morin, John Rebideaux, J. Tomlinson, J. Bastein, E. Gott, James Turvill, J. Bertrand, I. N. Lee, John Ryan, William Reid, Joseph Gote, Edward Cadarct N A. Coste, A. G. D. Ouilette, B. Young, W. Waldron, C. D. Brush, F. Elliott, A. Muckle, Thomas Boyle, H. Baudy, J. Pillow, Joseph Buford, Edward Honer, D. Masentelle, W. H. Maloney, James Honer, A. Bailey, S. Bertrand, Joseph Caldwell, George Gott, sr., J. D. Gibbs, George Fortier, H. Fortier, W. Woodbridge, P. Wright, C. R. Quick, P. Ferris, Joseph R. Ferris, T. Shay, Theo. Marentelle, Jacob Fox, Charles Cornwall, Frank Fox, H. H. Julien, George McLean, Lewis Wright, Joseph Wright, Ellis Wright, Jos. Bondy, Ira Pastorus, W. Craig, W. Dennis, C. E. Weldon, R. McCallum, J. Crozier, sr., D. R. Davis, W. Elford, D. Austin, T. Caya, D. Ouilette, William Edgar, A. H. Anderson, J. S. Banks, J. E. Turner, Edward Dunstan, William Johnston, H. Lane, George Thomas, Thomas Rush, John Brodie, James Oliver, J. M. Hicks, Fras. Delmore, William Edgar, L. Wigle, M.P., J. R. Wilkinson, E. Malott, P. Conover, E. Fritchell, M. W. Scott, Dr. Branton, John McGuire, W. H. Ryall, C. F. Cronk, C. E. Benlaugh, H. Wigle, John Cascaden, W. G. Fox, R. Gregory, H. Harris, John J. Malott, Henry Malott, Arthur Maynard, W. Wright, Dr. Allworth, Dr. H. Drake, J. R. King, James Doan, Sol Wigle, W. Longland, James E. Brown, T. T. Copus, Alexander Wigle, W. A. Greenville, D. H. McCoy, M. J. Wigle, H. Scratch, William J. Malott, John Avner, D. Wigle, Richard Eede, H. Granger, W. Raymond, W. C. Fox, J. Pearce, C. G. Fox, P. Gilboe, Daniel Fraser, W. Mullen, J. F. Millen, J. D. Mitchell, Edward Rogers, John Peterson, Charles Ryall, D. Ryall, John Barnett, George Wilcher, F. Isaacs, H. Smith, R. Shanks, N. Wigle, Z. Orton, J. Riley, George Whally, S. Duke, H. Ruthven, W. Watson, A. Hairsine, Thomas Reid, Joseph Imeson, J. E. Snyder, John Thompson, W. Imeson, Joseph Lamarsh, H. Pickle, John Whalley, D. McMullen, A. Coulter, G. Gulliver, George Irwin, Thomas Wilkinson, Robert Joliffe.

GLENGARRY.—Hon. Dr. McMillan, Donald MacMaster, Q.C., M.P., John McLennan, ex-M.P., D. A. McArthur, John A. McDonald, James Tomb, Archibald McPhee, R. R. McLennan, George Harrison, Malcolm R. McCuaig, Dr. Munro, Dr. Ferguson, John A. McDonald, A. J. Grant, Patrick Purcell, Dr. Cattanach, Thomas Wallace, Angus Campbell, Peter Delage, D. B. McDonald, H. R. McDonald, Donald McMaster, Alexander D. McDonald, D. H. McDonald, Hugh T. McDonald, J. B. Ostrom, Robert A. Wilson, James L. Wilson, John McKinnon, Donald McDonald, John Campbell, Alexander McTavish, Alexander Munro, Napoleon Gauthier, John Tobin, John McEwen, Hilaire Fillon, Alexander Smilie, John Kennedy, A. D. McRae, William Urquhart, John McDonald, Duncan McLain, Allan McLain, John R. Urquhart, John McMaster, Donald McPhee, Donald A. Cameron, Duncan Campbell, Roderick A. McLennan, Malcolm McLeod, Angus A. McPhee, Capt. Angus R. McDonald, John M. Campbell, John Cameron, jr., Allan McKinnon, Kenneth McLennan, Donald Grant, Alexander Grant, Archibald McDonald, Ronald McCulloch, Duncan McMillan, Donald McMillan, John A. McDonald, John A. Williams, Colin D. Chisholm, Duncan T. Chisholm, Neil K. McLeod, A. P. McDonald, Angus R. McDonald, Alexander Kennedy, Hugh Macmaster, John J. McMillan, Donald Robertson, Robert McMillan, Donald Cameron, Donald McCulloch, Donald T. McDonald, Alexander Robertson, Amide Decosse, Donald A. McDonald, George Timmons, John Hurley, Charles R. McDonald, Francis Trottier, John Kennedy, jr., Hugh McKinnon, Lauchlin McKinnon, Donald McCaskill, John D. McGillivray, Donald McGillivray, Simon Fraser, John J. McMillan, Robert McCormic, John McMarten, Rodger B. McDonald, Duncan J. McKinnon, Alexander McLeod, Peter Chisholm, Francis Tuckette, Adolphus Blais, Alexander D. McDonald, Farquhar McLeod, A. E. McRae, George Avo, Duncan A. McRae, Thomas McDonald, William D. McMillan, Christopher McRae, Alexander Chisholm, Donald W. McMillan, John A. McDonald, Angus McDonald, Donald R. McDonald, James McDonald, Johu J. McDonald, Norman A. McDonald, William McPherson, Alexander McLennan, Patrick Darrah, John B. Snider, Peter Stewart, William M. McPherson, John Ross, Dr. Harkness, Dr. Falkner, Alexander Leclair, Amelie Daust, Adolphus Laroque, Donald A. McPherson, Charles Westley, Donald McNickol, Duncan McQuier, Thomas McCabe, Thomas McAvoy, Donald Fraser, Thomas McDonald, Murdock F. McLennan, Charles McFadden, Duncan McDonald, Charles Craig, Robert Flanagan, John P. McDougald, Hugh Corbett, Donald McDonald, Allan F. McRae, Alexander S. McDonald, Roderick McPherson, Chris' topher J. McRae, John McCrimmon, John Togie, Lauchlin McDonald, A. D. McDonald, Roderick Cameron, Daniel Cameron, Andrew Fraser, Angus McLellan, Stephen Woods, Charles D. McDonald, James Bain, Angus R. McDonald, Angus McDonald, John Carrey, Angus S. McDonald, Angus A. McDonald, Alexander Fraser, Benjamin Clark, Alexander P. McDougald, Alexander C. McDonald, Duncan D. Grant, Dr. Hunt, E. Hunt, Joseph Tyo, John Angus Grant, David Fraser, Evander McRae, Charles McDonald, Alexander Gunn, Robert Blackwood, D. J. McDonald, Hugh McDiarmid, Donald J. McDonald, John A. Dickson, John B. Ferguson, Henry Ward, Farquhar Robinson, J. McGregor, Donald R. Grant, John McDonald, Samuel McDonald, John H. McDonald, Andrew Foulds, jr., Angus D. McGregor, Roderick Poriorrier, G. Gadbois, M. Rouson.

GRENVILLE (South Riding).—W. T. Benson, M.P., A. Carmichael, Joseph Stitt, T. H. Burton, D. Davidson, O. Dawson, A. Adams, M. Connell, W. J. Gamble, William Wallace, John Pearson, William Hopper, O. Tait, John Mellefont, John Dumbrelle, George Whitworth, Robert Johnson, Richard Cottam, A. Stacey, John B. Davis, Edward Reynolds, F. J. French, M.P.P., S. T. Boyd, H. W. Bennett, W. S. West, E. Jessup, James Cairns, G. T. Labatt, Dr. W. J. Jones.

GREY (East Riding).—J. Skelton, R. A. Riky, C. H. Baillie, John Madill, Hugh Carson, John Jelly, Simon Jelly, F. A. Campbell, D. Fisher, Dr. Rolston, Dr. Norton, G. R. Hannah, W. Calbeck, J. T. Hemstreet, R. L. Mortimer, Thomas McKim, Charles Addison, J. B. Dodds, Thomas Clarridge, Thomas Gilray, D. Henderson, C. Devitt, W. H. Dodson, A. Erskine, John Hutchison, James Elliott, James Nelson, William Fawcett, A. Freeborn, C. R. Sing, J. J. Johnston, H. Chisholm, N. Reid, M. Robinson, R. Kerr, James Bowes, James Burnett, William Ward, Dr. Handbury, Isaac Traynor, James Lamon, C. McDowell, J. W.

Morrow, W. T. Parsons, Joseph McArdle, D. K. McArthur, N. McColman, M.P.P., Robert Reid, Thomas Andrews, John Veitch, Joseph Rooke William Kerr, William Pringle, William Greer, Thomas Lowe, N. Smith, G. McAllister, Joseph Shaw, Thomas Shaw, John Gadoway, A. McGirr, J. C. Irish, Edward Potts, Francis Winters, J. R. Sing, H. McDonald, Thomas Brown, J. Ayling, William Hawthorne, T. S. Sproule, M.P., W. J. McFarland, William Lucas, John Lyons, G. M. Haskett, R. Askin.

GREY (North Riding).—M. Forham, A. M. Anderson, D. Creighton, M.P.P., James Masson, S. J. Lane, G. P. Creighton, John Creasor, D. A. Creasor, Samuel Platt, W. B. Stephens, Thomas Gordon, John Chisholm, James McLaughlin, John Rutherford, Henry Robinson, Capt. E. Dunn, Thomas Vickers, W. J. Creighton, William Heap, Hugh Taylor, H. H. Stephens, S. Spencer, Robert Taylor, Dr. John Barnhart, H. W. Jenkins, Alexander McLarne, William Johnston, Thomas Houth, Richard Daly, William Spencer, Thomas Mills, Fred. Plant, John Elliott, Samuel Whitman, William Walker, Robert Linn, Thos. Hudness, William Hewit, William Johnston, T. Chambers, William Norton, J. H. Delavee, John Marquiss, M. Somers, Carson Price, A. Freeborn, John Gillispie, Alexander Pringle, J. Sparrow, J. Milburn.

HALDIMAND.—J. Parker, William Ramsey, J. W. Forster, T. Strachan, J. W. Old, Richard Iuce, C. G. Snider, James Maddigan, E. S. Martin, Dr. Cameron, N. H. Wickett, John Scott, N. Garland, G. Cranston, D. Almas, William Higgins, H. McMarron, John Bell, P. Kenny, Robert Jepson, Dr. McKinnon, J. A Leach, M. Howard, R. E. Walker, H. B. Sawle, John Ryan, W. J. Clark, John Roper, Jas. Old, jr., F. Skelton, H. Warren, Dr. Green, Silas Avery, John Pattison, William Trotter, Edward Munroe, J. C. Perry, D. Kennedy, G. Moore, J. J. Smith, Thomas Isles, R. C. Cheswright, James McAlpine, R. Willer, Thomas Draper, S. Kuipe, T. Hazzard, R. Martindale, N. Mitchell, B. Marr, — Parsons, Dr. Gardiner, W. Mutchmore. J. Cochrane, Robert Smith, Thomas Smith, John E. Clark, George Clark, P. Young, William Ryan, James Ball, William Hull, Robert Walker, James Walker, B. McClung, John Sherlock, D. M. Turnbull, Thomas Flynn, M. McConnell, William Symington, John W. Hull, F. W. Young, S. A. Thompson, L. H. Johnson, Francis Hammond, S. B. Wylie, G. B. Stephenson, Joshua Parker, W. R. Shaver, William Ramsey, J. W. Forster, T. Strachan, James Bain, T. G. Gardiner, Dr. Langrill, Thomas Falls, Walter Jones, R. Walbrook, Joseph Seymour, A. W. Thompson. J. W. Holbrook, Robert Johnson, Joseph Hudspeth, G. A. Gibson, Joseph McGivern, John Perkins, R. Fleming, Alexander Tate, P. Babion, A. B. Miller, R. W. Rushton, R. J. Wingard, Joseph Martindale, R. Allen, Dr. Sherk, C. E. Bourne, H. T. Gardiner, G. Jepson.

HALTON.—Col. Clay, Dr. Webster, R. Noble, D. Lindsay, Edward Brain, William Burger, sr., William Burger, jr., George McMillan, Dr. Fox, Colonel Murray, Capt. Johnson, C. G. Murray, John Hainer, Alex. Cross, John Sproat, O. Robertson, Thomas Chisholm, A. Stark, R. Graham, S. K. Ruddle, N. L. Standish, S. Beaumont, Theo. Cook, Daniel Cook, D. Starrett, Joseph Cook, Richard Bell, Thomas Unton, David Cook, George Campbell, James Newton, Jonathan Lane, William Lane, John Newton, James Nichol, W. H. Shortill, R. Shortill, James Murray, John T. Elliot, John McGibbon, E. Chapman, Andrew Elliott, W. Elliott, D. Vickerman, D. Hutcheon, John Mason, William Holmes, Samuel McGibbon, William Easterbrook, John G. King, Benjamin Tuck, Charles Brown, W. C. Robinson, John Anderson, Alex. Robinson, T. J. Chisholm, John Askin, John Ford, Edwin Sitzer, William Pettigrew, W. C. Beaty, Henry Currigne, Wm. Ayerst, Jas. Biggar, Wm. Hager, H. M. Switzer, Asa Biggar, Wm. Raynard, Jos. Cullingsworth, G. C. McKindsey, Henry Watson, Dr. Freeman, N. Chisholm, S. Hannant, William Armstrong, Charles Knees, John P. Roper, Samuel Dice, D. McGibbon, John Hunter, James Lindsay, Ed. Lindsay, Charles Downey, J. W. Elliott, James Waldie, William Scott, J. Cartner, T. J. Starrett, Thomas Duncan, Dr. Stewart, William Clements, J. J. Wheeler, John Baird, D. Reid, John McDermott, T. Standish, St. M. Watson, Thomas Clark, W. J. Roe, J. H. Bradley, George C. Thompson, Robert Williams, G. L. Tizard, M. Felan, C. Armstrong, W. B. Chisholm, P. Doty, James Andrews, John Jon, John McGiffin, D. Chisholm, William Ferrah, John Bowerbank, Ed. Hilmer, John McKay, George Andrews, Charles Bradbury, T. T. Harris, W. H. Storey, D. Henderson, C. S. Smith, James Matthews, J. E. McGarvin, George Hinds, Joseph Fyfe, William Brown, R. Agnew, Dr. Richardson, Major Kerns, M.P.P., George Allan, J. C. Smith, R. Cole, D. McQuarrie, J. J. Burkholder, Lawrence Lowe, John Knitting, John Biggar, T. W. Jon, W. Y. Petitt, George J. Baker, William McDonald, C. C. Gibson, Alexander Coyne, James Bussell, John Cordingley, A. W. Peart, William Lucas, John Fothergill, W. G. Petitt, Thomas Alton, Daniel McLaren, E. Hunter, E. Corlett, Dr. Jones, George McKerlie, Thomas Watson, Edwin Dalton, John Dickson, A. B. Culloden, George Richardson, P. D. Scott, John Alexander, A. Patton, W. Herron, John Sanderson, J. Harvie, W. Bishop, Joseph Sanderson, A. H. Musgrove, J. Leech, J. Robinson, R. Evans, W. Yeo, Ed. Guest, J. Timmins, J. Hennings, G. Forsyth, F. C. Rodgers, F. Vanston, T. Watson, B. Gerry, J. Drewe, T. Kelly, J. H. Young.

HAMILTON CITY.—Alexander Turner, Alexander Blaicher, Ald. Morden, C. Barlow, T. Winfield, F. E. Kilvert, M.P., Thomas Robertson, M.P., Hon. James Turner, C. L. Thomas, Robert Irwin, W. E. Sanford, John A. Bruce, Richard Bull, W. Nicholson. G. M. Barton, A. McInnis, F. C. Bruce, A. E. Carpenter, John Milne, John A. Culham, J. D. Farmer, G. H. Mills, John Calder, W. G. Reid, W. Goering. F. A. Freed, John Pettigrew, Dr. Hillyer, R. R. Waddell, S. E. Gregory, W. H. Glasco, Dr. Ridley, George Roach, James H. Lottridge, W. H. Gillard, J. G. Bowes, J. Parkes, Josiah Bray, Robert Evans, C. Reneau, P. Volston, W. Handcock, C. R. Smith, William Murphy, R. Williamson, William Carey, W. Southand, W. H. Judd, Alex. McKay, John Kendric, F. H. Lamb, W. Gillespie, A. Gartshore, H. Martin, H. J. Larkin, J. H. Larkin, C. Foster, John H. Chappel, G. T. King, James Watson, M. Malone, E. S. Waterman, T. A. Mackay, R. S. Cooper.

HASTINGS (East Riding).—B. S. Willson, Alexander Robinson, James Collop, William Graham, John Aris, Nelson Lingham, William Sager, William Regan, Thomas Clark, P. R. Daly, J. S. Hamilton, James Youker, S. Palliser, J. Fairfield, James McMullen, Robert McMullen, William Sager, S. Alcombrack, S. Lazier, W. C. Farley, J. J. Farley, T. Farnham, D. Mullet, J. Caniff, W. H. Ketcheson, L. Jones, A. Jones, S. Clarke, W. Huffman, J. Balcanquel, J. McWilliams, R. R. Palmer, F. Brenton, A. P. Reid, D. L. Carscallen, W. Cluzie, C. Wilkins, O. R. Weese, P. McDougall, W. Doctor, J. Sutton, D. Hamm, W. P. Sager, W. A. Chapman, G. Hudson, jr., J. White, M.P., D. Hewitt, J. Wilson, S Hudson, W. R. Fargey, Wm. Gillespie, C McDavitt, E. N. Gould W. H. Melburn, J. Gillespie, J. Hicks, S. C. Emerson, Robert Chapman, J. McKim, J. Mather, M Shorey, G. Latta, W. H. Garrison, George Hall, G. McDavitt, R. Naylor, J. E. Campbell, A. Sutherland, W. Power, J. E. Kelley, W. Bird, J. Townsend, James Gay, R. Wickett, D. Wickett, A. Hamilton, A. L. Roberts, S Geddes, J. Creeper, M. Hill, A. McLarne, M. Campbell, R. H. Pegan, R. L. Lazier, J. Baldrick, J. Thompson, George Sherman, Thomas Deasy, C. Scanlan, A. Campbell, T. Curry, W.

V.

Kelley, C. Anderson, W. Mundell, J. Demill, J. English, J. Ray, W. Fripp, J. Skelly, D. McClarne, W. Beatty, R. Winters, Michael McCullough, T. A. Gordon, J. B. Jordon, R. Hamilton, S. Moult, D. Halsted, A. Collins, S. Lawrence, A. Coulter, J. Parks, R. Gibson, A. McGowan, W. White, R. Gordon, W. Graham, J. Graham, J. Finley G. Easterbrooke, C. Johnson, S. Baker, E. Elliot, J. Latchford, J. Clark, John Graham, E. Barber, R. Morton, W. Embury, T. Sproul, S. Good, Samuel Graham, Henry Monck, Frederick Daw, John Thompson, Robert Burley, Thomas Wright, Henry Waterhouse, R. Gordon, jr., James Beatty, Thomas Beatty, W. Sparrow, Amab Akey, S. G. Dafoe, jr., John Dwyer, W. Knowles, George Marsh, George Marlin, William Marlin, William Burley, jr., J. W. Wilson, S. Allan, R. Allan, Dr. Newton, George Stewart, W. Jamieson, J. McCullough, James Cameron, J. J. Richardson J. Fargey.

HASTINGS (West Riding).—A. Robertson, M.P., G. Denmark, William Sutherland, G. D. Dickson, Henry McIminch, H. Corby, T. Kelso, Dr. Tracy, W. J. Diamond, E. H. LaRoche, A. R. Dougall, W. B. Falkiner, H. Walker, J. C. Jamieson, A. McFee, Ald. Macoun, R. S. Bell, J. W. Loudon, P. P. Lynch, L. Quinlan, J. B. Joubert, J. Grant, James Walmsley, Sandford Johnson, J. W. Campion, James McCrudden, S. Burrowes, John C. Lake, James O'Brien, E. Hayne, A. McGinnes, H. C. Cronk, J. P. C. Phillips, F. H. Rous, James Peoples, A. T. Petrie, James Smith, J. H. Simpson, C. Bogart, George Sherry, J. C. Overell, John Brenton, James Nesworthy, W. P. McMahon. C. J. Starling, J. W. Johnson, S. A. Spangenberg, N. W. Lazier, G. H. Pope, John Panter, N. Lingham, W. B. Northorp, John Taylor, A. N. Reid, A. Bringnall, W. Y. Mikle, John Doyle, William Clarke, Samuel Kennedy, William Doctor, L. H. Henderson, D. Pitceathly, R. Bennett, A. E. Fish. S. Retallack, G. Wallbridge, H. Filliter, M. A. Dixon, Thomas Mills, G. A. skinner, E. F. Potts, William Templeton, W. Bullen, James Cummins, W. J. Northgraves, John Smith, J. P. Thomas, Dr. Willson. Dr. Gibson, George Sterling, S. Blackwell, W. J. Taylor, E. Britton, B. Rose. D. Morgan, Hiram Bell, R. Carr, James Anderson, Darius Green, Robert Juby, Stephen Tufts, W. Ward, D. Gaffin, Robert Hamilton, James Bird, William McCann, James Ritcheson, H. B. Smith, S. Dench, Harry Fenn, J. Gay, sr., J. Gay, jr., John Palliser, Thomas Green, George Greaves, Robert Fenn. R. Clark, John Hart. Thomas Leslie, Al. Ketcheson, Charles Aker, James Scott, Thomas McEwan, D. B. Ketcheson, Thomas Ketcheson, Charles Ketcheson, Charles Rose, C. Sills, William McCullough, Elias Ketcheson, M. Bird, W. Bird, J. A. Chisholm, G. S. Graham, Daniel Grass, E. Reid, J. R. Row, Henry Knox, Herman Knox, J. C. Rose, Ruliff Grass, James A. Chisholm, J. A. Consaul, Joshua Anderson, Alexander Beaty, Daniel Ostrom, Dr. Stevenson, B. Ostrom, T. Alley, W. Crouter, A. L. Crouter, George Chisholm, A. R. Gilbert, Dennis Carr, James Scott, Austin Hogle, Charles Taylor, John Young, M. Knox, George Knox, Charles Ostrom, George Ostrom, R. T. Graham, George Cleal, John German, W. R. Perry, A. S. Ward, George Potter, Wm. Reynolds, J. H. Garbutt, T. H. Blanchard, S. Young, T. D. Fairfield, Wm. Harry, B. Mallory, John Bush, Able Finkle, William McMasters, P. P. Pettitt, George Clark, W. D. Ketcheson, E. C. Ketcheson, T. Foster, W. R. Vandervoort, Peter Ford, W. W. Casey, Peter Miller, Frederick Ford, James Jeffrey, James Knox, Silas Green, Charles Scott, James H. Ketcheson, John Holden, Peter Grass, Burnham Mallory, Ezra Mallory, James H. Peck, John M. Allen, A. W. Hawley, J. W. Cunningham, William Shea, P. J. Patteson, Arthur Murphy, C. B. Saylor, Captain J. A. Porte, Captain J. A. Orr, A. M. Spafford, William German, Robert Hamilton, R. Loughead, James Crowe, Geo. Crowe, Robert Sanson, John Turner, Thomas German, George Graham, R. A. Barber, F. Cornwell, J. B. Graham, Thomas Ventriss, John Belch, C. F. Pelletier, E. Stoueburg, George Dench, W. H. Polipey, A. McWilliams, G. H. Gill, H. Meade, Henry Cunningham, George Simpson, Thomas E. Vars, A. Urquhart, D. R. Murphy, R. E. Bell, William Jeffs, R. P. Fidlor, Charles Flindall, J. F. Flindall, F. A. Hilton, J. W. Howe, J. A. Cleene, E. Hilton, W. T. Barker, D. McCauley, S. S. Gooding, James Kenney, H. Martin, J. Brooks, George Bartt, J. Lapointe, Robert Weddell, Thomas Burton, J. H. Nulty, William Reid, D. Daly, William Lyons, J. Rupert, J. McLarne, A. Parent, George Jackson, J. W. Hyde, L. Cruikshanks, Al. Knox, R. McKinnon, A. Flindall, John McDonell, Henry Gill.

HASTINGS (North Riding).—William Hilton, George Bleecker, Richard Campion, J. W. Pearce, J. Hamilton, A. W. Carscallen, G. McWilliams, James Wiley, J. Gladney, James Bailey, Hugh Jones, Thos. Warren, John Richardson, E. Maloney, M. Hilton, James Fidlar, John Downey, Charles Clairmont, T. P. Pearce, John Caskey, A. B. Ross, S. Ross, Thomas Monney, J. R. Hutchison, W. J. Allen, Robert Allen, W. Blaine, John McCoy, L. Einpey, James English, John Conlin, J. Blakely, C. Sandford, J. Robertson, J. Gillen, S. Curry, S. Rollins, J. Harper, James Whytock.

HURON (West Riding).—W. Campbell, S. Platt, James Mitchell, C. W. Andrews, F. W. Johnston, A. P. McLean, E. Campiai, Captain McGregor, Robert McLean, D. Doby, E. Beecher, P. McEwan, W. H. Ridley, J. C. Detlor, J. W. Smith, F. Jordan, George B. Cox, S. Dean, T. Troy, C. W. Andrews, P. Carroll, H. W. Ball, W. Lee, H. E. Johnston, R. Hays, Dr. Taylor, E. Graham, Dr. Holmes. J. Acheson, James Addison, James A. Reid, D. Cantelar, George Sheppherd, John Butler, W. McLean, F. F. Lawrence, Thos. Weatherald, M. Higgins, George Grant, T. B. Vanevery, M. Nicholson, Dr. Whitley, F. Pridham, Robert A. Stark, W. F. Welsh, H. Secord, E. Bingham, C. F. Strantel, C. Crabb, D. Currie, S. Andrews, G. N. Davis, James Bailey, P. Kelly, James Barr, Joseph Carter, John Enegle, C. Hamilton, J. Whitehead, A. Taylor, Joseph Goedmurpe, H. Martin, Joseph Beck, Isaac Fisher, W. J. Harris, A. McNeil, J. McDonough, R. Hamilton, Thos. Hussey, J. Whitley, A. C. Hawkins, Geo. Hawkins, R. Grovy, H. Chambers, W. Rickley, Jos. Hamilton, R. Webster, R. M. Racey, E. Corbett, W. H. Cooper, Geo. Hanley, Dr. Dowsley, D. Cantelon, John Allinson, T. C. Docherty, W. Smith, Thomas Cooper, E. Floody, George Anderson, A. M. Todd, J. Crait, S. Davis, W. Vanstone, A. Allen, James Potter, James McCallum, Robert Kelly, L. Netbery, Robert Medd, James Johnston, Robert Ellis, John Roberts, John Bowers, D. E. Munro, Joseph Whitley, G. Elliott, John Beacom, Henry Beacom, William Crooks, John G. Cox, James Peacock, Edward Acheson, J. T. Nattel, Chas. Middleton.

HURON (East Riding).—George Strong, William Carson, D. Wier, James Perkins, James Leech, William Evans, Anson Dolmage, John Williamson, John Kain, Benjamin S. Cook, Charles Wilson, Samuel Johnston, Thomas K. Boddy, H. W. C. Meyer, William Elliott, John Hanna, B. Willson, Thomas Bell, William Clegg, John Dinsley, Robert Cormyn, William Ellison, Dr. Bethune, Dr. Tamlyn, E. L. Dickinson, Alfred Roe, William McClymont, Thomas McClymont, William Johnston, Samuel Youhill, J. S. Smith, John Brennan, T. L. Jobb, Thomas Gregory, Charles Lloyd, E. R. Talbot, Thomas Farrow, M.P., James Hennings, James Timmins, A. Musgrove. W. Yeo, John Gardner, W. King, P. Thomas, R. Evans, G. Barton, J. Robertson, F. Irwin, T. Higgins, W. Job, P. Wells, J. Medill, W. Smith, W. H. Stewart, E. Guest, T. Stewart, W. Sanderson, T. Evans, J. Etcher, Andrew Patton, William Herron, John Sanderson, John Hooie, Robert Durion, William Bishop, Joseph Sanderson.

VI.

HURON (South Riding).—G. E. Jackson, R. Barber, R. Newall, S. Wallace, J. Pickard, M. McQuade, J. Weber, R. Elgie, W. S. Mundle, P. Dayman, Henry Colbert, John Rattenbury, Dr. Colman, J. Downey, W. Hawkshaw, Colonel Jones, F. Stephens, F. Neelans, D. Hogan, P. Speerie, J. Dorsey, W. T. Carroll, L. Murphy, Captain Dawson, George Sells, J. Stewart, T. Holemsted, James Able, C. Papist, W. Lee, J. Darwin, J. Evans, J. O'Sullivan, W. J. Sharmen, F. Case, George Case, T. Hays, James Hayes, C. Eygert, W. Morrison, J. C. Morrison, F. Morrison, B. O'Connor, Richard McKee, S. Scarlett, J. Johnston, J. Irwine, A. Boyd, James Hellen, J. Scarlett, M. Morrison, A. Morrison, James Ryan, J. Mobery, Henry Hamilton, R. Ferguson, John Berry, J. Swa'low, — McKillop, C. Dale, J. Bretton, J. Mills, Mr. Best, J. Lashare, W. E. Colwell, R. H. Ferguson, E. Dawson, E. R. Rutledge, Andrew Morrison, W. H. Cooper, E. Corbitt, M. McTaggart, George Hanley, J. Craib, Thomas Cooper. D. Cantelon, D. B. Kennedy, E. Floody, W. H. Simpson, Dr. Dowsley, Thomas Jackson, H. Beacom, A. S. Fisher, W. Renn, John Bell, H. Taylor, D. Reynolds, Dominick Reynolds, B. Churchill, — Barns, W. W. Connor, M. Morrisou, H. Wainright, J. Pollock, W. Meyers, Mr. Rutledge, G. Woods, J. Bailey, W. Graham, George Cassels, T. Simpson, D. H. Ritchie, W. Moffatt, J. Cook, J. Turner, J. Stewart, W. Edgar, J. Smith, J. Pettie, J. Gill, J. Happle, W. Hogins, H. Reynolds.

KENT.—Hon. Joseph Northwood, Henry Smyth, M.P., R. S. Woods, Andrew Hayward, Thomas Holmes, J. B. Pike, S. T. Martin, Matthew Wilson, Thomas Scullard, James Warren, John Matthewood, Napoleon Tetrault, D. R. Van Allan, T. H. Taylor, Nathaniel Massey, William Richards, J. L. Bray, H. J. Murphy, G. E. Richardson, M. D., Henry Nagle, John Knight, E. H. Hall, Charles E. Pagley, Edwin Jones, J. C. McNabb, William Baby, Caleb Wheeter, Robert Cooper, William Morley, W. G. Pennefather, Joseph Vaine, William Hea, J. R. O'Flynn, John Challoner, Edward Jordan, C. J. O'Neill, Isaac Smith, J. M. Northwood, John Haler, A. Berard, S. Stephenson, W. E. Hamilton, C. D. Williamson, Orrila Dolsen, Archie Lamont, Stephen Backus, George Wetherspoon, W. I. Martin, Henry Ball, C. H. Rose, Jacob Freistell, William Mansett, Hugh Stringer, W. G. Fleming, Charles Poile, James Richardson, William Northwood, J. S. Nicol, R. A. Hughes, William G. Betts, Thomas E. O. Hene, John Brennen, Samuel Glenn, Robert Black, John Rice, Thomas French, T. A. Smith, Hugh Kerr, Thomas Scullard, E. W. Seane, Edward Langford, Newton Elmets, George Merritt, Willard Merritt, Stephen Reid, Frederick Goodland, Henry Weaser, Alfred Ryall, A. McDonnell, Warren Bentley, T. A. Moore, James Moore, William Harper, William Tristram, John Tilt, John Leslie, Frederick Rice, Joseph Roche, William Johnson, John Morris, Samuel Heffernan, Wm. Ball, G. O. Scott, G. E. Young, H. A. Patterson, E. J. Roche, Warren Lambert, Thomas Callup, Alexander Ebests, John Pierce, Charles Crofts, John Schneider, C. R. Atkinson, Littleton Johnston, G. N. Atkinson, William Huntore, William P. Francis, James H. Oldershan, Alexander Gregory, John Carpenter, Augustus Pace, E. J. Degge, Dr. Sievewright, Thomas Sutherland, William S. Arnold, R. M. Northwood, James Mitner, David Park, William Singer, William Wing, Frank Robert, Alexander Dinnas, S. D. Radley, William F. Rushy, Frank Moore, Charles Williams, Andrew Rohan, Robert Halle, George H. Sexsmith, Ingram Taylor, James Whay, W. C. Wood, J. N. Henry, Jesse A. Henry, William H. Tighe, James Paul, William Sloan, C. Coatsworth, Henry Sales, Andrew Wilson, Henry Wilson, Thomas Taylor, John Warnick, William E. Bottoms, Boniface Dupuis, Moses Hudon, W. Still, Joseph Peltier, Thomas Gleason, William Gleason, P. T. Barry, George C. Marshall, Levi Marshall, Robert Kane, W. G. Cusack. Gibb Taylor, J. M. Taylor, W. J. Tichborne, James Little, James Toll, George Leslie, T. S. Arnold, Henry Young, J. W. Gibson, J. K. Morris, C. A. Williston, Alexander Elliott, John McMichael, James Buchanan, John Cameron, Joseph Muckle, Jas. Weldon, R. H. Black, W. G. Powell, John Little, J. G. Langford, T. R. Jackson, Thos. Coatsworth, William Clarke, David Hammill, Demetrius Holmes, John Shirton, David Hutchinson, Alexander Clark John A. Langford, George Langford, Frederick Arnold, Michael Arnold, David Arnold, James McMullen. Peter McMullen, Joseph McGarvin, John Van Horn, John Bedford, David Wilson, George McGarvin, Samuel McMahon, Dougald McNaughton, William McKenzie Ross, William Lane, Thomas Cean, C. A. Williams, Wm. Brown, Thomas Johnston, Albert Williams, Thomas Irvin, Joseph Payne, John L. Doyle, R. S. Toky, Peter Ferguson, William Irwin, James Cheswick, William Askins, John Lee, John Hunter, Geo. Francis, Arthur Walker, Frank Drury, Benjamin Evans, D. C. Echlin, G. W. Hatter, James Gilhula, Harry Kelly, A. D. Kersey, John Tearerne, William Higgins, Fergus Park, John Foxton, William Drew, Samuel Wellwood, William Wellwood, William Finlay, John McKeon, Timothy Dillon, Martin Dillon, Timothy Gilhula, Albert Mason, Horace A. Miller, John A. Ballagh, Garland Lethbridge, Thomas Marlott, Thomas Sullivan, James McPherson, Johnson Orr, Nathan Bell, Lawrence Higgius, Thomas Baxter, Peter Robert, Anthony Ouilette, Phillip Blair, Frank Bordeau, Timothy McQuean, Cornelius Purser, John Terry, Harry Pattinson, John Peel, William Willmore, Thomas Pollard, Samuel Montgomery, Barnabus Wemp, Matthew Coveney, William Trotter, J. G. Rose, William Bishop, T. Cullis, W. K. Merrifield, W. J. Slater, Hume Scott, William P. Killackey, G. W. Cornell, H. H. Anderson.

KINGSTON CITY.—G. M. McDowell, Hon. Dr. Sullivan, Capt. Gaskin, J. H. Metcalf, M.P.P., R. T. Walrem, T. H. McGuire, Dr. Smith, Dr. Mackenzie, G. J. Hobart, Henry J. G. Cunningham, Samuel Anglin, jr., John McMahon, Samuel Angrove, James Swift, E. Chown, G. M. Wilkinson, John McIntyre, Isaac Noble, James Wilson, George Richardson, J. T. McMahon, W. B. Savage, John O'Brien, E. Williams, J. Minnes, John Lovick, M. Doran, Charles Hatch, R. W. Shannon, James Quigley, C. F. Smith, S. J. Kirkpatrick, H. J. Wilkinson, J. Bastow, John Hauer, W. M. Drennan, H. Crothers, Donald McIntyre, Frank Tracey, John Jones, James S. Leith, T. J. Donoghue, Peter Bates, Captain McKée, William Snowden, P. R. Henderson, J. S. Henderson, Samuel Thornton, Thomas Gaskin, Philip Bajus, A. McConagy, J. S. Muckleston, Isaac Oliver, John Dodds.

LAMBTON (West Riding).—D. Mills, Joseph Case, J. McKay, James Halls, Jonathan Grier, D. W. Dulmage, J. Bowerman, Robert Thompson, John Glen, John Delbridge, Leonard Hunter, Thomas Coates, Robert Creery, Alexander Duncan, Henry Doufe, James Handford, N. J. Clark, William Buckingham, William Balkwell, William Taylor, Dr. Clark, Thomas Ellison, A. McDonald, A. Suller, C. Sanders, Joseph Ellison, E. A. Vidal, W. H. Hill, John Hanna, James McKelvey, William Farr, William Luscomb, Dr. Ward, R. E. LeSueur, E. S. Rowe, J. F. Elliott, Jacob Turnbull, James Lougheau, D. McCard, James Kelly.

LANARK (North Riding).—P. Reilly, J. S. Robinson, James Cowie, W. Bowes, J. H. Bond, Robert Needham, John Gemmill, John C. Stevens, Josepeph Rosamond, James Donald, John Monroe, A. Penman, George Campbell, William Lock, David Forbes, Allan Fraser, E. Mohr, A. Halpenny, Joseph Halpenny, R. D. Fetherston, A. E. Riddell, Richard Serson, George Fraser, Alexander Murphy, John Owens, William Wilson, John Moorhouse, Robert Story, James Shaw, William Green, Samuel Stevenson, M. D. Nagle, John Neal, D. S. Baird, John Howe, H. McBride, Edward Armstrong, George N. Kidd, James Wilson, John

VII.

Manion, John Cavanagh, Robert Clark, R. H. Armstrong, Patrick Garland, Alexander McDonald, William Atkinson, William Barton, William Bradley, Dr. Kidd, Dr. Groves, William McDaniel, James McGee, Thos. Hodgins, Adam Hodgins, William Rivington, William Reid, I. Halfpenny, William Ireton, William H. Sturgeon, Alexander McIntyre, sr., William Graham, Peter Reid, B. McGuire, William H. James, William Bailey, D. Guthrie, John Trainor, William Borrowman, James Herron, Robert Graham, Alexander Yuill, John Wright, S. S. Dickson, John Forsythe, William McKibbon, Henry Scott, William Lowe, jr., Robert Scott, Thomas Boal, sr., Patrick Monaghan, William Lowe, sr., H. H. Dickson, John Green, George Dack, Dr. Baird, John Givens, John Smith, John Houston, L. Dulmage, John Boland, John Dulmage, O. Banning, A. Teskey, Albert Johnston, Andrew Wilson, James Templeton, jr., L. McDonald, P. McDermott, Patrick McGregor, Thomas C. Foster, James McCann, John Rea, Archibald Stewart, Frank Coulter, John Watson, R. Young, William Hall, Peter Guthrie, George Pretty, Hugh Munro, John Munro, Archy Boyle, B. Rosamond, C. H. Sheard, Andrew Elliott, J. Jamieson, M.P., Thomas W. McDermott, William Thoburn, N. Bennett, C. H. Ferguson, William Baird, Dr. Raines, J. K. Cole, G. J. Clint, James Rosamond, sr., Andrew Kenny, Robert Scott, A. M. Greig, John Elliott, E. Leyden, William Willoughby, Dr. Burns, William W. Pittard.

LANARK (South Riding).—John Haggart, M.P., William Lees, M.P.P., H. D. Shaw, Robert Meighen, William Meighen, J. T. Henderson, Peter McLarne, A. J Matheson, F. A. Hall, W. W. Berford, Edward Elliott, William Hicks, William A. Meighen, John Wilson, Henry Moorehouse, Thomas Brook, George Kerr, C. A. Matheson, George Devlin, Dr. Grant, Dr. Munro, G. A. Consett, A. C. Shaw, William H. Radenhurst, Hugh Ryan, J. A. McLarne, W. J. Pink, T. A. Code, William Butler, Peter Hope, Benjamin Wright, A. B. Rudd, Michael F. C. Inderwick, Thomas Hicks, Thomas Hands, John Code, William Watson, John James, John Jackson, John McCue, Edward McLenaghan, Donald McPhail, R. Steadman, A. Armstrong, C. McLenaghan, George Poole, W A. Devlin, John Christie, Thomas B. Moore, Robert Smith, Arthur Bes', Geo. Oliver, Peter McKinley, John Poole, Henry Poole, John Acheson, Eph. Deacon, John Korry, George Buchanan, Joseph Perkins, Thomas Marks, James Warren, John Manion, S. Wilson, John Menzies, Richard Warren, Richard White, James Balderson, James Noonan, Richard Keays, John Dewitt, J. F. Thompson, Walter Cameron, Michael Bell, Richard Warren, J. M. Kenyon, Robert Allen, S. Wilson, George McMartin, M. Stanley, W. O. Sweeney, S. M. Barnes, Alfred Mills. John Splane, John Craine, R. Lewis, J. McGillivray, Ogle Crass, Dr. Acheson, F. W. Casey, J. R. Lavelle, G. F. Cairns, Alexander Woods, John Craine, jr., James Rath, S. N. Percival, J. Chambers, W. H. Jarvis, James Chambers, Peter Clarke, R. Livingstone, James Ferguson, John Ferguson, B. Cook, J. Poole, William Box, James Ackland, James Bothwell, S. Bain, W. G. Crown, A. W. Bell, W. Code, A. Graham, F. Hollingsworth, James Murphy, W. Kelly, D. G. Hamilton, J. W Hendry, John Huston, W. S. Moore, James McFadden, L. McCallum, W. R. McInnis, Jas. McIntosh, A. Nichol, T. Nagle, W. Pattie, John Summers, James Wauthorp, James Warren, Joseph Wilson, W. H. Wylie, A. C. Burgess, George Dummort, George Graham, Thomas Hodgins, James Hall, E. Hutchins, Dr. Wilson, A. McLean, A. G. Proud, Dr. Preston, H Robertson, W M. Summers, James Weeks, James Wilson, A. Wilson, E. T. Avison, D. Carmichael, W. W. Cliff, W. M. Dunham, H. N. Empey, G. G. Fulton. A. T. Hudson, J. Hawkins, Thomas Lever, C. B. Mansell, C. Munroe, J. McDonald, B. McNeely, W. Neelan, A. Parker, J. Scott, Alexander Steele, George Warren, L. R. Johnson, George Knox, J. Holland, — Sheppard, — Gardner, J. Stewart, T. Begley, A. C. Thicker, R. Cavanagh, George Kidd, P. Lowe, William May, R. Price, E. Code, S. G. Cram, W. Gosh, R. Griffith, T. Hawkins, H. Leach, J. Leach, R. Leach, Wm. Leach, J. McNeely, R. McNeely, James Nesbitt, M. Sterns, George Tackaberry, J. Salter, Thomas Nesbitt, J. McLenaghen, jr., W. McNeely.

LEEDS AND GRENVILLE.—H. Merrick, M.P.P., J. H. Merrick, M.D., R. W. Watchhorn, J. T. Depencer, J. Burchill, M. R. Church. M.D., E. H. Whitemarsh, E. Reel, Capt. P. T. Merrick, C. F. Ferguson, M.P., A. Blackburn, James Porter, George Taylor, William Bower, James Connelly, John Saunders, T. Kidd, John Rutherford. James Sanderson, William Kidd, James Malley, C. Richards, John Ferguson, B. Masher, S. Pearsons, Thomas Chester, J. Hughes, J. Spencer, C. Cook, J. McGilvery, F. W. Kassey, J. Lavall, A. Mills, W. Gilroy, O. Morehouse. W. Storey, E. McDonald, R. Goodfellow, Col. McCray, William Davis, A. Stewart, W. Hanton, S. Hode, S. Edgar.

LEEDS (South Riding).—D. Ford Jones, J. H. Whalen, S. McCammon, H. Green, R. H. Preston, M.P.P., W. A. Webster, J. Birmingham, J. P. Redmond, J. Herbison, Dr. Giles, James Gallagher, W. H Rorison, J. F. Earl, R. Blake. William Byers, John Singleton, George Taylor, M.P., Robert Brough, W. B. Carroll, Wm. McKenzie, M. Burns, J. B. Turner, D. Brophy, Dr. Meirick, J. C. Ross, T. P. Richardson, James Dempster, E. G. Hart, J. T. Green, James F. Watt, M. McIntyre, J. W. Campbell, J. H. Butler, J. Paul, J. T. Gallagher, R. Bell, W. H. Leggett, J. Whitmash, J. Bell, A. Bell, J. W. Preston, R. A. Preston, Benjamin Pett, W. Elliott.

LINCOLN AND NIAGARA.—John McLean, R. Clark, James Prior, E. Bradley, W. H. Wilson, J. F. Vanderburg, D. Lee, J. Rynail, John Petting, Alexander Spers, T. Bassett, W, H. Jones, D. Howarth, D. Scott, T. J. Stevenson, A. H. Bradley, W. L. Miles, J. Hamilton, Jesse Ness, J. B. Dolan, J. B. Smythe, A. Etchells. A. Summers, T. J. Walton, E. H. Phelps, S. R. Bradley, J. Bradley, A. Redhead, T. T. McArthur, J. Keating, J. Bassett, G. Gordon, W. Strong, J. Strong, C. Nester, D. Orth, T. R. Housser, J. W. Moyer, J. R. High, J. H. Orth, B. Martin, A. Meyer, P. Meyer, J. Konkle, J. Simpson, J. McLean, F. McGear, H. Mindabery, A. Simpson, James Hircitt, A. Hamilton, J. A. Cooper, A. Ward, M. Fields, Dr. Warran, P. Mills, Joseph Clement, H. Garden, John Knox, W. A. Thompson, Thomas Lampman, Thomas Hiscott, sr., R. Connors, J. G. Bernard, G. J. Miller, Joseph Walker, C. Canelman, A. Thompson, G. B. Wilson, S. Sherar, G. C. Clement, P. S. Second, C. Lowry, Joseph Lampman, S. J. Read, A. W. Wright, George Beatty, James D. Bennett, Joseph H. McCombs, Robert Kelly, W. S. Turline, William Hearle, Wm. Beatty, William Kerr, E. O. Henry, A. C. Couse, F. B. Rogers, B. Rogers, J. Oldham, Joseph Woon, J. C. Patterson, A. Culp, W. Virling, J. House, W. McCrum, Thomas Bell, A. A. Reavely, A. Merrett, John W. Fisher. J. Fisher, J. J. Broft, W. S. Madall, George Ryckman, J. H. Beatty, G. A. Camp, John W. Swayze, O. H. Lutz, Thomas Keyes, J. Durham, J. Warner, R. R. Secord, G. Steward, O. S. Secord, R. James, Ed. Hiscott, R. D. Irvine, C. Depotty, L. Bessey, J. Clift, J. Junkin, A. Read, W. J. Parnall, S. Parnall, J. Rebutner, T. J. Farmer, George May, A. Tenbrock, G. Ward, J. W. Johnson, J. A. Boyle, H. Boyle, T. Davis, B. Welstead, A. Phipps, S. A. Boyle, J. A. Ball, Al. Pay, J. Burtch, A. G. Hull, J. Vine, Mayor Smith, Ald. Goodman, W. Chaplin, Thomas Bate, Ald. McGeachie, J. Junkin, W. W. Greenwood, Richard Wood, H. Garden, G. B. Towers, Ald Dunlop, Dr. Klotz, Ald. Carter, Thomas Orr, Ald. Towers, W. B. Harris, Ald. Cuff, Richard Miller, Ald. McCarthy, W. Pattison, J. H. Ingersoll, T. R. Merritt, J. Carslile, G, C. Carlisle,

VIII.

Ald. McMillan, S. Montgomery, Ald. Elliott, E. A. Smyth, C. Sherwood, M. Moriarty, J. Hindson, D. D. Potter, W. D. Beadle, Dr. Clark, C. Chapman, D. C. McGuire, G. Wilson, J. Scott, J. Devanney, J. Fitzgerald, R. Peterson, J. W. Keating, M. Y. Keating, G. Cov, R. Howse, J. Hunniford, J. E. Beeton, J. A. Keys, D. G. Rowan, M. Swayze, Capt. Murray, L. Dorr, T. Holder, J. Marshall, W. McClorey, J. Albon, W. D. Magee, M. Kane, J. C. Eccles, T. Fitzsimons, A. Friesman, C. McDermott, G. Nicholson, W. J. White, G. Burtch, C. P. Camp, H. G. Hunt, T. R. Brownlee, C. Riordan, W. Chatfield, J. Hawkins, J. R. Seymour, H. P. Marshall, E. A. Jukes, G. Newman, C. H. Connor, J. Lewin, Alexander Stewart, J. Graham, D. Bryant, James Bird, William Shaw, James Wells, T. H. Taylor, N. A. McGregor, Dr. Greenwood, Dr. Sullivan, W. Campbell. J. Titterington, C. Stahr, H. M. Helliwell, J. Reid, Ed. Gardiner, B. C. Fairfield, Rev. O. J. Booth, Rev. J. G. Foote, E. W. Montgomery, T. Sullivan, S. Neelon, J. C Rykert, M. A. Ball, H. O'Loughlin, R. Stanley, N. A. Lindsay, C. P. Mills, W. McMaugh, R. Foster, J. C. Grobb, J. W. Grote, W. R. James, A. M. Macrea, C. Steinberg, J. Woods, S. Emmett, W. J. Smith, A. Bolden, Thomas Hastings, J. M. Lawder, J. A. Marquis, R Ratcliff, Thomas Beattie, Capt. McIlwain, John Sullivan, Ald. Gibson, Thomas Bullwant, W. A. Muttleberger, W. H. Brownlee, D. C. Plumb, W. A. Milloy, H. A. Garrett, R. G. Dickson, John Sando, Capt. Wilkinson, W. G. Donnelly, J. McDougall, J. H. Best, A. Bishop, Capt. Backett, R. Best, M. Lyons, John Ellston, W. H. Christie, F. Geddes, H. Pafford, Dr. Anderson, S. Callory, J. Thomber, F. H. Date, George Walker, H. Moyer, W. S. Moyer, J. Jarvis, G. Michner, S. Lindabery, S. Davies, J. O. Henry, G. H. Grobb, G. H. Walker, W. L. Kew, R. B. Patterson, W. S. Kerr, R. Book, M. Konkle, W. F. Zimmerman, G F. Fairbrother, R. O. Konkle, G. W. Tinlin, J. Durham, R. Walker, G. Parker, J. H. Zimmerman, D. Wiers, M. Grobb, M. Bark, G. A. Huff, R. S. Durham, T. Lindabery.

LONDON CITY.—T. McCormick, A. W. Porte, John Elliott, John Labatt, G. Taylor, W. P. R. Street, T. D. Hodgins, R. Bayly, Alexander Johnston, John Coote, A. K. Thompson, A. Cleyhorn, W. Johnston, A. O. Graydon, Josiah Blackburn, John R. Peel, Arthur Wallace, W. R. Meredith, M.P.P., W. J. Thompson, J. M. Cousins, Edmund Meredith, Thomas Beattie, Samuel Grigg, John Pritchard, W. Harwood, Upsill Ward, T. G. Lowe, W. McCormick, Joseph Percival, Nathaniel Reid, W. Percival, W. J. Reid, E. B. Reed, F. A. Fitzgerald, J. H. Flock, A. Gauld, T. H. March, John Cooper, Matthew Glass, Dr. Niven, H. Colerick, G. Watson, Dr. Brown, B. A. Mitchell, Dr. Moore, sr., R. W, Puddicombe, G. Nichol, Dr. Moorhouse, A. W. Woodward, Robert Smith, W. W. Fitzgerald, Bobert Boyd, W. D. Buckle. W. Dodson, W. Robinson, R. Southam, Dr. J. M. Smith, Charles Cox, W. Y. Brunton. J. D. O'Neil, John Tanton, Alexander Durdea, James Wright, John Rayner, Samuel McBride, R. Mountjoy, Alexander McBride, Robert Carrothers, T. F. Kingsmill, H. J. Boyd, James Macklin, Francis Foreman, Robert Kingsmill, Alexander McBean, W. McDonough, Charles Richardson, T. J. McDonough, Andrew McKenzie, J. P. O'Byrne, John Pittfield, J. T. Stevenson, W. Willis, R. McBride, J. R. Minhinnick, N. Ormsby, John Wolfe. John Arnold, W. R. Vining, P. Murray, W. Ferguson, Edward Fleming, jr., John Kincaid, C. B. Keid, N. Wilson, R. Howard, A. M. Smith, H. Burwell, James Taylor, Nicholas Wilson, jr., J. Pannell, A. Loughrey, Frederick Rowland, S. Trapp, John Geary, T. H. Carling, T. Aspden, George Macbeth, G. Wyatt, W. Wyatt, John Scandrett, K. J. Young, G. Priddis, James Priddis, M. Morgan, Martin Ferguson, C. A. Morley, H. G. Abbott, James Burns, G. Street, W. Elliott, G. Burdett, Simpson Mason, James Taylor, John Shopland, John Twohey, Alexander Sutherland, John A. Cousins, W. B, Winnett, Richard Winnett, John Puddicombe. W. McNeil, John Chester, Andrew McCormick, J. H Fraser, W. J. Imlach, J. J. Blake, John Fleming, Dr. Oronbyatekha, B. W. Greer, Charles Taylor, Job Cousins, C. B. Hunt, Alexander Aikman, C. A. Kingston, H. D. Long, Stephen O'Meara, P. F. Boyle, W. Milroy, Samuel Friendship, Edward Crossman, David Darvill, Edward Raymond, G. S. Birrell, A. B. Powell, P. Mulkern, W. Skinner, G. Riddell, Philip Cook, G. Rose, Dr. McGuigan, W. Wilson, John Bonner, G. McNab, John Boyd, T. Howard, Reuben Brummitt, Talbot MacBeth, H. Beecher, B. Cronyn.

MIDDLESEX (West Riding).—J. H. English, Col. English, S. R. Richardson, Alexander Johnston, John Folinsbee, W. Daniels, B. Hungerford. J. S. McCrault, P. O'Dwyer, Dr. Stevenson, Dr. Lindsay, C. Grist, James Wright, Dr. Nugent, A. Goodwin, D. W. Vary, W. J. Dyas, J. H. Lee, W. C. Moore, W. H. Meek, S. W. Shimbly, W. F. Snell, E. Woodbury, J. C. Diggins, J. Paine, C. Wood, Major Irwin. W. F. Fawcett, F. W. Meek, Dr. Hoare, Captain Mathews, C. Bixel, J. Robinson, T. Cawthrop, J. S. Loynes, E. Milner, F. B. Saxton, P. J. Alison, A. Carruthers, J. W. Drown, Dr. Evely, R. Williams, J. Barry, John Lenfestey, jr., James Lenfes·ey, S. G. Mungerford, James Gough, D. Harrington, W. Avery, W. Moody, George Urquhart, F. Robinson, J. Berden, W. M. Manigault, James Webb, James Copeland, R. Widdis, T. Hopwood, R. Pincombe, T. L. Armstrong, G. A. Mann, P. Welsh, W. Cross, R. Dumbrill, W. Cummings, C. Andrews, J. H. Evans, A. Stevenson. W. Cain, J. Alexander, F. Woodward, P. Fitzpatrick, Dr. Roome, Thomas Robinson, William Simpson, William Bilton, Joseph Shepley, Kirby Bilton, A. Adams, George Johnston, Aaron Burr, Harry McKune, R. Belford, D. H. Belford, A. Campbell, J.P., G. P. Dougald Campbell, H. G. Lindsay, Jas. Gamble, Thomas Pearce, Thomas Nagle, D. McKay, F. Bateman, E. Bateman, Dugald Lutch, Malcomb Campbell, James Ferguson, John Saxton, Charles Carroll, R. Williams, E. Degraw, A. McDougal, Hugh Turner, Duncan McKellar, D. McLean, John Bell, J. Howe, H. Howe, Samuel Ferguson, M. S. Lutch.

MIDDLESEX (North Riding).—Dr. Rollins, J. B. Carling, John Haukshaw, John Spackman. James Oke, Robert Saunders, George Willis, Dr. Lutz, B. V Elliott, L. Hardy, W. G. Bissett, R. Fariner, L. Thorne, Miller White, John White, William White, Thomas Abbott, T. Coughlin, M.P., H. Eilber, C. Coughlin, T. Yearly, P. Coughlin, W. Baker, C. Zwicker, William Fulton, T. Keyes, William Sanders, J. Sanders, A. Lary, J. Baker, P. J. Clark, D. Grant, G. Wein, R. Box.

MONCK.—D. L. McGlashan, S. W. Hill, J. Steele, Josiah Ward, Salom Vanevery, John McGlashan, Josiah Second, L. McCallum, M.P., Hosen Niece, T. J. Galbraith, A. McDonald, Jno. Murphy, A. Price, John Parry, W. D. Swayze, Charles Stevens, Henry Penny, J. R. Lalor, A. Boyle, Joseph Numby, R. F. Lattimer, William Edie, William Wilson, P. Johnston, C. T. Middaugh, Thomas Walters, Amos Baldwin, William Brown, E. Lee, Alexander Lattimer, George Vankeuren.

MUSKOKA AND PARRY SOUND.—William Gibson, E. F. Master, W. J. Sheppard, W. R. Beatty, John Gaina, D. Beatty, M, Rankin, T. S. Walton, A S. Smith, H. Brown, E. Hanes, J. H. Osborne, H. May, M. Fawcett, D. Cairns, D. C. Hahaffy, C. E. Mawdsley, S. Armstrong, F. W. Shaw, R. P. Perry, J. R. Higgins, W. C. Mahaffy, E. C. Roper, D. Srigley, S. C, D. Roper, F. G. Fauquier, R. J. Easton, G. McEachren, S. Clark, H. Swazze.

NORFOLK (South Riding).—Colonel Tisdale, A. McCall, Dr, J. Wilson, R. T. Livingstone, A. D. Ellis, Dr

IX.

Hayes, E. E. Ford, P. Mabee, A. N. Dunscombe, G. B. Jackson, George E. Curtis, George H. Luscombe, N. F. Sinden, Frederick Cope, H. D. Findlay, E. Matthews, J. C. Boyd, — O'Hendry, Joseph Brook, George Canfield, W. G. Pennington, William Wilson, Robert Hodgson, John Jackson, P. W. McGregor, John Nickerson, N. C. Ford, George Jackson, Thomas W. Walsh, John Dixon, Dr. J. F. Smith, William Wallace, James Jamieson, John Davis, Robert Law, G. H. Crysler, C. C. Kent, Neil McNeil, W. Nixon, H. Moore, H. Pope, Thomas Puzey, William Shand, Richard Stevens, Robert Waddell, C. McNeillidge, W. Rose, E. Gilbert, William Pope, Henry Robert, P. Lawson, O. Ansley, H. Ansley, Rev. H. Wilson, Henry McQueen, F. Morgan, James Riddell, D. Whiteside, Dr. Jolly, J. Stamp, Joseph Dunkin, Joseph McCall, Jas. Smyth, Dr. Kennedy, Robert Mabee, A. McLean, J. McKnight, E. M. Crysler, Dr. Tisdale, Thomas Roberts, Robert Ried, J. B. Wilson, A. Jamieson, S. B. Earl, H. Andrews, D. W. McCall, Thomas McCall, H. Cassels, Chas. Turvey, John Calvert, D. A. McCall, P. Rice, sr., George Price, John Caldwell, H. C. Gifford, Thomas Leedham, Thomas Howick, James McCrone, John Shaw, James Thompson, D. McInnes, William Dawson, C. P. Young, S. McCall, S. Kindry, J. Bottomley, James G. Secord, D. W. McCall, O. M. Smith, R. Shearer, A. Reid, John Machon, William Hunter, George Horton, W. C. Doyle, John Harvey, George Smyth, James Smith, C. W. Park, Dr. Stewart, S. N. Holt, James Hutchinson, R. Richardson, John H. Backhouse, A. Hutchinson, T. B. Dedrick, A. Dedrick, W. H. Barrett, Thomas Hutchinson, J. D. Price, A. M. Bennett, Dr. Pholan, George Cruise, J. L. Layman, O. Franklin, E. Tisdale, jr., E. Tisdale. sr., James Alward, N. Mansell, William Knowles, Thomas Barrett, J. R. Reid, J. Holtby, D. W. Boughner, Dr Tweedale, William Cowan, E. W. Siprell, M. Holmes, W. Morgan, C. Dickenson, M. White, J. Corner, C. Buck, J L. Buck, B. Birdsell, H. Walmsley, S. J. Graham, Robert Garnham, J. W. McGuire, James Boyd, M. Boughner, W. Stevenson, Joseph Collinson. S. Francis, H. Bradfield, H. Burrowes.

NORFOLK (North Riding).—John Allison, William Moulton, W. T. Boughner, John McClintock, R. F. Staples, John Bigham, Charles Wilson, Alexander Bell, J. Moulton, Thomas Naneckiville, Samuel Gregg, Samuel Nagle, Thomas Prouse, Robert Higham, James Bradburn, L. Walker, William Lawrie, Thomas Timnis, H. S. Teeter, Edward Lundy, J. C. Shannon, John R. Kestell, Dr. Merrick, Wilson McWhinnie, James Matthews, Ansley Heath, David Erwin, B. W. Thomas, William Armstrong, Bartholomew Hare, John Erwin, Jonathan Jull, John A. McLaren, John M. Lee, Nelson Clouse, Robert Coliver, William Heath, John Murphy, David Parney, John McNally, John J. Moore, Cosford Howey, Robert Erwin, Peter Banslough, Dr. L. C. Sinclair, P. Falls, John Thompson, W. S. Law, C. P. Smith, John Waterhouse, H. J. Caulfield, T. B. Tiltson, Joseph Luke, Peter Campbell, James R. Brown, Thomas Wood, Isaac Hogarth, R. C. Scott, T. Stoddart, Philip Andrich, J. N. Matthews, G. J. Rogers, James McKnight, Robert Wilson, Thomas Herron, Oliver Jarvis, R. M. Wilson, Edward Knight, William Ball, Elias Boughner, George Howey, Oliver Robertson, W. H. Teeter, Beckwith Sieton, Robert A. Clement, Stephen B. Pettit, James Robertson, James D. Clement, Henry Bartholomew, William Russel, John Blagney, John Cibbons, George Wood, George Hagerman, J. G. Bottomley, John Jull, Russel O. Snider, James W. Robertson, John Ostrander, John Burnett, Dr. J. M. Garvey, William Stilwell, J. C. H. Herron, James W. Whiteside, William Sandham, John Connor, John Langohr, W. A. Ferguson, Robert Powers, Robert Stoddart, Louis Voigt, Samuel Wilson, Thomas White, James L. Cowan, Roger Crysler, James Cowan, Dr. W. Mackay, Alexander Turnbull, Robt. Quance, William Mackay, Henry Wilkinson, Peter Quance, Jacob Lovereen, John Shepherd, Perez Dean, Philip McKim, John Richardson, John Armstrong.

NORTHUMBERLAND (West Riding).—A. Campbell, Benjamin Jackson, James Barnum, Major Rogers, Dr. Boyce, W. Mulholland, Josias Gillard, George Hares, John Stanley, Charles Gifford. George Wickes, Richard Croft, E. McIntosh, jr., D. Egleson, James Teney, S. Vanderburg, J. Coyle, John Thackery, John Braithwait, J. J. Muirhead, A. Sherar, G. Guillet, M. P., R. Mulholland, M.P.P., R. R. Pringle, J. V. Gravely, D. H. Murnaker, A. I. Hewson, I. A. Polkinghorne, H. F. Holland, H. B. Crusoe, J. R. Barber, T. O'Neill, E. H. Fogarty, I. Y. Cruikshanke, W. Battell, Dr. H. A. Craig, John Fetherston, John Purser, H. Tye, C. Elliott, M. B. William, R. Lunn, T. Rettallick, James Crossen, H. McKechnics, Thomas Hoskins, sr., G. W. Livingstone, R. Winch, E. A. McNeill, Charles Gifford, Robert Scarf, George Wickes, William Rosevar, M. Rosevar, R. Croft, J. Green, M. Dean, W. Noble, Samuel Pruser, jr., B. Bonskill, W. Ough, James Smith, D. Watt, jr., Thomas Moore, N. Smith, W. L. Burnham, Charles Garbutt, Robert Lowden, Henry Rosevar, E. Rowe, Edward Morton, William Drope, sr., C. H. Thompson, Henry Brown, D. McIntosh, jr., D. Eagleson, James Terry, S. Vandeburg, A. Patterson, I. C. Rosevar, A. Campbell, B. Jackson, Alexander Hall, H. Battell, W. Usher, Dr. Boyce, W. Mulholland, I. Gillard, J. Barnum, Major Rogers, George Hare, Joseph Doncaster, John Standley, Joseph Grosseau, John Stewart, James O'Brien, William Muirhead, John Mulholland, William Beatty, John Braithwaite, John Coyle, John Thackeray, W. Gregg, J. J. Muirhead, A. Shearer, Joseph Rosevar, Col. Boulton, Dr. H. A. Craig, A. E. Munson, B. McAllister, S. E. McCarthey, I. H. Hamilton, Dr. T. Rowe, Edward Phillips, H. Lye, C. White, John Greenwood, R. Lunm, John McCaughey, A. Barr, W. A. Deering, G. Guillet, M.P., R. Mulholland, M.P.P., H. F. Minaker, J. Vance Gravely, Mayor R. R. Pringle, J. A. Polkinghorne, R. H. Holland, H. B. Crusoe, James R. Barber, T. O'Neill, James Crossen, E. H. Fogarty, William Battell, Dr. Craig, M. B. Williams, John Purser, A. H. McDonald, A. J. Hewson, J. Roddick, R. Lunn, John Featherston, Thomas Retallick, J. F. Hamilton, J. Y. Cruickshank, George Featherside, George Vosper, Robert Wilson, W. W. Hooey, H. E. Barr, E. Gordon, W. Porter, W. Salisbury, John Mulholland, W. Jones, G. W. Bruce, R. E. Fier, H. N. Coates, N. B. Gash, S. G. Livingstone, H. W. Williams, H. W. Peck, J. F. Cochrane.

NORTHUMBERLAND (East Riding).—H. S. Casey, John Haig, J. Ketchum, E. Tuttle, F. McGuire, William Johnson, Dr. Willoughby, W. L. Payne, C. Head, James Cochrane, H. Hicks, D. L. Simmons, J. D. Silcox, J. G. Rosamond, W. W. Webb, Thomas Wannamaker, Robert Clark, John Lean, William Clendinning, Jas. Stanley, D. Ewing, Dr. Richards, W. H. Boyce, A. M. Hamilton, R. P. Hulbert, D. S. Pickworth, James H. Shinkle, Rev. W. Buchanan, O. Lessard, John Shinkle, Thomas Blizard, A. Speirs, W. German, R. Armour. George Flemming, W. E. Kemp, James Young, John Kelly, M. J. Doyle, J. B. Richards, W. Gerow, H. P. Gould, John W. Phillips, G. L. Duncan, William Pickworth, W. H. Cochrane, E. Cochrane, J. G. Murphy, W. Wade, A. P. Delaney, John Goodfellow, D. N. King, J. M. Cowan, Henry Belford, John Dusenbury, Alexander Anderson, Charles Ross, A. Wessels, J. A. McColl, W. W. Crews. H. McQuaid, John Abbott, Adam Young, J. Pilkey, A. Flemming, James Gulvin, D. Johnston, William Stillman, George Anderson, G. Bedford, — Hume, James Demondie, A. L. Colville, D. Waters, S. S. Thorue, Joseph Townsend, Dr. Byarn. R. W. Turner, P. Kennedy, H. Foulds, John Peters, P. Brennan, F. Foulds, Dr. O'Gorman, J. A. Howard.

ONTARIO (North Riding).—Robert Rowland, R. S. Webster, William Nelson, Allen Gray, Alexander Hardy, J. Blanchard, James W. Umphrey, John Scott, — Hagarman, Ed. Taylor, John Madill, Thos. Cain,

X.

W. Barton, Ml. Umphrey, Wm. Sinclair, Jas. McPherson, E. H. Herring, Allan McPherson, Thos. Coyne, J. S. Wardell, J. S. McPherson, Jas. Glendening, Hy. Brethour, R. Beard, Wm. Colquhoun, Jas. Brain, Wm. Taylor, Thos. Tran, Wm. Walker, Jas. Ruddy, Jas. Doble, Jno. Edward, Ed. Edward, Jas. St. John, sr., Richard Penhall, M. Gillespie, A. J. Sinclair, Dr. Gillespie, H. Wilson, C. McClelland, R. Wallace, John Twohey, J. J. Risdon, J. McArthur, J. Nutting, W. Foster, R. Gilbertson, A. McFadyen, J. Reynolds, A. W. Cooper, W. Tarbox, D. H. McRae, Thos. Cooper, Alex. Later, B. H. Johnston, W. Robertson.

ONTARIO (North Riding).—C. H. Davidson, Frank Madill, J. A. Proctor, B. Madill, G. R. Proctor, A. Hamilton, Jas. Gordon, John Harrison, Thos. McCullough, H. Waller, J. Duncan. H. Musgrove, W. McRae, sr., Geo. Suter, Robt. Gibson, Laura McKay, Angus McDougall, Donald McTaggart, F. W. McRae, Geo. Drake, Alex. McNeil, Wm. Bain, Archibald Currie, Angus Gillespie, Thomas McEachren, Wm. Skinner, Wm. Brain, Hugh Stoddart, James McCaul, N. Gordon, Thomas Treleaven, T. C. Hodgkinson, C. A. Paterson, John McRae, Charles Galloway, Alexander McRae, Reeve; James Donnell, W. Westcott, F. McCuaig, Frank McRae, J. P., F. B. Brown, John McArthur, E. H. Cameron, P. D. McArthur, Alex. Cameron, D. Gillespie, R. T. Turner, W. Osborne, Peter Walls, Jas. A. Bell, Chas. Thompson, John Kennedy, Dan. McBride M. Brennan, William Daly, William Glassford, Ronald Sillers, Andrew St. John, Aaron Madill, John Murray, J. S. McMillan, Robert Hodgson, Charles McArthur, P. McDougall, James White, S. Parsons, Ed. Tisdale, W. Hamilton, W. Campbell, Jas. White, jr., Wm. Martin.

ONTARIO (South Riding).—D. Burns, D. Wells, F. C. Brown, Thomas Downey, H. E. Derby, Thomas Hodgson, George Matchell, J. Higgins, Lewis Luke, D. McGee, J. Hyland, W. Smith, B. McQuay, F. W. Gibbs, D. C. Downey, Dr. Bogart, J. H. Long, H. Jeffrey, J. C. Wesley, Wm. Burns, John Smith, C. Fox, Dr. Gunn, N. Ray, Col. O'Donovan, Wm. Barnes, Thos. Deverell, U. H. Billings, Joseph Rutledge, J. B. Dow, R. H. Lauder, J. Stanton, U. R. House, L. Sebert, L. Armstrong, J. Farquharson, C. E. Ray, D. Whitney, J. A. Watlin, L. Fairbanks, Thos. Lawlor, Thos. Dow, Thomas McCann, Wm. Thompson, Dr. Adams, G. Gibson, John Spurill, J. Newport, J. O'Donovan, Jos. Pearn, J. B. Powell, Joseph Black, D. O'Leary, C. E. Gross, W. Granger, E. J. Johnston, M. Collins, G. McGillivray, John Fothergill, W. Alguire, George Hickingbother, D. Galbraith, L. Hoack, W. H. Crosby, John Bernard, H. Howell, N. F. Patterson, E. Magee, H. Parnis, C. Dawes, S. Bruce, Orr Graham, Dr. McLinton, James Prince, H. Charles, J. Cork, J. Lawder, T. S. Corrigan, U. S. Parish, James Boxall, J. Thompson, T. V. Raines, C. Henderson, B. F. Ackerman, J. Wright, A. Reynolds, J. Nicharry, F. M. Yarrold, James Graham, John Adams, L. Savage, C. Hood, John Miller, S. Stephenson, A. Johnston, J. Mitchell, J. Baxter, P. Gorman, John Cuthbert, T. C. McAvery, D. Burrell, R. Miller, J. Lery, E. Boone, J. Linton, T. Moody, T. Barnett, William Cochrane, J. McCreight, V. Glenn, W. Pitt, A. McKay, J. Lawrence, Joseph Hartip, W. Sadler, T. Lay, J. Lawton, B. Brynal, Wm. Smith, A. Wheton, William Magee, John Sleigh, B. Graham, W. Mitchell, C. Mitchell, T. Mitchell, N. Stevenson, A. Perkins, J. L. Jones, Frank Jones, S. Jones, J. Hartip, William Musgrove, J. A. Douglas, F. Smith, H. Graham, John Graham, John Bell, James Hoyle, Thomas Poucher, R. Miller, jr., Dr. Freel, J. Linton, William Jones, P. Larkin, J. O'Shea, Robert Kinnon, John Burk, George Levy, C. Percy, George Gibson, George Lery, jr., Thomas C. Johnston, William Davitt, R. Jackson, S. Lankin, A. Hubbard, William Goodwin, William Vinty, Thomas R. Smith, B. Gibson, J. Corbett, J. L. Smith, J. Crawford, Thomas McBrien, S. Medland, E. A. McBrien, J. Vipard, D. Burns, W. Main, R. Main, W. McBrien, F. W. Hodgson, J. Stephenson, H. H. Spencer, J. Medland, Thomas Stephenson, Thomas Cluin, R. Moore, —. Fitzgerald, T. Burt, J. Reed, W. F. Cowan, W. H. Gibbs, W. Coulthard, W. H. Thomas, W. T. Dingle, T. M. Shirley, C. A. Jones, J. S. Larke, T. W. Gibbs, R. S. Hamlin, John A. Carswell, E. B. Morgan, Joseph Gould, William Warren, H. Finnemore, T. H. McMillan, C. Scott, R. Dillon, M. Western, C. Law, P. Wall, W. Lang, O. C. Rowse, E. I. Rowse, H. Lang, Dr. Belt, J. Ray, J. Woon, W. Deans, C. Williamson. John Jeffrey, T. G. Hawthorn, O. McNider, W. J. Hare, Charles Crysdale, William Stephenson, Joseph Craig, James Pellow, John Carter, John Warr, J. Brooks, W. H. Warner, W. T. Atkinson, L. English, John Gibson, R. Kirkpatrick, A. E. Luke, George Annand, M. Brooks, H. B. F. Odell, A. Hall, Mr. Lee, Mr. Leek, John Derry, A. Hinds, M. Kirkpatrick, John Wilson, jr., James Wilson, W. H. Hunter, F. Warren, A. Carswell, John Hyland, William Luke, C. N. Vars, George Rice, W. H. Holland, John O'Regan, George Gould, C. Kirby. John Thornton, C. H. Sweetapple, S. Sleep, Edward Carswell, T. Cornish, W. H. Stanton, Rev. A. B. Demill, James Cochrane, L. Prudholm, Arthur Farewell, George Pedlar, Thomas Pinder, W. Hodgson, H. Bickle, G. Blight, J. Morrison, C. Caulder, W. Robb, Dr. Warren, A. Darlington, J. Wood, H. Meen, J. Pherrill, W. Bowles, M. Phreney, John C. Day, James Walker, R. Clay, H. Langford, W. H. Bryant, J. McBrien, S. S. Williams, E. Hodges, W. Verslake, G. Medland, William Hoar, A. Duff, H. E. Derby, George Bickle, John Davis, A. Wilson, T. Wilson, J. Ronty, Major Hodgson, J. C. Fox, John Mothersill, Richard Robins, Charles White, William Cleveden, George Annard, H. B. Odell, John Bartlett, Isaac Higgins, Reuben Hamlin, James Jenkins, Henry Robbins, Richard Luke, Thomas Luke, George Bechel, J. Hurrey, J. Hyland, Tim Leonard, John Brooking, D. McGee, William Batty, William Bain, J. Horn, Wm. Brusher, William Dunn, George Hyland, H. B. Howard, William Unwin, J. Thomas, Henry Davis, Joseph Street, John Lankin, J. Ross, W. Hazelwood, J. Hazelwood, J. Stock, J. Martin, H. Howden, George Minty, Walter Hodgson, C. Hodgson, William Bright, William Thompson, John Moffatt, Thomas Noffal, James Harper, S. Williams, C. Allens, William Howden, William Brent, John A. Nackerville, J. Ashton, A. J. Smith, C. Ross, William Smith, J. D. Howden, R. D. Power, Robert Hodgson, F. Richardson, William Richardson, M. Gaskin, L. Grass, W. H. Browne, J. Goodman, William Beith, Thomas Perryman, C. Stuback, Thomas Wilerston, F. Garfitt, William Blyth, S. Roberts, James Smallcomb, George Wichett, James White, Robert Wilerston, P. Christie, Joseph Bairn, D. Christie, E. Link, G. Lawton, E. Christie, N. J. Browne, William Crosier, C. McLane, Thomas W. Porter, A. Eurchman, N. Costello, William Foster, F. Elliot, R. Strath, James Wilson, Joseph Bryant, Phil. Whitney, James Caruthers, James Compton, George St. John, John Stobel, H. Gregg, E. Alton, William Stoven, John Howsan, S. Douglas, J. Dewer, J. Murton, James Gregg, William Real, Joseph Burton, D. Perkins, Robert Branson, James Burrs, George Byers, John McLeod, Ed. Newton, S. Graham, William Scott, James McFarlane, James Gibon, James Broad, Robert Muron, William Marks, James Baird, John Caulder, John Lamb, Solomon Wilson, A. Beattie, John Miller, W. H. Parks, James Long, William Spence, John Martin, William Weir, John Bryce, Fethis Epter, John Bell, James Strong, James Baird, D. Wheler, J. Coates, George Jackson, Robert Johnston, James Kilpatrick, James Browne, James Dobson, Joseph McConnell, W. C. Heard, S. W. Christian, John Rolph, James Holtby, Wm. Pearson, N. Bates, Edward Stickney, Thos. Choalin, John Parker, John Saunders, William T. Christie.

ONTARIO (West Riding).—J. A. McGillivary, George Lolley, George Gray, J. P. Galloway, E. R. Anderson, R. Etwell, Wm. Hogg, Jno. Noble, George Hobson, R. R. Hubbard, T. M. DeGeer, William Ruddy.

XI.

James Nokes, George Sharp, T. Bolster, sr., R. J. Butler, James Peters, sr., W. Johnson, sr., W. Hamilton sr., James Richards, Jno. Bascom, J. A. Sinclair, J. N. Towle, M. Vicars, William Low, William Johnston, jr., H. S. Peters, J. Blight, A. S. Hardy, Dr. Nation, George Evans, S. B. Todd, Jno. Fogg, H. H. Cook, Jno. McCullough, R. W. Gilpin, Jno. Whitney, H. T. Johnston, William Henry, C. Kelly, R. Doble, R. Nelson, W. Worthington, M. J. Malone, James Madill, C. Conway, H. Madill, F. Mooney, L. Lapp.

OTTAWA CITY.—Joseph Tasse, M. P., C. H. Mackintosh, M.P , Ald. Desjardins, Al'. Laverdure, Ald. Durocher, A. D. Richard, William McEvels, H. Robinson, Captain Bowie, Alexander Forsey, E. Morel, J. A. Pinard, M. Durocher, Thomas Keough, George Goodwin, G. J. O'Doherty, J. Goulden, D. Deslorges, J. B. Ariel, James Brown, L. A. Oliver, J. B. C. Dunn, Ed. Lablanc, J. S. McCracken, P. Baskerville, Ald. Heney, M. Starrs, John Casey, P. H. Chabot, T. Lamey, N. A. Savard, John Crawford, D. Morin, Louis Gratton, W. O. McKay, Ald. Swalwell, Thomas Birkett, J. L. Richard, E. Chevrier, Alexander Chevrier, L. J. Lussier, Dr. Valade, Oscar McDonell, John Cawthray, J. Reardon, William Howe, James Warnock, H. Robillard, Ald. Erratt, Ald. Willans, William Cowan, William Davis, M. P. Davis, T. W. Currier, Emmanuel Tasse, S. Borbridge, William Kerr, John Stewart, H. G. Roche, John Bruice, F. McCullough, Dr. Coleman, R. Montgomery, T. Cundell, S. Rogers, Dr. McDougall, G. A. Harris, H. Meadows, W. Borthwick, G. H. Taylor, E. Mahon, George Howe, W. H. Baldwin, A. Chatfield, C. T. Bate, F. Clemow, D. O'Connor, Dr. Grant, Charles Magee, H. F. MacCarthy, J. W. McRae, Dennis Murphy, J. A. Gouin, John Graham, A. Stewart, F. J. Boswell, H. J. Boswell, A. S. Woodburn, A. Ferguson, Ald. Cox, Ald. Lewis, Ald. Cherry, William McKay, J. Latchford, T. Butler, H. Alexander, J. Barnes Dunn, J. Johnston, A. Woodcock, L. L. Grison, W. Beckett, J. Currie, William Mosgrove, W. A. Allan, Alexander Grant, William Stewart, Wm. McCaffery, P. C. Anclair, Joseph Kavanagh, M. Kavanagh, A. J. Christie, Jos. R. Esmonde, Dennis Egan, John McKenna, Charles Brennan, E. C. Barber, C. S. Shaw, F. R. Bysche, E. Dupois, Dr. Church, John Rochester, J. R. Booth, W. G. Perley, Ald. Gordon, Ald. Whelan, J. B. Abbott, John Baskerville, E. McGillivary, C. Gagne, W. R. Baldwin, T. J. Richardson, G. R. Kingsmill, Hugh Alexander, R. D. O'Brien, McLeod Stewart.

OXFORD (North Riding).—William Lark, William Donaldson, William Moysey, R. Woon, Daniel Lark, George Hargett, Alexander Marks, Henry Glavis, Thomas Rowe, James Holloway, John Session, Daniel Dougherty, Henry Jolve, Jos. Hutchinson, Conrad Seltive, John Peacock, Timothy Stanby, Dr. Clement, William Thompson, Al. Harwood, John Mulvin, John Donaldson, John Blair, George Walker, Hugh Frazer, R. D. Innes, J. W. Tate, Charles Young, John Blair, Elijah Cody, Dr. Adams, Captain Goodwin, Dr. Duncan, John McConkey, Thomas McConkey, Robert Innes, John Barwick, T. Wilford, Samuel Wallace, Jos. Stevenson. W. B. Wilson, Thomas Chambers, William Virtue, Isaac Thompson, John Glavis, Henry Chesing, Thomas Hart, Thomas Alger, Thomas Dent, Henry Huntingford, R. W. Buss, Charles Burns, William Crosley, Arthur Tew, Adam Oliver, Elam Martin, Joseph Long, Charles Miler, Captain Williamson, Francis Galbraith, George Clark, David Maynard, George Eandicock, Thomas Boles, C. A. Minna, George Harrison, D. French, John Pollock, J. G. NcNee, Samuel Toil, Dr. Sparks, John Towit, A. S. Shepherd, C. Brock, Hugh Kennedy, James Potter, John Potter, Charles Wilson, R. Martin. Joseph Fletcher, J. Covinting, F. Hayward, William Grey, Alexander Finkle, J. Pyke, John Barwick, A. W. Francis, J. B. Doyle, James O'Rourke, Dr. Thrall, Dr. Swan, W. H. Millman, D. M. Pirsey, S. G. Burgess, R. Burgess, M. M. Nisbitt, William Muir, William Wilson, S. Tregant, H. Martin, Henry Hill, James Mapson, M. Stewart, J. G. McKay, Charles Eltom, A. K. Roomer, S. Clarke, Edward Chambers, John Hart, James King, James T. G. King, William Bishop, William Whitcomb, William McKay, William McIntyre, Joseph H. Nillis, Robert Williams, R. Woodruff, B. Sheppard, William Maynard, W. Heyden, J. A. Spracklin, Angus Dent, Robert Hall, George Gordon, John O'Neill, Jarvis Thompson, Joseph Blackburn, George Harwood, John Glendenning, John Pascoe, M. Fury, James Gamlin, F. K. Chaplin, G. Hamon Grime, J. G. Eddington, A. A. W. Hastings, John Barwick, William Donaldson.

OXFORD (South Riding).—H. S. Anderson, Jno. Henderson, D. A. Kirk, William Strode, H. J. Adams, L. F. Bungay, E. C. Cook, Dr. Hill, Dr. Curdy, Dr. Sutherland, W. H. Stinson, G. C. Sutton, J. A. Tidy, George Walker, W. R. Brown, J. H. Robinson, Thomas Tims, Thomas Taylor, John Downing, S. Gregg, Jno. Coventry, John Fishlee, Edward Jarvis, J. S. Henderson, Alexander Bell, Thomas Henderson, J. W. Chambers, James Mighton, James Haylow, J. L. Peers, D. Chambers, A. McClenegan, M. Walsh, Dr. Williams, Henry Rowland, A. Allen, G. Cramer, W. Sudworth, Thomas Henderson, W. Holcroft.

PEEL.—Abraham Black, James Richey, John Breaden, Herald Scholfield, Arthur B. Harris, Thomas Goldthrope, Gaylord Grenious, William C. Oughtreed, Charles G. Hamilton, George Grafton, Chas. Lynn, Daniel M. Sharp, John Davis, Samuel Richey, Charles Pallett, John Curry, Deazley Graham, Alexander Griffith, Thomas Pallett, Francis Shaver, Robert McCarter, William A. McCulla, James Hamilton, Sir M. Parker, Eli Crawford, Rev. Father Cassidy, Rev. Father Morris, R. P. Campbell, A. F. Campbell, Westley Wright, Thomas O'Shaughnessy, William Webb, C. Robinson, William Andrew, — Lawrence, Jas. Campbell, Charles A. Schillar, James Jackson, Nathan Elliott, Thomas Graham, George Cheyne, William Tilt, Johnston Goulding, George Gooderham, Alfred Adamson, George Crozier, John C. Crozier, Clarence Conover, Wm. Crozier, Alex. Mitchell, Wm. Magrath, Thomas Newman, Joseph Rogers, James Sprowl, Samuel Wolf, Aran Gummerson, William Hopkins, Hugh Kee, George McLelland, John Price, A. Brunskill, John W. Beynon, Dr. C. Y. Moore, B. J. Juston, S. Vasbruder, R. Blain, J. J. Manning, Captain Miller, James Thurston, Alex. Blakeley, John Thomson, John Appleby, Allen Laughead, John L. Leary, James McCracken, Robert Steen, Nathaniel Steen, Joseph Armstrong, George Evans, Joseph Graham, Young Moore, Thomas Reed, William Bell, William Price, James Alderson, William J. Arnott, John Beatty, Thomas Fogerty, Samuel Cantling, Henry Carten, Wm. Graydon, John Graydon, W. Justin, J. McClure, Wm. McKenzie, John C. Rutledge, Robert Ramsay, Thomas Ballinger, Edward Rutledge, Isaac Wiley.

PERTH (North Riding).—E. Garting, C. Schaffer, H. Schencker, Wm. Burton, W. D. Weir, C. Witle, W. Wilson, R. Martin, George Hess, Dr. Michener, George Draper, H. B. Morphy, A. St. E. Hawkins. John Sutherland, Robert Roth, George Tilliax, John Gable, R. Woods, B. B. Sarvis, Dr. Philip, William Hess, Dr. Dingman, B. Bothwell, H. H. O'Reilly, William Binning, J. Livingstone, jr., Adam Hess, H. E. Karn, R. H. Henderson, J. Lee, R. Kemp, W. Mitchell, William Elliott, D. D. Campbell, John Binning, Dr. Burgess, George Towner, S. Bricker, G. J. Collins, George McKiever, Owen Wilson, Wm. Welch, J. Watson, Adam Torrence, A. Large, James Carson, John Martin, Moses Lang, John Watson, W. B. Freeborn, Thos. Maywood, John McKee, James Roe, James Gibson, Wm. White, Ed. Anderson, Michael Franscombe, Richard Strong, Wm. King, John Willoughby, Alex. Kennedy, Thomas Greer, James Moffatt, D. Scrimgeour, J. Q.

Monteith, S. S. Fuller, A. Caven, J. M. Moran, C. F. Neild, J. D. Riddell, Thomas Patterson, Thos. Burr, H. T. Barker, J. R. Woods, J. G. Smith, J. Abraham, T. Hagerty, Dr. Hanavan, S. R. Hesson, M.P., J. M. Johnston, S. Long, G. W. Lawrence, John Corrie, John Stewart, J. M. Liddell, J. O'Donohoe, W. Guy, R. Larmour, M. Cleary, W. H. Winstone, J. Robb, G. T. Jones, John Pearson, Fras. Rushton, W. H. Coulton, Peter Brimmer, P. Shibert, Charles Elligsen, Wm. Sykes, Thomas Kelley, P. H. Kelly, S. Henry, E. Brodhagen, D. A. Dempsey, Andrew Kuhry, Wm. Baumbach, Robert Hanna, Patrick McDonald, John Jacob, F. Ullerich, Jacob Ney, George Leversage, Thomas Hanson, D. L. Caven, D. Matthews, John Clark, E. J. Beattie, H. Sheard, H. Symons, T. I. Knox, James Alexander, J. G. Alexander, Joseph Henderson, M. Harvey, Dr. Hamilton, Young Coulter, A. W. Fetherston, James Irwin, George Richmond, Samuel Rce, John Stevenson, S. S. Rothwell, Thomas Fullarton, James Boyd, Thomas Carter, Wm. Sweeten, C. McKenzie, James Smith, W. Jackson, Thomas Later, John Mann, Wm. Gibson, H. Hasenpflug, H. Schnenker, William Burton, W. D. Weir, C. Witte, C. Shaffer, W. Wilson, E. Gartung, Emil Hess, William Stevenson, H. T. Cutler.

PERTH (South Riding).—H. F. Sharp, James Clark, G. F. Robbins, Dr. Hall, K. Waring, M. Hart, R. T. Gilpin, H. A. L. White, E. S. Smith, Jos. Thompson, J. B. Abbott, T. D. Stanley, S. Fraleigh, W. H. Gilpin, J. Shamholts, J. W. Guest, Robert Guest, W. Moyles, James Chalmers, A. Carman, George Spearin, Wm. Adams, W. V. Hutton, John Bartlett, J. H. Carter, E. A. Hogg, Dr. Harrison, J. W. Cathcart, Wm. Coleman, Robert Eaton, Richard Gleeson, Thomas Bennett, Wm. Dunseith, John Hudson, David Murray, Francis McCracken, Robert Stewart, Joseph Stafford, Dr. McKay, David Marriott, Jerry White, George Lyons, H. O'Dett, Dr. Guest, James Whitson, Rev. Jas. Hannon, J. Willard, M. J. Beam, Dr. McCullough, Henry Monteith, Nelson Monteith, Wm. Douglass, jr., C. McNamara, Arthur Robb, W. A. Monteith, John A. Thistle, M. Steele, R. A. Buck, Samuel Monteith, David Mills, Joseph Case, Thomas Coates, I. McKay, Robert Creery, James Halls, Alexander Duncan, Jonathan Shier, Henry Doupe, D. W. Dulmair, James Hanford, Ichabod Bowerman, N. J. Clark, Robert Thompson, Wm. Buckingham, John Glen, Wm. Blackwell, John Delbridge, Wm. Taylor, Leonard Hunter, John McCurdy, James Burns, John T. Crawford, W. J. Campbell, G. D. Lowrie, Wm. Dickenson, Wm. Graham, A. Sawyer, Joseph Mieghan, John Burns, Neil Maloy, Richard Francis, John Cole, Wm. Hanson, James Gourlay, Francis Standeven, J. Dougherty, J. Skinner, J. W. Cull, R. W. Keeler, James Wilson, Thos. McClay, Wm. Etty, H. McIntyre, sr., A. Dent, Alex. Thompson, W. R. Davis, H. McIntyre, jr., William White, G. Skinner, W. S. McCullough, Jno. Broderick, Frank Carling, G. Davidson, S. R. Stewart, Fred. Goebel, R. Babb.

PETERBOROUGH (West Riding).—John Carnegie, George Burnham, M.P., J. E. Hammond, Jas. Stevenson, F. O'Meara, G. W. Hatton, T. M. Willan, George Hilliard, M.P., A. P. Pousette, W. H. Moore, E. Phelan, Rev. B. Clementi, John Douglas, E. Green, C. W. Sawyers, R. Muncaster, G. W. Hall, Joseph Buller, John Dogherty, H. Lebrun, E. A. Peck, H. Rush, R. H. Green, W. H. Robertson, T. Cavanagh, C. McGrath, E. Dunford, Wm. English, L. Potvin, H. Letellier, J. Corkery, P. Cunningham, Joseph Barbeau, Jos. Breault, S. Payne, W. E. Whitehair, P. McDonnell, M. O'Donnell, H. C. Stapleton, James Hope, John Baptie, A. Sawers, R. P. Boucher, Charles Stapleton, E. J. Toker, T. Rutherford, Wm. Logan, John E. Belcher, John Craig, M. Faucett, Hon. R. Hamilton, W. H. Hall, Wm. Lasher, J. G. Macklin, J. G. Macdonald, George Noble, W. H. Rackham, Wm. Trotter, A. Vinnette, Jos. Wilson, Wm. Detcher, J. McClelland, W. A. Kelsey, B. Shortley, C. S. Wallis, Wm. Cluxton, L. F. Carpenter, George Webber, R. W. Thompson, Joseph Sproule, Terrice Guerin, Wm. Logan, P. Heffernan, John Garvey, R. A. Morrow, A. Williams, Thomas Kelly, John Sawers, James Kendry, Dr. Burritt, A. Hall, W. H. Wrighton, J. E. Hammond, S. Masson, T. Laplante, J. Hackett, M. Giroux, A. Elliott, James English, W. Snowden, H. Owens, N. T. Laplante, H. Phelan, T. E. Fitzgerald, H. Libey, H. Best, James Picard, T. McGrath, A. Comstock, James Stewart, Geo. Stethem, T. Sabin, J. McNamara, H. C. Winch, Wm. Croft, H. Charman, John Lynch, Dr. Halliday, A. St. A. Smith, Dr. Kincaid, Wm. Langford, R. Rowe, D. Breeze, John Delaney, jr., Wm. Fitzgerald, F. W. Hilliard, F. Mason, John W. Miller, T. M. Croley, W. McCall, John Parnell, C. Rutherford, C. Wynne, Jas. Wason, A. Dawson, H. Robinson, A. McNeil, G. W. Hatton, H. Long, G. W. Rubbidge, R. W. Errett, John Brownlee, Joseph Huston, B. Laurin, W. H. Chamberlain, Col. Poole, J. W. Alford, A. Gibson, John Bell, John O'Mara, W. Garbutt, John Preston, Alex. Scott, J. Hetherington, Geo. Chalmers, E. Fitzgerald, M. Galvin, C. Blewett, S. Nicholls, J. Trennum, J. Northey, sr., Charles Moore, Robert Rossborough, D. Costelloe, G. W. Fitzgerald, L. Davis, Joseph Miller, Samuel Nugent, P. Young, jr., Alex. Fitzgerald, E. Bulmer, W. Blewett, H. W. Pearson, W. Pearson, R. Harrison, Alex. Roseborough, Samuel Roseborough, John Moore, James Bennett, James Brealey, Matthew Johnson, G. McKee, James Hawden, John Harper, J. J. Greene, R. Waterman, J. K. Moore, Capt. Dundass, Joseph Foster, Robert Dunlop, Thomas Armstrong, Wm. Collins, J. J. Bennett, Samuel Bennett, James Brown, A. Young, R. Parker, R. Morse, H. Waddell, W. McAllister, W. Huggan, Joseph Clark, J. M. Willan, J. W. Lucas, W. Greer, R. Lang, sr., Wm. Embuson, Thomas Telford, J. Cadigan, Thomas Sullivan, Robert Calvert, D. Shanahan, P. Brick, P. Costello, M. O'Reilly, Alex. Clark, George Rivington, M. Doran.

PETERBOROUGH (East Riding).—R. C. Strickland, Frederick Barlee, Isaac Garbutt, sr., John Dinwoodie, B. Eden, J. Moore, J. Horner, W. J. Sanders, J. Blewett, J. Nelson, G. W. R. Strickland, F. Dinwoodie, A. I. Wright, J. Rogers, William Cox, sr., J. Griffin, J. P. Strickland, Dr. Armour, J. Cooper, Giles Stone, H. J. Le Fevre, W. J. Wallace, T. Recroft, R. Chapin, Isaac Watson, sr., A. Wilson, R. Hill, James Morrison, L. Stone, John Sutton, Sparham Sheldrade, T. Grieve, L. Steele.

PRESCOTT.—P. Garreau, J. A. Macdonald, P. Labrosse, J. Boileau, E. A. Johnson, L. Charbonneau, Simon Labrosse, M.P.

PRINCE EDWARD.—M. McQuaig, D. B. Solmes, John Abercrombie, Adam H. Taylor, Hamilton Lepero, L. B. Stinson, E. Merrill, R. Clapp, T. C. Demill, James N. Bolter, W. H. Cotter, S. J. Cotter, J. B. Cronk, R. A. Brooks, G. Allison, Isaac Crow, P. F. McQuaig, J. N. Carter, Thomas E. Owens, W. J. Conger, George O. Alcorn, James Walmsley, George E. Fraser, N. Walt, Thomas Waring, J. F. Dougall, R. A. Foster, David Macaulay, J. S. McQuaig, Maxwell Lepere, A. A. Corkindale, James Love, Dr. Evans, J. Heffernan, H. V. Carson, F. White, Thomas G. Carson, Cornelius Clapp, George Ballie, G. J. Chadd, J. B. Garratt, D. C. Clarke, D. S. Hicks, T. J. Howard, Dr. E. Kidd, H. Mandeville, Hugh McCulloch, Thomas Mongard, R. Noxon, M. Osterhout, L. B. Stinson, W. Lane, A. C. Dulmage, D. McGibbon, John Fegan, Samuel Clapp, N. Hudgins, Z. Polmateer, N. Hicks, D. Clinton, W. Clinton, J. B. Ruttan, M. D., S. Savage, Alva Platt, John Rillis, R. P. Niles, R. C. Reynolds, John Young, P. C. Vanhorn, James Calnan, H. H. Huyck, George Chadd, R. A. Norman, A. H. Saylor, A. B. Saylor, R. Saylor, A. Huyck, John

XIII.

Bull, R. Burr, J. Terwilliger, Donald Ross, E. B. Hazzard, S. J. Bowerman, Parker Young, Joseph Redmond, E. Gerrow, John Abercrombie, James Gibson, John Kenny, P. Bond, John Gibson, R. F. Hubbs, John Prenyer, Allen Caven, John Caven, Alexander Shannon, P. Macaulay, P. McMahon, A. Dame, Angus Stanton, M. Harrison, George Hulbert, Richard Dame, J. Heffernan, T. D. Noxon, N. Cooper, N. S. Demill, Parker Young, George Martin, Elias Young, John Waring, James Walmsley, Thomas Walmsley, Robert E. Clark, C. A. Macdonald, J. G. Murray, W. Boulter, R. B. Turnbull, John Welbanks, James C. Wilson, Charles S. Wilson, L. Vance, R. Gourley, J Mottashed, Jacob Fralick, James Fralick, B. Aylesworth, Thomas Ker, Angus H. Harrison, Henry Van Black, James Ker, Thomas Ker, C. J. Bongard, A. Davidson, T. L. Connors, E. Powers, James Carson, R. Miller, jr., Joseph Miller, R. David, W. Ker, Joseph Pearson, John Byers, James Porter, M. Marsh. W. Delong, W. R. Dempsey, W. Peck, E. Walbridge, W. E. Anderson, W. A. Brickman, Jno. R. Anderson, John Anderson, James Anderson, A. R. Hunt, J. E. Glenn, J. Robertson, J. H. Osterhout, J. Johnston, W. Anderson.

RENFREW (North Riding).—John Dunlop, Robert De La Hay, Robert Coburn, Jno. McDonald, Jno. De La Hay, Dr. Rattray, James Murdock, W. B. Coleman, James Bulmer, Robert Bulmer, W. Wallace, jr. Alexander Frazer, A. T. Mansell, S. A. Huntington, H. R. Wigelsworth, F. Weedmark, Dr. Channanhouse, C. W. Boland, James Bowes, M. Andrews, James Rowan, Robert Martin, Joseph Biggs, Thomas Deacon, P. White, M. P., T. H. Burritt, M. J. Gorman, Archibald Foster, Dr W. W. Dickson, H. W. Perrett, W Beatty, R. G. Scott, U. H. McKimm, W. R. White, Edward Clarke, D. C. Chamberlain, W. J. Douglas, A. Dunlop, W. H. Deacon, M. Howe, R. C. Percival, W. B. McAllister, James White, J. J. O'Meara.

RENFREW (South Riding).—Michael Galvin, B. V. Stafford, J. Butler, J. A. Macdonald, J. Harvey, D McNamara, A. Campbell, W. W. Sterling, E. Harrington, W. Allan, H. A. Devine, James Curtis, S. Whelan, R. Proctor, J. Maloney, A. J. Morrow, Michael Ryan, W. Richards, W. Gorman, R. Turner, W. Foster, J. C. Williams, A H. Johnston, A. Duff, J. Murphy, A. Barnet, P. Devine, M. J. O'Brian, P. Kelly, James Carswell, C. Enright, Michael French, C. J. Scott, P. McRea, J. Clark, M. Fitzmaurice, J. J Devine, J. R. McDonald.

RUSSELL.—Pierce Mansfield, James Stevenson, John Tylter, James Spratt, W. Mansfield, R. McDonald, W. Graham, H. Robillard, W. Helmer, R. Wilson, Joseph Quesnell, O. Richer, R. Doran, J. Whiteside, H. Tompkins, W. B. Dickinson, M. M. Annable, P. H. Cassidy, D. H. Eastman, John Askwith, N. W. Clark, Robert Cummings, Robert Clark, B. Rathwell, J. J. Smith, W. H. Lowrie, W. R. Dickinson.

SIMCOE (North Riding).—James Hamilton, John McBride, F. Hewson, James Leatch, W. Bourchier, Archibald Drown, Henry McCutcheon, James Bridges, Archibald McDearmid, Joseph Stinson, John Gray, Thomas Robinson, jr., Neil McEachren, Dr. Kirkland, Charles Lawrence, John Bell, W. H. Cross, Arthur Clark, W. J. Watson, William Forgie, E. B. Sanders, John Algee, John D. MacMadely, C Todd, N. Grose, William Harvey, D. Ellis, Henry O'Neill, R. Leadley, C. F. Waller, D. Garvin, James Johnson. John Kent, W. J. Orr, Dr. Oliver, S. S. Saunders, H. H. Strathy, B. Hinds, R. King, sr., G. A. Radenhurst, James Anderton, F. E. Pepler, M. Shanacy, F. J. Brown, J. Scroggie, T. Lennox, T. Kennedy, S. Wesley, F. Edwards, E. H. Williams, E. Burns, T. Purvis, J. A. McCarthy, R. R. Holt, R. K. Parkes, T. Long, G. Moberly, C. Gamon, F. Telfer, Dr. Campbell, J. Rowland, T. A. Brown, R. Brudette, J. McLean, James Mitting, J. Lindsay, W. Swain, Capt. Wheeler, A. Wheeler, A. Dudgeon, C. Cameron, C. Stephens, H. Trott, C. McDonnell, A. Lockerbie, Alex. Clark, P. Doherty, D. Fleming, D. Stephen, D. McGuire, T. W. Brady, W. A. Hogg, A. Cameron, Wm. Switzer, M. Harkin, Isaac Carter, W. Scott, William Miller, Joseph Johnston, John McKay, John Lott, Edward Mackay, Oliver Carson, J. Carlton, William McKay, W. J. Flack, J. McNaught, Dr. Wylie, M. Carlton, Arthur Clark, T. W. Fair

SIMCOE (South Riding).—W. Stewart, Dr. Armstrong, W. Fisher, Captain Sutherland, R. W. Booth, Dr. Modill, J. C. Hart, W. MacWhinney, Captain McClarn, Jos. Colborne, W. J. Parkhill, M. P. P., R. S. Campbell, Thomas Hand, John Murphy, Thomas Raburn, M. Colquhoun, R. Gallagher, J. W. Norris, M.D., John Stewart, Dr. Buchanan, Col. R. T. Banting, C. Cook, J. Boddy, Wm. Black, J. A. Campbell, W. R. Coleman, E. A. Fawcett, O. R. Ferguson, George T. Fisher, John Rainey, John Ross, John Lennox, William Crispin, Reuben Mathews, Frank Ross, Henry Sloan, J. W. Sloan, Robert Sproule, A. Gregg, John Beatty, S. Coulter, A. Edgar, C. Grose, B. Hill, H. Grose, J. P., George Wallace, H. Grose, jr., G. P. McKay, M.P.P., Dr. Callighan, T. Connelly, William Howie, James Hunt, J. A. Stewart, Stewart Wright, John Hopkins, S. T. Reynolds, James Black, Isaiah Wilmot, Ed. McConkey, James Reid, William Latimer, R. Leonard, H. Purvis, J. L. Burton, John Dodson, M. J. Hamlin, E. A. Little, A. Campbell, C. Palling, W. P. Soules, William Lennox, John Blackmore, Joseph Huggard, R. Wilkinson, H. Lennox, J. W. Armstrong, J. W. Fennell, William Metcalf, Jno. Robinson, George Webb, William Webb, George Duff, Wm. Dinwoody, Jas. C. Chapman, D. Dunn, W. H. Davis, I. T. Lennox, J. T. Fletcher, William McBurney, Wm. Cunningham, James Donnell, T. W. Lennox, John Lennox, Thomas Scythes, Robert Tegart, George McGirr, John Cobourn, John Graham, sr., John Graham, jr., John Gallagher, M. N. Stephens, Richard Ludlow, Richard Baycroft, J. O. Rogers, William Bellamy, Copeland McGill, Thomas Madill, A. J Rogers, Robert Wade, Michael Irwin, Joseph Kidd, John Cumberland, James Gilmore, James Martin, John Martin, Isaac McCleary, Robert Murphy, William Foster, Robert Heany, Joseph Kidd, James Brett, Henry Baycroft, W. McDermot, C. Cooke, W. H. Hammell, M P.P. James Morrow, Samuel Cavener, Noble Greenaway, P. Durham, J. P., R. W. Lawrie, Thomas Greenaway, James Dilane, J. N. Bond, George Gordon, George P. Hughes, William Potter, Robert Calhoun, L. Rodgers, Amos Train, v. Hastings, W. Atkinson, W. P. Roberts, John Lowrie, T. E. Williams, H. Ledgerwood, Thomas Morrow, D. A. Williams, A. W. Burke, T. Milligan, James Tegart, S. Turner, James Potter, Joseph Abernethy, John McManus, Joseph Thompson, Richard Coffee, jr., Thomas Abernethy, James Manning, E. T. Turner, P. Craig, D. Green, J. Ferguson, R. Manning, Robert Adams, William Carter, Joseph Wright, Walter Evans, A. Lilly, sr., N. Morrow, W. Skelly, D. Lowrie, J. Pearson, J. S. Hammill, Robert Cairns, George Hays, E. A. Rose, M. Martin, W. Fenton, James A. Scott, J Early, J. Stewart, James Hammill, Thomas Atkins, W. Cairns, J. Melross, Alexander Brolley, James Murphy, Alexander Lilly, jr., John Colwell, George Averall, James Bennett, E. Tomlinson, Joseph Mulligan, Dr. Law, S. Ward, Thomas Baycroft, Robert T. Banting, J. Woodcock, Charles Barting, Major Jones, J. Willoughby, Thomas Mills, E. Bell, A. Gilroy, N. Kirby, J. English, W. McKnight, T. Strongman, George Irwin, Robert Hannah, A. Maynard, Julius Rodgers, John Bell, T. Mitchell, James Banting, P. H. Stewart, George McClean, T. S. Patteison, John Glassford, R. Hannah, F. Averall, James Coulter, John Campbell, M. Goodwin, Robert Nixon, George A. Jebb, James Hipwell, W. Stewart, James Spindlee, C. Armstrong, Robert Scott, William Graham, Richard Coffee, jr.

XIV.

SIMCOE (East Riding).—W. Copeland, John Williams, James Dinnan, T. Marchildron, Amos Dean, Geo. King, Robert Perry, B. S. Campbell, W. Lawson, W. Beaty, J. McDermott, F. H. Holland, H. T. Switzer, A. Burton, J. B. Howell, James Freeborne, D. H. Williamson, W. H. Bennett, P. E. Kidd, M.D., C. M. Peters, William Kelly, J. Keating, Charles McGibbon, W. F. H. Thompson, H. Thompson, J. T. Crawford, A. B. Thompson, G. F. Marter, Jonathan Tasker, Robert Nicholls, Alexander Later, J. A. Miller, E. Prouse, C. W. Riley, W. Holden, B. H. Johnston, E. Cox, G. H. Corbett, M.D., Charles Corbould, James Quinn, G. J. Booth, John McCosh, J. W. Slaven, G. J. Bolster, A. W. Gordon, C. E. Grant, Arthur Reeve, G. H. Hale, W. J. Gilpin, George Whitten, Charles S. Elliott, M.D., T. J. Decatur, D. L. Sanson, Charles E. Hewitt, James Reide, T. W. Armstrong, P. Burnett, J. A. Ardagh, M.D., S. James Millard, H. Sinclair, William Edwards, Andrew Clarke, W. Turnbull, Isaac Passmore, William Dunn, Robert Jupp, A. R. D. Paine, R. Murphy, James Morris, Thomas Moffatt, Thomas B. Campbell, Albert Fowlie, D. McGill, John McGuire, John A. Stephenson, Thomas Whipps, D. Strathearn, P. Strathearn, A. Spring, D. Miller, James McDermott, G. Bentley, G. Cunningham, A. P. Robinson, W. O Black, T. Plunkett, R. T. S. Drinkwater, T. H. Drinkwater, A. Hewitt, A. Kerr, A. Millichamp, B. R. Rowe, W. Campbell, W. Teskey, John Gray, M. Leith, J. Teskey, George Badger, John Ball, A. Craig, W. H. Kent, George Wright, R. Graham, H. Overend, Robert Hipwell, George Caswell, W. Edgerton, N. Ryan, W. O'Brien, George Raikes, H. M. Clarke, John McCloud, C. Atkinson, H. Shaw, J. Baskerville, J. Steele, James Ross, D. Allingham, George Crawford, William Greenshields, S. L. Lawrence, S. Jeremy, William Seymour, James Mawdsley, J. Hipwell, H. Barnhart, W. M. Kelly, J. B. Plunkett.

VICTORIA (South Riding).—Jno. Dobson, F. D. Moore, J. R. Dundas, S. Irwin, A. Hudspeth, E. D. Orde, J. Kennedy, Dr. DeGrassi, J. W. Wallace, J. McSewin, J. B. Smith, M. Dean, Dr. Coulter, R. Leary, Dr. Poole, G. Ingle, J. C. Rodden, R. Sylvester, J. W. Diament, Robert Sylvester, J. D. Flavell, A. Wray, J. Duck, T. E. Bradburn, M. O'Halloran, J. L. Winters, J. Gallon, Thomas Mitchell, W. White, E. Veith, R. Touchburn, J. H. Southern, S. Cornell, W. Blackwell, W. Jordan, J. Blackwell, R. Bryons, A. H. Melville, J. D. McMurchy, Jno. Blackwell, H. Walters, P. Brady, J. Ireton, S. Burn, J. Marks, J. D. Graham, J. Maunder, J. Begley, A. Culton, N. McMurchy, G. A. Jordan, J. C. Grace, J. H. Lemmon, J. Pyne, A. A. J. Soanes, J. Finlay, W. Jackson, J. Bryans, P. Duck, H. Jackson, sr., J. T. Currins, J. Ellis, J. Jordan, T. Hoey, T. Fee, M. Hoey, R. Agnew, I. Feir, J. McLean, A. McKay, W. Meagher, W. Skuce, T. Simons, J. Peyell, W. Brown, W. Reynolds, J. McArthur, D. Moore, C. McLean, W. N. Rea, J. Hawkins, J. Patterson, T. Collins, A. Feir, A. Simons, J. Twohey, P. Fisher, Thomas Stephenson, I. McNeely, Dr. Norris, S. English, sr., J. Agnew, sr., A. McQuade, J. Johnston, W. Delane, J. Brown, D. Toole, H. English, J. Bannan, W. Gardner, W. Wilson, W. R. Lang, D. Balfour, W. Adams, H. Toole, F. Fee, W. Best, T. H. McQuade, J. Adams, H. Jackson, T. Magee, J. Groves, G. Moncrief, W. Crowley, G. Elliott, R. Eagan, A. Faulkner, B. Downey, G. Switzer, G. Guiry, E. McColl, J. O'Brien, G. Mulcahey. W. Delane, jr., J. Guiry, W. Franks, J. H. Boat, J. Lowes, J. Carlin, D. Story, J. H. Cassidy, G. Gartly, J. Ashmore, J. McFeeters, C. Thurston, C. Fairbairn, A. Finlay, J. J. Rapley, T. Corbett, F. Kelly, J. Bell, R. Thurston, W. Hunter, R. Steele, T. L. Davies, F. Hopkins, W. Dobson, W. Wray, J. Brandon, W. Hetherington, R. Wilkinson, J. K. Hetherington, J. Long, J. Fell, jr.,— Brandon, W. Lysle, G. Justice, H. Dunn, W. Brown, C. Austin, W. Thurston, R. Kennely, J. J. McCullum, J. Lithgow, J. Duggan, J. Dobson, S. Pogue, A. Knox, J. Lamb, J. Thompson, W. Hetherington, jr., P. Warren, R. Warren, J. Johnston. D. McCammus, J. L. Read, Dr. Bonnell, J. Thompson, E. Bottum, W. Boyd, M. M. Boyd, J. Simpson, J. Petrie, J. Moore, J. Kelly, T. Sleman, J. Glenny, J. Wallis, Dr. Vrooman, W. H. Pogue, J. Sloan, J. Moffatt, A. Casey, W. Stewart, W. Jerwood, W. Ellis, H. Sharp, W. Brown, W. Banks, J. Thorndyke, S. Dundas, M. Webster, Dr. Jeffers. M. Thorndyke, T. Grimstone, J. Kinney, W. M. Thorndyke, W. Bunker, T. Foster, T. Robinson, W. Thorndyke, T. W. Dodds, J. Thorburn, D. McDougall, D. Ferguson, G. Haackie, R. Ramsay, I. Argue, J. J. Fee, J. McKinnon, J. Black, J. Trelevan, J. S. Cruess, A. Smith, R. Irwin, Dr. Cornwall, George Lamb, Dr. Higinbotham, S. English, jr.

VICTORIA (North Riding).—James McArthur, William Jordan, Rev. W. Logan, [James Head, J. Draylin, J. A. Aylmer, Dr. Lowe, Thomas Roberts, R. Macdonald, S. Swanton, J. Simpson, F. Sandford, W. H. Simpson, C. H. Cunningham.

WATERLOO (North Riding).—R. Morison, Dr. Morton, J. H. Moyer, S. J. Ferris, A. Knight, Thomas Miller, Alexander Miller, William Beggs, J. R. Williams, C. Heimbrick, Jno. McKee, George Ruler, P. Huffner, A. Steis, J. L. Kroetsch, M. Kraft, D. Savavas, Jac. Dunke, Jno. Ruppell, A. Sheriff, Jac. Pepler, H. Kranz, M.P., Alexander Miller, P. E. W. Moyer, J. M. Scully, H. M. Andrews, J. S. Hoffman, E. A. Lyons, H. Knell. E. P. Cornell, W. R. Jaffray, William Oelschlager, J. E. Neville, James Gibson, George H. Lang, Jno. Gildner, Jno. A. Mackie, George Rumpel, J. R. Eden, H. C. Hilborn, B. H. Unger, R. Smyth, William Ross, F. Knell, J. E. Seagram, S. E. Moyer, Jac. Conrad, Dr. Bingham, J. Kalbfleisch, A. Rockel, C. Froehlich, C. Huether, L. Kuntz, Isaac Hoffman, C. Bricker, A. Merner, Paul Fink, T. Walter, V. Otterbein, Dr. Vardon, W. Roos.

WATERLOO (South Riding).—Jacob Ratz, Louis Penn, Otto Klotz, Jacob E. Klotz, E. A. Boye, John Braid, George Chapman, Dr. McIntyre, William Kerr, Dr. W. Lovett, Thomas Hammett, A. B. Cowan. T. H. McCallum, A. Warnock, D. McKenzie, Walter Willison, J. M. Irwin, George Hespeler, John Culter, Samuel Cherry, Dr. Duck, George Pattinson, George Clare, Thomas Cowan, G. T. Strickland, Hugh Thompson, James Thompson, Laurenes Shinner, D. Howell, Thomas R. Smith, Thomas Todd, E. Daniel, John A. Cornell, William Millar, Samuel Merner, J. Groff, J. R. Feich, Jacob Wahl, John Culham, John Lorentz, Lewis Hahn, A. J. Blackely, Absolam Muma, H. R. D. Brown, W. R. Plum, J. P. Johnston, James Cunningham, J. Ernst, Louis Ritz, A. J. Brewster, Thomas Telfer, C. Heldman, W. E. Ellis, James Wilson, William Cowan, A. Cranston, Walter Guggesburg, Allan Bowman, Charles Nispel.

WELLINGTON (North Riding).—Dr. Clarke, William Nowdy. E. L. Clarke, W. H. Lingwood, John Alexander, L. H. Clarke. W. R. Tiffin, Richard Johnson, A. M. Clarke, Dr. Standish, W. J. Jennings, Robert Shields, J. T. Lacy, R. Irwin, C. Fois, John Watt, William Long, R. Lowry, J. Robb, S. Caswell, M. Haller, E. J. O'Callaghan, Dr. Henderson, William Clarke, B. B. Johnston, Capt. White, John Buschlen, M. Martin, C. Green, William F. Johnston, Dr. McMahon, T. J. Neil, James Tassie, John Rogers, M. Donnelly, J. Hampton, James Ellis, T. Ryan, Alexander Shelton, H. Wilson, M. D. McGregor, E. Murphy, John O'Brien, J. A. Wilkinson, Thomas Clarke, R. Knox, Dr. Cotton, William Kingston, E. C. Wood, W. Trimble, E. C. Perry, John McLaren, A. Reddish, James Mannell, M. Schneider, G. Benning, T. R. Wood, W. H. Smith, T. A. Craig, J. C. Johnston, W. R. Scutt, R. F. Taylor, S. Graydon, R. Davey, James Culin, J. M. Watson,

XV.

James Moumahan, J. Maben, R. Harvey, R. B. Somerville, William Taylor, Dr. Cowan, Alexander Gillies, W. C. Boddy, H. Leighton, Frederick Wieland, George Preston, Dr. Harvey, George Leighton, John Collison, Joseph E. Davis, William Boyd. J. Jackson, R. Fallis, John Gillespie, Thomas Hunter, G. Bennett, W. B. Jelly, H. Lipsett, B. Field, H. Field, James Golden, Thomas Durkin, John McLean, Richard Bugg, J. J. Johnston. Robert Stephenson, John Fair, T. O. Stauder, William Smith, C. Hefferman, William Ternan, M. M. McMarten, C. C. Groen, James Phelan, James Fraser, H. Fergusson, Robert Martin, F. Mitchell, George Church, I. H. Quirk, Joseph Halley, E. Bristow.

WELLINGTON (Cen're Riding).—M. Anderson, J. C. Morrow, James Mun, J. F. Paterson, J. W. Green Armytage, Dr. G. O'Reilly, John Beattie, James Pattison, J. J. Craig, T. Hughes, W. Speirs, B. McMahon, John Tindal, T. Sherwood, John Jacob, T. A. Gale, F. Dalby, Thomas Biggar, F. Smith, Thomas Gordon, J. C. Johnson, Martin Schneider, M. Fox, H. S. Mitchell, W. Salter, W. Tindale, Joseph Thomson, William Beatty, John Mair, John Wissler, J. H. Broadfoote, James Reynolds, W. Aldordice, John Cunningham, James Cushing, P. Shea, W. Robb, Joseph Nesbit, M. McLinter, William Short, H. Roberts, William Waddick, Charles Strangeaway, Alexander Ewing, F. Cassidy, W. McDermott, R. Burns, Dr. Tambylin, R. Kennedy, R. Black, William Gibson, William Campbell, J. A. Hanna, J. C. Ross, Thomas Hanna. S. Farrell, George Banks, Peter Burns, James Keeley, T. Martin, W. H. Hunter, James Johnston, James Hewitt, Geo. Robinson, J. T. Walker, John Buchanan, James B. Reid, R. Henderson, D. Connell, Alexander Cotten, R. Donaldson, D. Smith, M. Smith, S. Reid, John Preston, John Fairgreave, John Wilson, James McGowan, James McKee, James Simpson, W. Patterson, T. Hamilton, John Hamilton, George Robinson, William Redman, James Mann, John Hillis, Geo. Swan, John Collins, A Baker, John Smith, John Kearns, W. McPherson, R. J. Sturgeon, W. Cornelius, Thomas Holt, James Cross, John Connolly, Thomas McManus, James Burns, G. H. Lewis, James Clarke, J. McGowan, George Stewart, Robert Johnston, G. Burns, W. McDowell, John Ought, A. Griffin, Samuel Boyle, John Palmer, H. Cameron, William Bruice, William Long, Thomas Thompson, John Robinson, William Johnston, R. Harrington, William Woods, Thomas Mannill, S. Armstrong, S. Velle, M. Dochurty, A. Bullard, James Daziel, A. Morrow, William Armstrong, A. Maxwell, F. C. Stewart, J. Gilchrist, J. S. Leighton. John Crozier, John Kearns, R. Hewitt, W. L. Walsh, Joseph Foster, James May, — Mercer, — Robinson, John Fox, J. M. Bennett, A. Hustin, John Walter, John Mole, — Riddle, C. Smith, — Barker.

WELLINGTON (South Riding).—James Goldie, W. Bell, J. A. Wood, A. H. Goodeve, John Harris, A. B. Petrie, Dr. Keating, J. L. Murphy, F. J. Chadwick. H. Vincent, J. H. Deitz, W. Noble, J. A. Nelles, James McAstocker, Charles Raymond, J. B. Armstrong, Jos. Heffernan, E. H. Maddock, Dr. Herod, Peter Kerr, W. H. Cutten, M. Bancroft, W. H. G. Knowles, Peter Anderson, A. McQuillan, J. Conway, J. Hallett, J. A. Kidner, George Robbins, Thomas Griffin, H. Gummer, J. C. Chadwick, A. O. Buchan, W. Hearn, St. George Scarlett, George Norris, T. P. Coffee, S. D. Hill, George Williams, J. J. Hazelton, Jno. Moore, Jno. Reid, W. Jenkinson, James Hewer, F. K. Sweetnam, C. Davidson, G. Tappenden, G. Chamberlain, Thomas Ellis, Dr. Morrow, J. H. Hamilton, D. Brandon, P. Downey, Ald. Coffee, Ald. Hall, Ald. S. B. Skinner, Ald. McDonald, Ald. Hatch, Ald. Lamprey, Ald. Burns, Ald. Roche, Ald. Finlay, Ald. Walker. Ald. Goldie, M. Sweetnam, A. Blyth, F. McQuillan, E. V. Thompson, sr., E. V. Thompson, jr., Theo. Vale, M. O'Connor, Thomas Henderson, J. Goetz, W. West, M. Caraher, J. Neustadt, George Porter, B. Metcalf, J. Atkinson, J. R. Thompson, Robert Conway, Martin Cassin, H. Arkell, Jno. Illes, J. Scott, James Anderson, Jno. C. Moore, Peter Barrett, Patrick McGarr, E. Eagle, W. Leslie, — Rudd, jr., M. Sprenham, Charles Martin, Alexander Smith, Captain J. Kennedy, James O'Brien, M. McCann, D. Shoreltz, T. Copeland, H. Hortop, H. Carter, Jno. McQueen, James McQueen, Robert Jestin, J. Tovell, Charles Gerow, W. Duffield, Charles Bernard, N. Synnett, Captain L. Carberry, A. McMurchy, G. A. Lacy, Francis Gray, Thomas Sutton, W. Smith, Henry Smith, Thomas Bingham, Jno. Harper, William Green, Jno. Leason, S. Gregson, Jno. H. Reed, James Millar, Dr. McNaughton, Peter McGill, A. McMillan, D. McMillan, R. Anthony, C. Webster, James McDermott, W. Conboy, C. H. Walker, James Arthurs.

WENTWORTH (North Riding).—H. Drummond, H. A. Drummond, W. A. Drummond, Charles Drummond, P. Downey, M. Downey, James Downey, Charles Emery, A. Eaton, James Fowler, Frederick Fields, W. H. Featherston, W. D. Flatt, R. Featherston, H. H. Featherston, J. W. Fowler, S. J. Gallagher, Wm. Gallin, Edward Harris, George Harris, D. Herron, George F. Hill, William Hislop, James Higginson, James Law, R. Little, James Little, R. Lyons, L. Langton, Ed. Markle, James Mitchell, James Mullock, L. Mullock, John Mitchell, James Mackay, William Mackay, John McDonald, W. Nicholson, John Nicholson, jr., George Nicholson, John Nicholson, C. Newell, J. S. Nicholson, Thomas Nicholson, T. Organ, J. W. Ryckman, S. W. Ryckman, William Rose, W. Ryckman, S. Speck, J. Springer, F. Anderson, W. Ashberry, J. Alderson, jr., George Alderson, John Alderson, Thomas Alderson, J. W. Burton, R. Burton, E. Burton, J. Beatty, G. Bennett, W. Bennett, W. Baker, R. Bradley, J. Blagden, E. Blagden, B. Blagden, jr., John Blagden, J. Burton, P. Burton, W. Carroll, P. Carson, Joseph Carson, James Carson, W. Cairnes, H. N. Crooker, S. Campbell, G. W. Campbell, W. Campbell, D. Campbell, George Cartwright, F. Draker, D. Doyle, F. Dawson, George Eaton, W. Edgar, T. Edgar, J. T. Eaton, M. C. Eaton, J. Eaton, T. H. Eaton, Am. Eaton, A. Eaton, G. Fielding, A. Freeman. Arthur Freeman, Joseph Ford, N. Fulton, B. Gunby, T. Galloway, C. Galloway, H. Gastle, J. Hunt, R. Hamilton, James Hamilton, C. Hamilton, J. Kerr, T. Le Messurier, J. Livingstone, J. H. Livingston, W. Mahon, M. McCovick, J. Nixon, G. S. Nicholson, A. Newell, J. Paine, E. Pepper, W. Paine, A. Patton, George Perry, W. Rusk, J. B. Smith, James Sullivan, W. Simpson, R. Sparks, S. E. Tausley, S. Tausley, S. S. Tausley, A. Tweedle, J. Vance, W. J. Vannorman, C. Vannorman, A. Warner, George Walker, D. Whitley, M. Alger, James Alger, Jos. Alger, Edward Alger, J. Beatty, A. Bannatyne, D. Brown, T. Cartwright, P. Cronin, M. Sager, William Robb, John Gamble, W. Misener, William Boyle, Robt. Thompson, S. Larmon, James Vroman, John Pitten, J. Baker, Thomas Head, D. Patterson, H. Armstrong, R. Lowry. A. McKnight, Joseph Boyle, R. K. Kernighan, John Brant, D. Bell, J. B. Plaston, D. Wray, M. Costolo, F. J. Armstrong, Joseph Taylor, Joseph Parker, A. McKellar, John Harbottle, George Bickell, Robt. Patterson, D. McCormick, E. McNicholl, W. J. McGuire, James Mills, T. Purdy, T. McNicholl, M. Sullivan, George Patterson, James George, Charles Patterson, N. Vansicle, Matthew Sullivan, Michael Sullivan, Jas. A. Sipes, John Culham, John A. Cornell, S. Willard, D. A. McDonald, John Hammond, O. McGinty, John Ireland, John Allen, Charles Boyle, George Baker, P. Creen, H. Clark, John Cleaves, S. Cook, M. Doyle, D. Davies, J. C. Eager, Edward Fields, George Foster, Samuel Green, William Gallan, Thomas Little, L. Mullock, J. Metzgar, Dr. McLaren, Dr. McGregor, W. Radford, sr., D. Stock, W. Stock, J. T. Stock, W. R. Wilson, M. Atkinson, L. Bauer, N. Bowen, A. W. Brown, James Crane, M. Crane, G. W. Colton, R. Cutler, A. H. Cumming, W. Cookoo, C. Daly, M. Daly, R. Donaldson, R. Ferris, D. Fonger, V. E. Fuller, J. Gallagher, Thomas Hunter, J. Hodge, W. Hall, Alexander Henderson, William Hopkins, W. R. Hall, W. G. Hall, J. Ireland, Robert Ireland, George Ireland, John Jackson, C. Klodt, C. H. King, T. Kirby, J. A. Kennedy, Aug. Leather, W. B. Leather, Thos. Lacey, V. Little, J. Mullen, P. Mutter, Thos. Marriott, Jno. Marriott, J. McMichael, Wm. Norton, W. B. Reid, W. Ross, J. F. Read, Jas. Smith, W. Schojan, R. Smiley, J. Smiley, J. Stewart, P. Stewart, T. B. Townsend, T. Attridge, Jno. Allen, Geo. Bradt, F. Buttenham, Chas. Baxter, J. Bradt, J. R. Blanshard, T. Blanshard, S. Crooker, R. Carey, J. Carey, G. W. Carey, W. Cloyd, H. Clappison, W. D. Curtis, R. T. Wilson, T. J. Bell, Jno. Bertram, Jno. Wilson, S. Lennard, H. Bertram, J. M. Barton, P. O'Connor, Jas. Dickson, T. Cartner, Jno. Maw, W. Cowper, Jos. Black, Geo. Fielden, T. Hickey, Geo. Ball, G. W. Bennett, S. J. Lennard, W. Babcock, T. Byrne, W. Graham, John Kerwin, C. McCardel, D. H. Nelson, F. J. Collins, John Enright, J. F. Smith, W. Hardy, A. R. Wardell, George McDermott, John Poole, James Webster, Thomas Wilson, P. Brady, Alexander Bertram, H. Bickford, Dr. Walker, H. Crowe, C. Fry, P. K. Gain, J. J. Grafton, H. C. Gwyn, R. McKechnie, W. G. Smyth, Jos. Brown, M. R. Thomas, M. S. Wilson, James Wilson, Henry Wyld, P. Ray, jr.; F. Ray, John Burk, W. Finlay, William Wordley, J. Simpson, Thomas Johnston, H. Edworthy, G. Hayes, Thomas Curtis, H. Sheridan, R. Watson, W. Weir, Thomas Weir, Robert Weir, W. Waygood, J. Walker, jr., J. Cornell, T. Duffy, W. Dougherty, C. Duffy, M. Foley, H. Foley, W. Foster, T. Foley, T. Garvin, M. Garvin, F. Gray, E. Hurren, J. A. Hunt, J. Hunt, E. Hunt, J. C. Hood, P. Hood, W. Hood, A. Hood, W. Kerr, J. O. Kerr, O. Livingston, Jno. Maddaugh, T. McKenna, P. McCarthy, A. Nicholson, A. Smith, James Smith, Andrew Smith, James A. Smith. George Sheed, A. Sinclair, T. Savage, J. Savage, B. Sullivan, R. Sheridan, Jno. Sheridan, M. Peebles, Alfred Jones, J. Brennan, K. Wishart, W. J. Morden, G. M. Smith, T. Connell, J. Ryckman, Dr. Witherall, Owen O'Connell, M. Fraser, W. Bullock, jr., James Stutt, Dr. Stutt, T. Morden, C. Morrison, James Taylor, sr., James Clark, Charles Foster, George Smith, Sol. Ryckman, Alexander Brown, jr., W. Green, F. Miller, J. Webster, sr., M. McGinn, J. Maloney, A. Ross, J. Markle, J. T. Hourigan, Edward Freel, J. Rutledge, P. Enright T. O'Brien, P. Green, D. Sharpe, R. Speck.

WENTWORTH (South Riding).—D. W. Camp, W. H. Morgan, Martin Lally, George Cann, Watson Muir, Jno. H. Traviss, W. Nevills. Robert Topp, Murray Nelson, Iradeus Nevills, Robert Shepherd, M. McDougall, Ross Petitt, Robert Glover, J. D. Lutz, Thomas Lowry, S P. Stipe, Valentino Mott, Harry Bovant, Jno. W. Kerr, Joseph W. Jardine, F. M. Carpenter, A. G. Jones, Murray Pettit, Andrew Carpenter, Richard Onance, W. G. Fletcher, William Ptolemy, E. J. Duffy, C. D. Potts, Joseph Bates, Wilcome Man, James Reed, M. J. Donohoe, A. French, A. G. Muir, W. H. Nelles, S. A. Nelles, Jacob Book, H. Anderson, Thomas Hunter, G. C. Pettit, George Cline, J. H. Leeter, A. H. Pettit, John Grout, Jonathan Carpenter, H. H. Anderson, D. W. Camp, W. H. Morgan, George Cain, Watson Muir, M. W. Dalton, A. W. Dalton, H. P. Bridgeman.

YORK (North Riding).—W. S. Ramsay, John Kay, D. Brooks, Levi Miller, William Ardill, Thomas Ough, John Roseman, R. Long, William Harold, Luke Gibbons, J. A. Sharpe, Samuel Mosley, Joseph Hollingshead, J. S. Boddy, John Boddy, L. Vanostrand, George Evans, jr., T. W. Stephens, W. H Thorne, D. T. Wilson, Henry Isaac, Dr. Britton, Dr. Howe, Richard Park, Robert Mallory, Francis Boulton. J. G. Tinline, John Hogan, W. M. Sibbald, T. C. Sibbald, W. B. Perry, James McClure, John Harty, M. B. Faughburn, George Bishop, G. L. Stevenson, W. I. Stevenson, W. B. Linton, W. R. Vivian, W. H. Major, Jno. Donnell, R. Donnell, Dr. Sibbald, Angus Ego, W. M. Sibbald, H. Park, J. R. Stevenson, R. S. Hill, James Anderson, George Evans, Jno. Kay, M. Umphrey, H. McDonald, C. Reynar, Charles Laviolette, C. B. Paget, H. Corner, D. W. McDonald, D. Sprague, C. Traviss, W. L. Marshall, George Hamilton, J. Hamilton, Jno. Boag, Josiah Willoughby, M. Hodgius, Patrick Connell, Jno. Parks, D. Brooks, F. Sprague, D. Wilson, Jno. Purdy, Wilson Stoddard, Robert Stewart, Robert M. Lawrence, Thomas Edmanson, Jno. Boddy, John H. S. Boddy, Robert Fennell, William Fennell, James Lawrence, R. B. McCartney, Frank Dowler, Edward Garrett, John Armstrong, Samuel Lukes, Mark Scanlon, Dr. Stephenson, Dr. Taylor, Dr. Porter, Thomas Dewson, William Barry, J. T. Sproule, Gipson Cook, James St. Clair, William Wilson Stoddard, Frank Stewart, Mr. Wilson, Dr. Forest, Frank Wood, Walter Rogers, Jno. Stubbs, William Sullivan, Mr. McNelly, George Pool, Thomas McBrien, Wilson Scott, Samuel Heilly, Matthew Heilly, J. M. Barry, B. Barnard, William Goodwin, James S. Boddy, William McCausland.

YORK (East Riding).—Robert Melburn, Benjamin Morton, George Digby, J. J. Cosgrove, Charles Coleman, Captain D. C. Burk, J. A. Huntley, Joseph Davids, R. H. Crew, Richard Holman, Martin O'Grady, F. Thompson, Joseph Brown, John McQuarrie, Mr. Alman, Mr. Nettleton, James McGee, Frank Boston, Matthew Chester, Dr. Winstanley, Mr. Hewitt, William Gray, William Lee, John Lee, Louis Fitzgerald, W. E. Playter, J. L Payter, W. H. Salmon, Richard Cosburn, William Tustin, James Young, David Mathers, Nathaniel Rudd, Mr. Dunn, Henry Stoddard, Duncan McNair, Thomas Bennett, James Walmsley, D. Ryan, R. Elgie, R. G. Playter, William McGill, Hugh Wilson, William Tabor, Robert Rogerson, Alexander Moffat, John Taylor, Mark Barker, Richard Fursey, David Chapman, James Simpson, Charles Baxter, Ed. Gledhill, William Wakefield, William Brown, George Woods, Wallace Carson, George McCormack, Henry Mason, Arthur Beattie, Charles Kerswell, Francis Langrill, John Zegman, James Dean, Samuel Dean, Robt. Brown, Joseph Francis, John Alcott, Henry McCrea, Arthur Woods, Thomas Davidson, Lawrence Baldwin, Reuben Pugsley, Thomas Sabin, William Brunskill, Robert Johnston, Robert Cook, Alexander Quinton, Robert Drury, A. L. Wilson, George Brown, T. H. Ince, Mr. Monck, Edgar Jarvis, W. H. Eddis, Edward Manton, John Hoskins, Alfred Hoskins, Frederick Clark, George Denby, Robert Lawrence, Michael O'Halloran, J. H. Smith, James Woods, Samuel McBride, James Hopkins, William Douglas, George Robinson, James Childs, Robert McBride, John Morgan, J. Fulton, Hamilton Mercer, Thomas Williams, Matthew Pearson, William Long, Henry Duncan, Charles Watson, James Hogg, John Watson, John Burk, Robert Janes, Ed. Burk, George Beasley, James Chadwick, Charles Goldwin, Solomon Turner, John Hutchison, George May, Robert Hunter, Ed. Armstrong, Samuel Martin, Thomas Patterson, John Laidley, Thomas Lambert, Mark Watson, John Bell, Robert Myers, George Long, George Scarce, Luke Phelen, William Johnston, John Coates, William Lawson, Richard Drury, Robert Madill, William Middleton, John Whitaker, Chas. Stewart, William Stewart, David Duncan, John Weldrick, J. T. B. Lindsay, Joseph Bales, David Birrell, Thomas Humberstone, Dr. Richardson, George Hope, William Street, John Finch, Frank Gilding, Samuel Dingel, Frank Bickford, R. R. Waterhouse, A. Andrews, Æmelius Baldwin, Thomas Crean, Thos. Williamson.

YORK (West Riding).—Jacob Bull, James Conron, sr., Dr. Charlton, W. J. Conron, Edward Eagle, Robert Flynn, David Maquire, David Rowntree, William Tyrrell, Thomas R. Wadsworth, Oliver Willy, Dr. Walker, Peter Frank, Colonel Gracey, John Abel, R. A. Cortisson, John Elliot, C. W. Edwards, Gilbert Gilmour, William Hay, Henry Keys, James Mounsey, T. F. Wallace, Daniel McKenzie, William Farr, Oliver

XVII.

Prentice, Alexander Locke, John Rowntree, Alexander Rogerson, George Wallace, Thomas Woolley, Amos Maynard, David Stewart, Captain Wallace, Rowland Harvey, A. E. Keffer, Andrew Collins, Archibald Gallanough, Charles A. Holmer, James McDonnell, George Charlton, Thomas S. Cook, Michael Fisher, George Keffer, James Osler, Joseph Keffer, J. C. Steele, Aaron Oster, Richard Vanderbury, Fullerton Gibson, Alexander Gibson, William Crowley, J. S. McNair, William Glass, Charles Kirkland, James McWilliams, Robert McCaffrey, James Vanderbury, C. Creasor, John Marsh, Joseph Rumble, Robert McNair, William Hart, Duncan McMullen, James Sherman, William Taggert, John A. Sinder, James McNeil, Thomas Matthewson, Alfred Rupert, William Robinson, R. B. Orr, James Oliver, Daniel Kinnie, Neil Malloy, David Blough, William Sheardown, George Watson, Alexander Cameron, Alexander Malloy, Daniel Malloy, George Cooper, William Kyle, Jno. Richards, Peter Franks, Henry Marsh, Jno. Sindner, Thomas Walkington, George Wilson, George Smith, Thomas Oliver, Daniel Malloy, jr., John Blough, Thomas White, Joseph Burkholder, Richard Brown, John Bennett, Charles Palmer, J. W. Devons, William Darker, John Fenwick, Hugh Ferguson, Charles A. Gough, William Hutchinson, Charles Keffer, John Kaiser, George Moodie, James Marshall, Charles McNeil, John Watson, Alexander McNaughton, Jacob McKay, George Toffer, Robert Robb, Malcolm McTaggart, W. Stewart, Daniel Sullivan, John Brown, Richard Willis, William Shunk, John McLean, Donald McArthur, Archibald Cameron, Andrew McNeil, Alexander Cameron, Thomas Cairns, John Harvey, Dugald McMurchy, Thomas Cousins, John Kerr, Hugh Kennedy, John McNaughton, Thomas Jarrett, Thomas Smyth, sr., Thomas Kersey, John McDonagh, Thomas Smyth, jr., Hugh Kennedy, Michael Lelles, jr., Robert Hollingshead, William Hemphill, James Cherry, Robert Robinson, John A. Beamish, David Elder, William Farr, Pierre Fletcher, Gavin Lauria, Alfred Mussen, Samuel McClure, W. McClure, Peter McNaughton, R. N. Taylor, H. Peters, Thomas Richardson, John Wray, Joseph Weatherill, John Wright, Isaac Crosby, J. Brown, S. Savage, William Powel, John Powel, Benjamin Brillinger, William Sanderson, John Sanderson, James Reynolds, M. Teefy, M. H. Keefler, John Hart, John Duncan, John P. Bull, John Brimer, John Canewan, Ed. Conley, James Fullerton, I. Gilbert, John Kerr. Ed. Lindner, P. Langton, Peter Malbery, Allan Royce, I. Grogan, John R. Bull, John Todd, Thomas Gilbert, I. P. Ross, Jas. Hislip, Andrew Watt, George Dracoff, George Carter, David McComb, Richard Yateman, Charles Yateman, S. T. Humberstone, A. G. McTavish, Abraham Wilson, William Clarke, John Golding, John Brackey, Jas. Carruthers, Robert Clark, Francis Watson. John Stewart, Wilson Clarke, John Clarke, James Stewart, A. W. Duncan, Thomas Jackson, John Woods, James Keyes, T. F. Pratt, A. Anderson, Frank Baby, William Boake, D. W. Clendenan, Albert Foxwell, Walter Foxwell, David Kennedy, G. Logan, S. N. Lasher, Robert Harris, Ed. Williams, Robert Ward, Richard Coe, James Kennedy, George Weisman, George A. Bull, E. W. Bull, Donald Cameron, James Duncan, William Duncan, Abraham J. Griffith, James Griffith, William James Smithson, W. John Smithson, Henry Walsh, Joseph Hislip, John Bryant, A. M. Bryant, John Clarke, Alex. Clarke, John Duck, James Eastwood, sr., J. Eastwood, jr., John Eastwood, Samuel Eastwood, Robert Eastwood, James Elford, sr., J. Elford, jr., Charles Gibson, Benjamin Goldthorpe, John Kay, David Kingsberry, James J. Kenny, W. Lennox, Hugh J. McNeil, John L. Noble, Fred. M. Noble, Charles Northcote, William Peeler, S. Plunket, Samuel Richey, William Simpson, George Simpson, William G. Simpson, Francis Tremayne, Matthew Canning, J. W. Clarke, J. W. Coultes, Robert Coultes, sr., James Carry, John D. Evans, Robt. Garbutt, Wm. J. Gracy, Jos. Gracy, jr., John C. Ide, Henry T. Ide, Thos. H. Ide, John P. McConnell, Thomas Musson, John Newlove, William Newlove, John F. Newlove, Joseph Patterson, Matthew Peacock, J. Peacock, jr., Thomas Ranger, William Scott, John Strong, Alexander A. Waries, Richard Walker, George White, sr., George White, jr., Joseph N. Wood, George T. Wood, Arthur F. O. Wood, Samuel R. Wood, James Allen, Patrick Bannon, Samuel Bryans, William Clayton, Francis Cornish, Meade Creech, Joseph Creech, William Darling, Richard H. Evans, M. Farrell, Edward Harris, J. B. Kaiser, Henry Lever, Joseph McClinchey, William A. Muston, W. H. Scott, Thomas W. Smith, George Smith, Charles Ware, William S. Canning, Andrew Coulter, James F. Duffy, Richard S. Geddes, James H. Gracey, George M. Hill, James F. Hill, Isaac Jobson, Samuel Johnson, George M. Lyons, William T. Madill, George Middlebrook, George M. Middleton, John Middlebrook, Robert Priesly, sr., Thomas Ramage, Ira Shibley, Thomas Taylor, James H. Taylor, William R. Wadsworth, James Bayes, Henry Beamish, John Calhoun, James Carruthers, Matthew Codlin, James Ella, David Frost, jr., Thomas Griffith, Richard Johnson, James Kellam, R. H. Kellam, John Love, Jesse Mabee, Michael E. O'Brien, Thomas Peters, Charles Peters, Isaac Plowright, William Riley, George Rowntree, James Rowntree, Alexander Sangster, Dr. T. Savage, Samuel Smith, David Stewart, Arthur Watson, William Wood, Robert Wood, John W. Wray, J. Wray, Wm. P. Atkinson.

The constituencies of Bothwell, Cornwall and Stormont, Grey (South Riding), Middlesex (East Riding), Middlesex (South Riding) and Welland appointed delegates to attend the Convention, but although we have written for lists of those gentlemen who attended, up to the hour of going to press they have not arrived, and consequently do not appear in this Appendix.

The two lists given below arrived too late to appear in the alphabetical order.

LAMBTON (East Riding).—A. C. MacKenzie, Jacob Rogers, William Phippin, Captain Gattis, D. Menluimick.

LENNOX.—J. J. Watson, A. F. Holmes, T. E. Howard, Allen Oliver, W. N. Doller, Elijah Shon, Uriah Wilson, Charles Fraser, Luke Spafford, George Parrott, Isaac Aylesworth, Nelson Lapum, Jesse Amey, R. R. Finkle, Robert Filson, R. A. Fowler, William Charters, D. Vandewater, Captain Chalmers, J. C. Carscallen, A. C. Parks, Thomas V. Sexsmith, H. Vankoughnet, Henry Harris, P. W. Dafoe, George Gordanier, John Gordanier, James Metcalfe, Zephaniah Groomes, J. G. Woodcock, T. G. Carscallen, T. G. Davis, Ed. Lapum, William Saul, Alexander Henry, Donald McLiver, William S. Detlor, James H. Downey, James M. Sexsmith, J. T. Grange, M. Pruyn.

www.ingramcontent.com/pod-product-compliance
Lightning Source LLC
Chambersburg PA
CBHW030401170426
43202CB00010B/1446